The
Designer's Apprentice

Automating Photoshop®, Illustrator®, and InDesign®
in ADOBE® CREATIVE SUITE® 3

Adobe

Rick Ralston

The Designer's Apprentice:
Automating Photoshop, Illustrator, and InDesign in Adobe Creative Suite 3
Rick Ralston

This Adobe Press book is published by Peachpit.
Peachpit
1249 Eighth Street
Berkeley, CA 94710
510/524-2178
510/524-2221 (fax)

Find us on the Web at: www.peachpit.com
To report errors, please send a note to errata@peachpit.com
Peachpit is a division of Pearson Education

For the latest on Adobe Press books, go to www.adobepress.com

Copyright © 2008 by Rick Ralston

Project Editor: Becca Freed
Production Editor: Tracey Croom
Copyeditor: Jill Simonsen
Tech Editors: Adam Pratt, Matt Neuburg, and Bill Cheeseman
Proofreaders: Joanne Gosnell and Cathy Lu
Compositor: Kim Scott, Bumpy Design
Indexer: Rebecca Plunkett
Cover design: Charlene Charles-Will
Interior design: Kim Scott, Bumpy Design

ISBN 13: 978-0-321-49570-9
ISBN 10:   0-321-49570-5

9 8 7 6 5 4 3 2 1

Printed and bound in the United States of America

For Julie A. Wilson
Wise, sensual, and sublime, she is the real magic.

Acknowledgments

I could not have even contemplated writing this book if it were not for Julie A. Wilson. She is my mentor, my friend, my partner. She opened the door to a new life in which something like this is possible. She pushed me to follow this dream, and for that I can never repay her. She cared for our farm and animals for the too many months it took to write this book, and she never complained. She gave me invaluable feedback on and corrections to the text. And her photography graces this book almost literally from cover to cover, helping me bring my ideas to life with grace and beauty.

I would like to thank Rebecca Freed for being my editor. Although I wouldn't have blamed her had she tossed this first-time author out on his ear, she gave generously of her time, experience, knowledge, and skill. Not only did I rely heavily on her expertise, but I blatantly stole her insights whenever I could and am at present peddling some of them as my own. Thank you, Becca, for everything.

Thank you also to my acquisitions editor, Pamela Pfiffner; to Adam Pratt at Adobe; and to Bill Cheeseman, Cathy Lu, Matt Neuburg, Rebecca Plunkett, Jill Simonsen, and Dori Smith for technical assistance. Props to Charlene Charles-Will, Tracey Croom, and everyone at Peachpit Press for being kind, understanding, and professional.

Thanks to my mother Jo-an for giving me a love of books and encouraging my artistic aspirations. Thanks also to my sister Julie and brother Jim for their support, and for not getting mad when I didn't call.

Thanks to Joanna Colrain for helping me be a better human being. Thanks to Patricia Dreame and Bonnie Dreame for support and encouragement, and to Tom Cox for an ocean of coffee and a river of ideas. Thanks to everyone at Coke.

A big zagharoot to Troupe Hameeda. I wrote a great deal of this book listening to them dance late into many a beautiful Georgia night.

Rick Ralston
June 2007

Contents

Introduction

Do something once, it's creative. Do something twice, it's repetitive. Do something three times, and you can probably automate it.

—*Adrian Woods, Technical Art Lead, Microsoft*

Many years ago I produced a monthly shipping schedule for a worldwide shipping company. It was a freelance job that I worked on at night in the dim corner of our basement apartment bedroom. I received messy text files on 5 1/2-inch PC floppy disks. Out of self-defense I taught myself how to automate text cleanup in a DOS text editing program (which was all I had at the time). And when finished, I transferred the file to a Mac, where I did the layout in PageMaker. From there, I learned that I could add style tags to the text as part of the automated cleanup phase. Once imported, PageMaker would apply the correct typographic styles and tabs to the text based on those style tags.

At that period in my life I had very little free time. Everything I could automate, every minute I could wring out of the process, meant I had more time to spend with my wife and enjoying life. As a result, automation had a direct, personal, and meaningful impact on my life. With the knowledge you take away from this book, it could have the same effect on yours.

The Purpose of This Book

I've long been frustrated by the lack of adequate documentation and holistic discussion of graphics automation. Composed of disparate and disconnected parts, graphics automation is a topic usually served up with such a narrow focus that I'm left feeling as if I were looking at the subject through a peephole, seeing only bits and pieces here and there. To make matters worse, much of the existing documentation either assumes you know more than you do or is so mired in technobabble that you feel the author's intent must be to confuse rather than inform.

Another problem I've encountered is elitism—the attitude that if you're not an expert, you have no place at the table, no right to ask questions, and certainly no right to make mistakes. Thus, if nothing else, I want to make it clear that beginners have just as much right to learn about and apply graphics automation as professional designers or programmers.

That said, graphics automation resides in a zone between geeks and creatives. So far, the winds have blown geek-ward, but I wanted to do my part to take the practice in the other direction, making the zone more habitable for creative types. Graphics automation doesn't have to be difficult to understand or apply; it's only made so by the disjointedness of the existing references and training materials.

My aim, then, is to round up graphics automation instruction under one roof and to offer it in the plainest language possible. I won't tell you, however, that under this roof the topic exists as a unified whole. Instead, the different kinds of automations form what resembles a dysfunctional family: Sometimes quarreling, sometimes uncommunicative, the various members (together and separately) still somehow manage to do wondrous things.

Nor will I tell you that this book promises to cure all of your graphics automation ills; no book could. Instead, it's a start—a primer that will provide the grounding you need to appreciate the field, apply it to your own challenges, and explore it further on your own. Graphics automation is fun, exciting, and a challenge. It involves creativity and problem solving and stretching your abilities. There's always something new to learn and very few hard-and-fast rules—making it a playground for those whose imaginations are captured by it and an effective tool for anyone who wants to save time and money on graphics projects.

Adobe's Creative Suite serves as a natural hook on which to hang graphics automation's hat. Its three design applications—Photoshop, Illustrator, and InDesign—are the most used applications in the graphics field as well as some of the most easily automated. Adobe, in fact, has long supported automation in its applications—from scripting (including three different scripting languages) to actions, data-driven publishing, and some server-based applications. And because these applications have become industry standards, they enjoy the support of third-party developers and a robust user community.

What You'll Learn

Moving from the theoretical to the practical, this book is divided into three parts: automation concepts, tools, and projects. The concepts provide a foundation on which to build your understanding; the tools give you the means to automate; and the projects demonstrate what's possible.

While creative types often have a hard time embracing automation—thinking the topic is foreign to their world and experience—I hope to show that this is *not* the case, that graphics automation is both essential and as familiar as breathing. Indeed, the concepts you apply in graphics automation are concepts you already apply in your everyday life.

Developed separately and for specific purposes, graphics automation tools (each of which has its own strengths and weaknesses) are far from an integrated group of applications. That said, the better you understand them *as a group*, the more effective you'll be in approaching and solving automation problems with them.

The four chapters that make up the projects section demonstrate how you can put into action the concepts and tools you learn about in these pages. Think of these projects as Tinkertoys that you can dismantle, study, and reassemble to make into something new entirely. Projects should never be taken literally; instead, they should simply point you to possibilities.

Who You Are

So who are you? If you're reading this book, you're likely to be a creative professional in graphic design or photography—or both. You are (I would hope) curious and open to trying new things, and have a penchant for solving mysteries. It doesn't matter if you're young or old as long as you enjoy tinkering and experimentation.

You will need a good understanding of at least one of the applications covered (Photoshop, Illustrator, or InDesign) to get the most out of this book. A desire to learn, however, is paramount; the rest will follow.

If you're self-employed, you'll understand the need for efficiency. When time equals money, automation is key, allowing you produce jobs faster and more accurately so that you have more time to design and work on client relationships. You might also explore data-driven publishing as another revenue stream.

If you work for someone else, automation will make you a more productive employee. (Just make sure that increased productivity equates to raises and promotions!) It also frees up some of your time for more creative tasks.

If you have creative people working for you, this book should give you some ideas on how to save labor costs by making your employees more efficient. As a side benefit, when they are freed from some of their drudgery, your employees will be more content. And you'll be able to feed them higher-ticket design work.

Downloadable Files

Most of the files used in this book's projects are posted at www.peachpit.com/apprentice. To download them, go to the Web site and register the book. You can see more of Julie A. Wilson's photography at www.zumedia.com/j

If you'd like to contact me, you can do so at apprentice@zumedia.com.

I

Concepts

Automation surrounds us, in many forms. Robots might be the first thing that springs to mind, but automation is also in imagery we see, sounds we hear, and actions we take. No matter how complex automations may appear, they *always* consist of a trigger that starts the process, something that's being acted upon (or input), the actions themselves (or commands), and the results (or output). When viewed as these four elements, automation isn't really very mysterious.

In fact, automation is probably more familiar to you than you realize. Just think about your morning routine to understand how basic automation is to our existence. We are a bundle of bodily automations, habits, instincts, and rituals. Our hearts beat, our lungs breathe, our bodies move, all thanks to automation. We multitask, rely on instincts, and habitually make our morning coffee *just so* because automation is there, underlying and supporting us. We could not get through 10 minutes, let alone an entire day, without it. It is us—body, mind and spirit.

1

Of Mice and Brooms

An Informal Introduction to Automation

Come, old broomstick, you are needed,
Take these rags and wrap them round you!
Long my orders you have heeded,
By my wishes now I've bound you.

Have two legs and stand,
And a head for you.
Run, and in your hand
Hold a bucket too.

—From The Sorcerer's Apprentice *(Johann Wolfgang von Goethe)*

Just about all of the information you need to understand automation is contained in the "Sorcerer's Apprentice" sequence of the 1940 Disney animated classic *Fantasia*—really. To help you understand, here's a quick recap of its plot: Sorcerer exits to run a few errands, leaving his apprentice (played by Mickey Mouse) to fill a basin with water. The mouse sees an opportunity and uses his boss' incantation to bring a broom to life to do the chore for him. Broom quickly fills basin but won't stop. Mouse applies ax to said broom. But instead of ceasing and desisting, the single broom becomes an army of brooms, marching on to fill the now-overflowing basin and flood the room. Mouse panics and is surely doomed. Sorcerer returns and restores order. Sorcerer shoots stern look at mouse, but all's well that ends well. *Finis.*

While Walt Disney meant the sequence as a cautionary tale (*do not call upon powers you don't know how to control*), I see it as a classic automation problem. Think of the incantation as a list of commands, or a program. Here's what it looks like in outline form:

1. Give broom life.
2. Make broom perform the following tasks repeatedly:
   a) Fetch water
   b) Pour fetched water in basin

But Mickey has made two serious mistakes when it comes to automating the task at hand: 1) He didn't indicate that the broom should stop fetching and pouring once the basin is full (in automation—and programming—this is called an *endless loop);* and 2) He didn't instruct the broom to return to its original inanimate state. Here's what the outline might look like with those instructions added:

1. Give broom life.
2. Make broom perform the following tasks until basin is full:
   a) Fetch water
   b) Pour fetched water in basin
3. Return broom to its former lifeless state.

The "Sorcerer's Apprentice" sequence illustrates another important aspect of automation—*magic*. When you watch an agent you've built do things on your behalf—making decisions and delivering something it would have taken you forever to do—it's hard not to feel like the Sorcerer. You take some lines of text and blow a little life into them, and away they go to do your bidding. This feels like magic to me, and it never, ever gets old—a great motivator for exploring and mastering automation.

In this book, we will define *automation* as a set of editable commands that a computer can execute to accomplish a task. In my analogy, I've used the word *automation* rather loosely to refer to both the field of automation and the software functions themselves. Thus, I'd like to introduce *agent* as the term for the software process. Agents can take many forms, such as a script or Creative Suite action, but as we'll soon see, they share the same structure. And at their most basic level, they all perform the same function.

Although agents may look complicated, you can always break them down into the following components:

Trigger. This is the action that sets the process in motion—for example, double-clicking an icon.

Input. This is what the automation acts upon

Commands. These are the steps required to accomplish the goal.

Output. This is what the agent produces.

In the Apprentice's case, the trigger is reciting the incantation to get things going; the input consists of the broom (since it's the thing being acted upon); the commands comprise the fetch-and-pour routine; and the output is a basin filled with water to the correct depth. No matter how big and bewildering an agent is, you can always break it down into the above-described four parts. Keeping this structure in mind can help you retain your bearings as you analyze or create an automation.

Alternative Ending

For the sake of argument, let's suppose that Mickey was able to pull off his magic and get the broom to haul water. What benefits would he enjoy? For starters, he would avoid the drudgery of performing a mindless, repetitive task, freeing his mind and skills for more profitable endeavors. A mind enslaved by repetitive work cannot soar; ergo, a happier, more productive mouse would be the result.

If the broom were properly automated, there would be less spilled water and thus less clean-up for Mickey. Maybe the Sorcerer wouldn't slip on the cobblestone floor; maybe the grout between the cobblestones would last longer; and maybe—just maybe—Mickey's clothes would stay cleaner. You begin to get the picture.

Let's take his automation one step further. What if the agent were automatically triggered when the water in the basin dropped below a certain level? Mickey would never have to think about the water level again. As a result, he would be less stressed, and there would likely be less friction between him and his boss (since there would always be water). And once Mickey got the broom thing down, couldn't he conceivably apply the same agent (with a little tinkering) to taking out the garbage, bringing in firewood, or any number of other chores? I'm sensing a promotion for Mickey…

Understanding these automation concepts will help you apply automation to the situation at hand. You may be using different tools, but they'll employ the same structure: trigger, input, commands, and output.

Now imagine that instead of hauling water to a basin, you need to process a set of images sent to you via e-mail for a monthly newsletter: You would need to detach the images from the e-mail, open them in Photoshop, resize them, downsample their resolution, change the color space from RGB to CMYK, apply the Unsharp Mask, rename each file with the current date and sequential numbers, and put the whole shebang in a new folder with an appropriate project name and date. And you need to do this with 15 images a month. How long would it take to perform these tasks manually? It took me 45 minutes—with no interruptions. In contrast, it took me less than 10 minutes to accomplish the same tasks using an automation agent—and during the entire 10 minutes I was busy working on another project.

And what if you were to make a mistake while performing this mind-numbing series of tasks? There's additional time involved in catching your error and repairing the damage—and that's if you're lucky. If you don't catch your error and the newsletter goes to press with the mistake, your job could be at stake.

There's also the problem of transition time: It takes mental effort to prepare for a complex, multistep task; initiate it; stay on track; and not lose your place. Each time you're interrupted, you must refocus, find your place, and get back into the swing of things. Sustained focus—which these types of projects require—can cause mental fatigue, which can produce distractibility. And distractibility can lead to even more interruptions. And multiple interruptions only compound the problem.

But automation suffers from bad PR, often evoking black-and-white images of car assembly lines or HAL trying to asphyxiate his crewmates in *2001: A Space Odyssey*. Well, here's some good PR: The automation tools you'll be using with this book can be adapted for use with iTunes or GarageBand or video editing software (**Figure 1.1**). Automation is used to create Billboard's music rating charts. Pixar uses automation to create animations and render its movies. U2 uses automation to create its light shows. NASA uses it to build

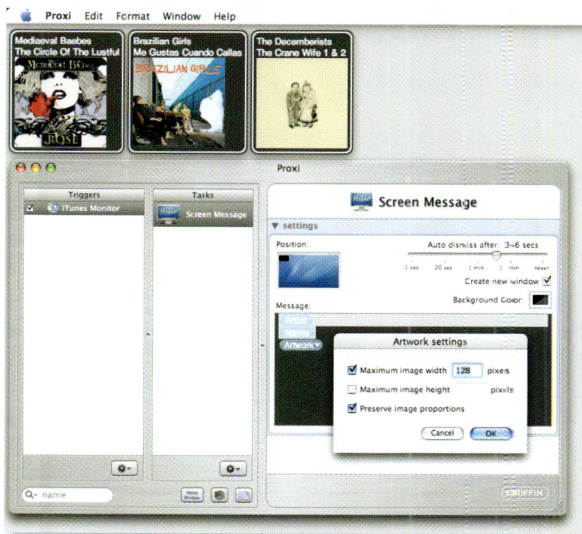

Figure 1.1 *The free Mac application Proxi lets you quickly set up an automation to display currently playing iTunes song titles, artists, and album artwork on your desktop. Three songs are shown at top and the Proxi workflow is below.*

maps of Mars. And you know what? You probably already use automation in your daily life and don't even know it. Do you run through the same routine every day to get ready to leave the house? That's automation. Your alarm clock is the trigger, and you're the input. Getting out of bed, showering, and eating are some of the steps, and an alert, clean you walking out the front door, keys in hand, is the output. It's just another form of automation.

You get to decide whether you want to dip your toe into automation or do a cannonball into the deep end. You can make extraordinary things happen with just five lines of scripting or by building an action in less than a minute, but you can also build full-fledged applications that communicate through the Web and consult databases. You can automate one thing on your desktop or the workflows for an entire graphics group. Getting started with automation is not like starting out with a huge, difficult-to-learn program: Because the process is modular, you can proceed at your own pace, using automation to save five minutes out of the day or making your living by creating automations full time.

Best of all, you can get started for free. Creative Suite is set up to handle scripts and Actions right out of the box. In addition, many free agents are available online, which you can then edit and build upon. Later on, if you decide to go to the next level, you can purchase more robust editors and applications.

So let's get to it: What kinds of things can you automate in Creative Suite? A better question might be what *can't* you automate. In general, you can automate just about any task you can perform manually, plus a few other processes—and all of them will be carried out with greater speed and accuracy. Here are some of the things you can do using automation in the various Creative Suite applications (keep in mind, however, that this is not a definitive list; *there is no definitive list).*

Photoshop. Create files, resize images, apply filters, save in different formats, batch-process folders of images, trigger actions based on events, build multiple versions based on template files, and apply copyright information to multiple files.

Illustrator. Create and edit objects, create and edit text, change attributes (color, position, and so on), find and replace, use Illustrator's data-driven templates, output in different formats, and print and save files.

InDesign. Merge data from text files to create file iterations, export stories or pages, search and replace text, clean up imported text, build calendars, and build catalog pages (**Figure 1.2**).

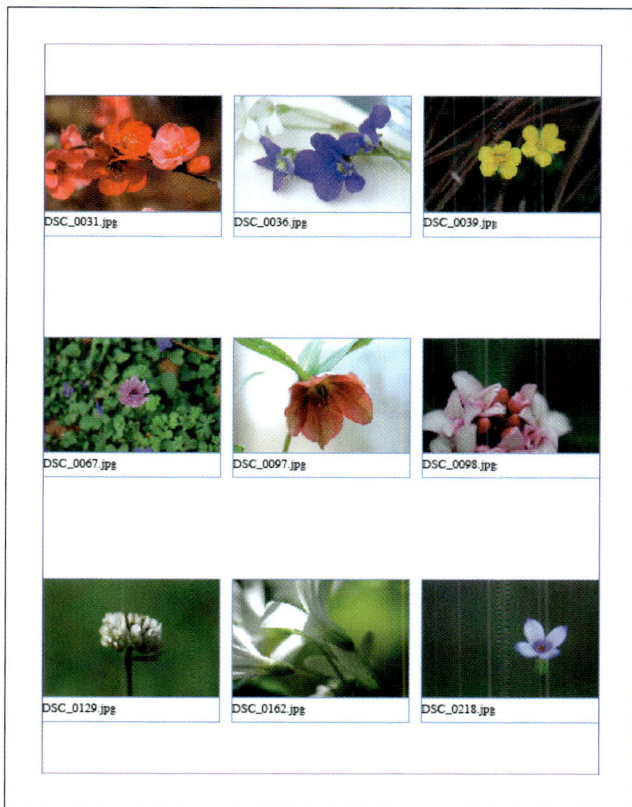

Figure 1.2 *Using a JavaScript included with InDesign (Adobe InDesign CS3 > Scripts > Scripts Panel > Samples > JavaScript > ImageCatalog.jsx), you can create this contact sheet in roughly 12 seconds.*

Now, think about how you could string these individual operations together to make a workflow. Using scripting, for example, you can make two or more programs work in concert—which means that you could edit an image in Photoshop, place it in InDesign, and then output it as a PDF to a watched folder (more on that later), which in turn could send the file to a server halfway across the world. *Amazing stuff.*

To the Laboratory

Automation exists to free you, not enslave you. Your skills are too valuable to be wasted hauling water, as it were. If you work for someone else, that person will benefit, certainly, but it is a shortsighted boss who then uses your saved time to shackle you with even more repetitive work. If you find yourself in this situation, quit immediately and don't look back. Automation is a tool, not a weapon; it exists to ease our workloads, not turn us into automatons. If a tool imposes a condition rather than solves a problem, we're reduced to powerless mice, begging the brooms to stop.

As you pursue your automation tasks, remember that play is essential. Graphics automation is far from an exact science, and many times exploring a few options will hand you the key. If you're of a certain bent, finding the solution to a problem may seem like solving a mystery. There will be clues and evidence (and some red herrings), and it's your job to piece it all together. This may sound strange to you now, but the rush you get from solving that mystery is addictive. Play and explore and try things. It's through this process of discovery that you'll learn new techniques and find solutions you never dreamed of. Just be sure to back up regularly and don't put single-copy files at risk.

You are now the Sorcerer. Think of this book as your workbench and imagine yourself working in your own laboratory. Different animation types surround you like so many potions and beakers bubbling over Bunsen burners. Mix and experiment. Get your hands dirty. Burn a hole in the floor. With a little imagination, a bit of patience, and a willingness to experiment, automation will become your Apprentice.

2

I, Automated Animal

The Robot Within Us

Detective Del Spooner: Can a robot write a symphony? Can a robot take a canvas and turn it into a beautiful masterpiece?

Sonny: Can you?

—*From* I, Robot *(Isaac Asimov)*

Imagine that you've just woken up: You're standing at the bathroom sink about to uncap the toothpaste. You don't hold the tube up, look at the cap, and wonder how it works. You don't try to figure out which way to turn it or what to do with it once you've uncapped it. You don't have to calculate how much pressure to exert on it so it doesn't slip in your grasp. You do not consciously have to give it a thought—in fact, you're probably thinking about something else altogether while you look at your funny hair in the mirror. The uncapping instructions are stored in your brain, there for accessing whenever you need them.

Now imagine that you're driving to work, cruising along listening to the news when suddenly some idiot pulls in front of you, making you swerve into another lane. In that moment—just after your brain registers the danger but before you take evasive action—here is what you do *not* do. You do not make a mental list of the pros and cons of a variety of different maneuvers. You do not plot strategies. You do not call your significant other so that he or she can weigh in on the matter. You act swiftly and without a lot of thought.

As you start to turn the wheel, you don't have to consider which direction to turn, how fast and far to rotate the wheel, or how hard to depress the brake. You don't have to increase your heart rate or release adrenaline into your blood stream or any of the other physiological things that your brain and body do to get you ready to face or flee danger. You don't have to shut all other thoughts out of your mind so that you can concentrate on the task at hand. And the curse words probably spilled out of you without much thought either.

You do all of these things automatically—that is, *without* thinking. The instructions are there (inside you) because you've stored them through experience or instinct. All your brain has to do is access them from memory, loading and running them in the same way a computer program is "run."

We humans are automated to the gills. Without automation, we couldn't reliably uncap our toothpaste in the morning, nor would we be likely to survive the drive to work. We also could not walk or chew or breathe. We couldn't string together the few words it would take to convey even the simplest thought; in fact, we couldn't even create the words.

Despite this, many people feel that automation is somehow outside the experience of being "human." We point at robots and think, "That's where automation exists—outside of me, outside of my experience." And because we regard automation as foreign, we're not interested. Or we fear a loss of control. Designers in particular can be hesitant to hand over control (*cough, control freaks*)—a statement I make with love in my heart because I, too, am a designer and know well that fear.

But it's a fear we must shed because as humans, we rely on automation in the most basic sense. Without automation, we would not have had the time to produce languages, art, scientific research, or even civilizations—all of the things that get to the heart of being human.

Body

To demonstrate how essential automation is to the human condition, I designed an informal experiment that simulates taking control of one of my automated bodily functions. Adult hearts beat somewhere between 60 and 70 times a minute for our entire lives. They speed up when we're in danger, slow down when we're at rest, and compensate for every nuance in between. We generally don't have to give this system a thought—that is, our heartbeat is *automated.*

The Heartbeat Experiment

For my simulation, I wrote a script to show what life would be like if we had to manage our heartbeats (for the full text of the script, see Appendix 1, "The Heartbeat Script"; the audio file is also available for download from www.peachpit.com/apprentice). See **Figure 2.1**. My little script creates an audio file in which two-syllable color names are randomly spoken 60 to 65 times a minute for about 10 minutes (trust me, that's about all you can stand). I then copied that audio file onto my iPod, plugged in the headphones, and headed outdoors on a beautiful fall day. The two syllables of the color names approximate the double-beat of the heart; I chose the color names because I liked the way they sounded. In my simulation, when I heard a color name through my headphones, I repeated it aloud. Since the order of color names spoken was random, I could not anticipate, and therefore mentally automate, the routine; I had to pay attention to the process. In other words, I was putting forth the mental effort required to make my own heart beat.

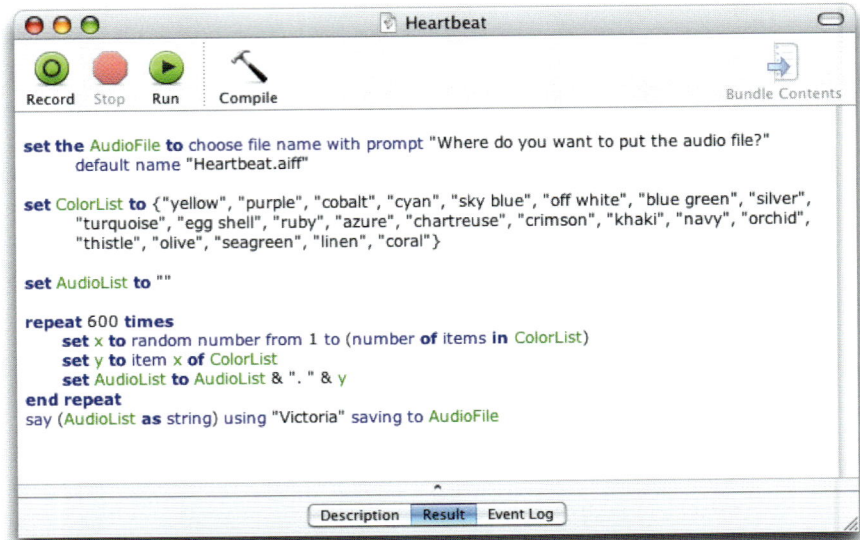

```
set the AudioFile to choose file name with prompt "Where do you want to put the audio file?"
    default name "Heartbeat.aiff"

set ColorList to {"yellow", "purple", "cobalt", "cyan", "sky blue", "off white", "blue green", "silver",
    "turquoise", "egg shell", "ruby", "azure", "chartreuse", "crimson", "khaki", "navy", "orchid",
    "thistle", "olive", "seagreen", "linen", "coral"}

set AudioList to ""

repeat 600 times
    set x to random number from 1 to (number of items in ColorList)
    set y to item x of ColorList
    set AudioList to AudioList & ". " & y
end repeat
say (AudioList as string) using "Victoria" saving to AudioFile
```

Figure 2.1 *This short AppleScript produces a 10-minute-long audio file.*

Picture me wandering about my yard talking to myself. My mind is theoretically engaged in the task of making my heart beat. What else could I do at the same time? I found that I could pet a cat, pick up a cat, walk around (itself an automated function), take the shovel from my wife and dig in the flower bed (ignoring her long-suffering looks as I loudly blathered on), and move some landscaping logs. Not much else.

Here are the things I couldn't do: I couldn't engage in a conversation, do long division, compose a poem, tell a joke, paint a picture, or wax philosophical. I couldn't transcend the maintenance of just one bodily task to do the kinds of cognitive activities we consider "human." I wouldn't have had the time. To explore the concept further, I didn't have to consciously control the muscles it took to pick up the cat (so I didn't, for example, use too much force and throw her over my head). I didn't have to think about how to make my legs move. In fact, if I suddenly had to flee some danger, I probably could not have given enough attention to escaping if I had to increase my heart rate to keep pace with my bodily needs. I probably would have died in the effort, either by not managing my heartbeat properly or by being overtaken by whatever was placing me in danger.

And that's just my heartbeat. Think about breathing, blood pressure, pupil dilation and constriction, digestion, saliva production, and the multitude of other processes deep in your body that are responsible for fighting infections, cell division, and maintaining chemical levels. There's no end to it.

A Bear Steps into the Room

You're sitting quietly, flipping through a book in your living room. Your body is at rest, chugging along at a fairly slow pace. Suddenly a bear steps into the room. (I imagine it walking on its hind legs, but use your own imagination.) Your body is about to automatically undergo an enormous change to prepare you to either take on the bear or lunge through the other door. Everything that happens takes place automatically—and without these automatic responses, you'd be at a huge disadvantage, bear-wise.

In this sequence of events, the first thing you do is stand up to prepare for whatever action you're about to take. At this point you would simply pass out if your body did not automatically compensate for the drop in your blood pressure. While your brain is frantically trying to figure out what to do, your body swings into automated action. Your pupils dilate for better vision. Blood is diverted from your gastrointestinal tract and sent to, among other areas, your skeletal muscles. The bronchioles of your lungs are dilated, and you're now able to take in more oxygen. Your heart rate goes up while your saliva production goes down (resulting in dry mouth). Your adrenal glands dump adrenaline into your blood stream, and your blood-glucose level increases.

You are now literally loaded for bear. All of this bodily automation is within you so you will live another day and have the opportunity to propagate your species. Our bodies are too complex for us to run on the conscious level, so we must rely on automation for our survival.

Mind

We've now seen that many biological processes are automated to keep us alive and freed up for complex tasks. Some higher brain functions, however, are also automated—at least to a degree.

Habits

Instructions like those we use to uncap the toothpaste are stored in a fist-sized part of the brain called the basal ganglia (which is nestled under the cortex). This is where higher thinking occurs, according to research conducted by Ann M. Graybiel of the Department of Brain and Cognitive Sciences at Massachusetts Institute of Technology. More commonly referred to as habits, these instruction sets are called up out of memory and run much like a computer automation agent.

According to Graybiel, our habits give us the freedom to respond to novel situations. These stored instructions—which Graybiel calls "chunks"—permit us to carry out some actions with barely a thought. This is automation, and these "chunks" are our automation agents.

Instincts

What we commonly refer to as instincts trigger emotions, produce the startle reflex, and imbue in us the drive to survive. These are not learned responses; instead, instincts are stored somewhere in our brains and are triggered in response to various stimuli. They are not interpreted by the conscious mind and therefore tend to be immediate, swift, and strong. Because they are unmediated, these instincts, or instructions, can seem to come out of nowhere—as if set in motion by someone or something apart from ourselves. These instructions are our system-level automations.

Multitasking

We're all pushed to do more than one thing at a time, both in our jobs and in our personal lives. Can we work on a report and answer someone's questions over the phone simultaneously? Can we watch the evening news and fold clothes all at once?

Take the proverbial joke about walking and chewing gum at the same time: It illustrates that we're constantly multitasking. While we're driving we think

about a project we've just been handed that morning. As we listen to someone talk to us, we're formulating our response. And when we're walking with a
friend, we're also engaging in conversation with that person.

If we weren't able to automate one or more of these tasks, we'd have to do
everything—and I mean *everything*—sequentially.

Spirit: Rituals and Repetition

Humans often find repetition comforting on a spiritual level—and sometimes
that type of repetition (which often takes place without conscious thought)
can resemble automation. Take, for example the mundane ritual of me making and drinking my morning coffee. The sheer repetition and sameness of
it gives me a small comfort, a momentary safe harbor from what I imagine
to be the trials of the day ahead. I can go through all of the steps it takes to
grind and brew the beans and then drink the coffee without giving it much, if
any, thought.

Is this automation? I must admit I'm a bit uncomfortable implying it is—a dis-
comfort, I believe, that stems from the idea that automation is somehow dehumanizing and dispiriting. Automation is dehumanizing, the thinking goes,
because it somehow negates the essence of what we feel makes us human. It's
dispiriting because spirit is what we define as that essence. Because automation has no soul, it's thought to be outside the human experience.

But in practice, spirituality and religion are rife with repetitive actions—the
repeated recitation of religious texts or mantras, the repetitive motion of
walking meditations, the Sufi spinning of the Whirling Dervishes, the highly
structured and repetitive rituals of religious and spiritual services, rites, and
ceremonies.

Many of these activities are performed over and over until they're carried out
without thought—which is exactly the point: to put the body or logical mind
in a kind of holding pattern so that we don't have to care for them. This in
turn sets us free to transcend to loftier thoughts and experiences.

Repetition also provides the comfort of the familiar: We're soothed by the
knowledge that we won't have to deal with the unexpected for some period
of time.

Free to Be Human

It is my contention, then, that automation is at the very heart of our "human-ness"—which is not to say we should behave more like robots. Instead, we should look kindly on our internal automations. Without them, we would not have the time or energy to aspire to any of the qualities we cherish as humans. They are what make humanness possible.

Automation does not provide the answer to everything, just as the application of logic can't solve every problem. It does, however, help us get on with the task of being us. And isn't being us hard enough? Can't we use all the help we can get?

II

Tools

Graphics automation tools for Creative Suite (including actions, scripting, Automator, data-driven publishing, server-based applications, and third-party programs) might seem like a motley crew. Each has its own goals, routes, and hidden powers—and weaknesses. As a group, though, they form an incredibly flexible and adaptable toolkit.

You could do worse than an action (in Photoshop or Illustrator) as a place to start exploring graphics automation. Actions contain the essence of a great graphics automation tool. They are fast and easy to build, maintain, and troubleshoot, and they serve up their structure in a beautifully simple set of stacked boxes. Each box is highlighted as it plays back what you have told it to do.

All of these tools seek to mimic a human's actions and thinking, only faster and more accurately. They enact these processes on files, whether they have recorded our physical actions or we have programmed them. They are, fundamentally, our robots.

3

A Call to Actions

Creative Suite's Native Automation Tool

Action is eloquence.

—*From* Coriolanus *(William Shakespeare)*

Actions are Creative Suite's version of application macros—mechanisms that record and play back the steps a user performs manually. Able to act on both single files and (in Batch mode) multiple files, actions are easy to create, edit, and use, and they provide a great introduction to automation.

Actions are perfect for smaller automation routines that don't require a great deal of customization, such as a typical Photoshop workflow of resizing, cropping, and changing the resolution and color space of a small batch of images. Using an action, you can quickly and easily record the steps you perform manually for the first file and then automatically play the action back for the remainder of the images.

You can also halt actions and allow user input. And since actions can trigger scripts (and scripts can trigger actions), actions can communicate (to some degree) with other applications. Actions are available in Photoshop and Illustrator but not, unfortunately, in InDesign. (Some reasons for this are that page layout tends to be less repetitive than image preparation, and InDesign has its own automation tools that handle some of what actions do.)

To create an action, you simply open the Photoshop or Illustrator file you want to use and then open the Actions panel, push the Record button, and perform whatever tasks you wish to automate. When you're finished, push the Stop button. When you want to apply those same steps to another file, all you need to do is choose the action from the menu in the Actions panel and press Play. What can be even more useful is the ability to apply an action to an entire folder of files as a batch.

Occasionally, you'll need to edit an action to correct small mistakes or adapt it to new workflows. To do so, you simply drag and drop the action's steps (or commands) to change their order and double-click to modify them. You can also save actions to a file so that you can share them with colleagues or friends.

Actions are perfect for throwing together quick automations: They aren't nearly as difficult to create and maintain as scripts, and thanks to their ability to process batches and pause for user input, they can serve as flexible and powerful automation agents.

The Reflecto Action Tutorial

As you proceed through this tutorial, you'll learn how to write and edit your own actions by creating a Photoshop action that produces an image reflection (like the effect that's used in a lot of Apple's advertising and marketing materials). The effect makes an image appear to be sitting on a shiny surface (**Figure 3.1**).

Figure 3.1 The finished product of the Reflecto action. You can adjust the length of the reflection in the action.

For this tutorial, you'll be working with the Layer Comps.psd image, which is located in Photoshop's Samples folder. Save this file as Reflecto.psd in your documents folder. Once you've done this, hide both the "text" and "votive" layer sets (by clicking the Eye icons next to the layer names in the Layers palette) and flatten the image (Layers palette > Flatten Image). You should now have an image that's 4 inches wide by 4.24 inches high at 100 pixels per inch. You can copy and paste any image you like into this file for the tutorial—just make sure to flatten it before proceeding; if you fail to do so, the action won't work. Save this image as Reflecto.psd.

Creating a New Action Set

Begin setting up your action by creating a new action set—which you can think of as a folder that will contain different actions. Sets are useful both in organizing your actions and when it comes time to save them (since actions can only be saved in sets). To open the Actions panel (if it's not already open in Photoshop), choose Window > Actions. To create a new action set, click the Actions panel menu arrow and choose New Set. Name this set Reflecto Set (**Figure 3.2**).

Figure 3.2 *To access the Actions panel menu, click the menu icon in the top-right corner.*

Creating a New Action

Now it's time to create the Reflecto action. To do so, go to the Actions panel menu and choose New Action (**Figure 3.3**). In the New Action window that appears, name your action Reflecto and make sure that Reflecto is selected in the Set pull-down menu (**Figure 3.4**). When you click the Record button, Photoshop will begin recording most of your mouse movements and menu selections into this new action; it continues to record until you click the Stop button.

Figure 3.4 *The New Action window.*

Figure 3.3 *To create a new action,*
from the Actions panel choose New Action.

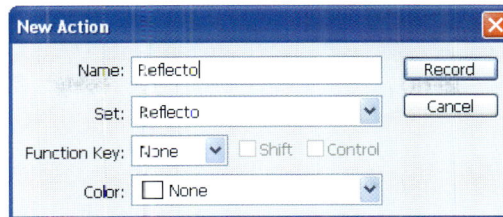

Recording the Action

Here are the steps you'll record to create the Reflecto action.

1. Double-click the single layer named Background, and in the New Layer
    window that appears rename that layer Original.

    The Background layer is a special kind of layer: As such, it cannot contain
    transparency or be moved from its position at the bottom of the layers
    stack. By renaming it, we're converting it to a regular layer.

2. Set the canvas size (Image > Canvas Size) height to 120% with the anchor
    at the top center (**Figure 3.5**), and then click OK.

    This will give you the space at the bottom for the reflection.

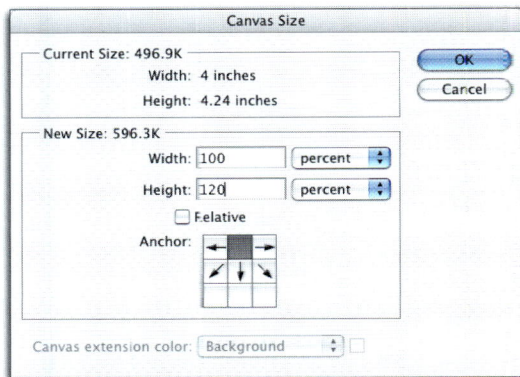

Figure 3.5 *The Canvas Size command gives the image space at the*
bottom for the reflection. You can change the percentage or make it
an absolute size by specifying pixels or inches.

3. Set the canvas size again to give the image a nice border by giving it 115% for both the width and height, and set the anchor in the middle (**Figure 3.6**). Your image should now look like **Figure 3.7**.

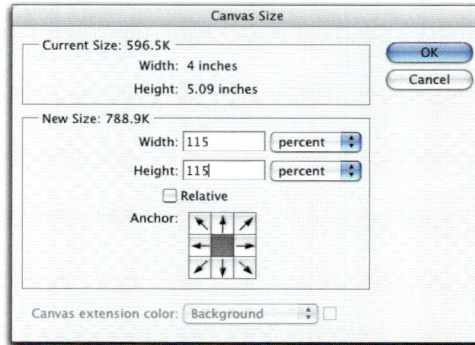

Figure 3.6 *The second Canvas Size gives the image a border. Specifying percentages makes this action more adaptable to other image sizes. Using absolute measurements would restrict this command to the size of the tutorial image.*

Figure 3.7 *The Reflecto tutorial image after setting the second Canvas Size.*

4. Create a new layer (Layer > New > Layer), double-click it, and name it Background. Now drag it below the Original layer (**Figure 3.8**).

5. With the Background layer still selected, fill it (Edit > Fill) with black (**Figure 3.9**).

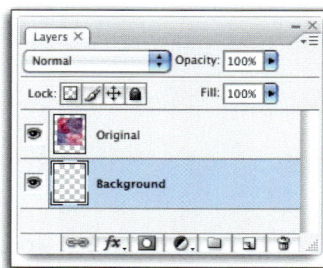

Figure 3.8 *After creating and naming the Background layer, click and drag it so that it appears under the layer named Original. Note that you could have also created the new layer by clicking the second icon from the right at the bottom of the Layers panel (the one that looks like a turning page).*

Figure 3.9 *After completing Step 5, your image should look like this.*

6. In the Layers palette, click the Original layer to select it, then duplicate it (Layer> Duplicate Layer) and name it Reflection.

   This layer will eventually become the reflection at the bottom.

7. With the Reflection layer still selected, flip it (Edit > Transform > Flip Vertical). Then, using the Move tool, drag this flipped layer until its top snaps to the bottom of the Original layer (**Figure 3.10**).

8. Using the slider at the top of the Layers panel, set the opacity of the Reflection layer to 60% (**Figure 3.11**).

   This will give you a nice reflection, but you still need to make it fade out toward the bottom of the image.

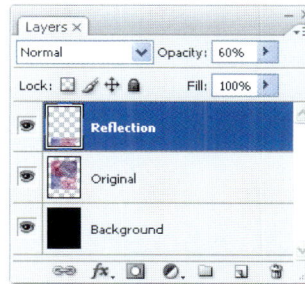

Figure 3.11

Figure 3.10 *You can start to see how this effect is coming together. The flipped duplicate layer will, with some tweaking, become the shiny reflection.*

9. Create a new layer (Layer > New > Layer) and name it Gradient.

10. Press the D key.

    This will reset the Foreground and Background swatches to the default black and white.

11. Select the Gradient tool, making sure that Linear Gradient is selected (**Figure 3.12**).

12. With the Gradient layer still selected, click in the Document window with the Gradient tool, starting about a quarter-inch from the bottom and dragging up to where the Original and Reflection layers meet (**Figure 3.13**).

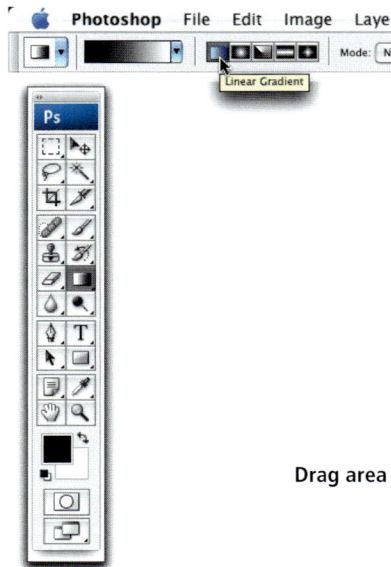

Drag area

Figure 3.12 Note that the action does not record you selecting the Gradient tool, only the gradient you draw. Make sure you select Linear Gradient from the Tool Options bar.

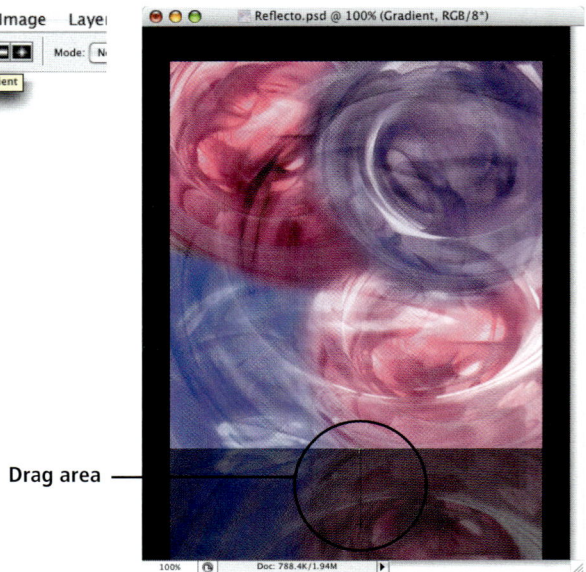

Figure 3.13 Using the Gradient tool, I started about a quarter-inch from the bottom and dragged up to where the two image layers meet. You might want to adjust this for a larger and stronger reflection.

13. In the Layers palette, set the Gradient layer's Blending Mode to Multiply (**Figure 3.14**).

14. To halt recording, click Stop.

Congratulations—you're finished! The Reflecto action should look like **Figure 3.15**.

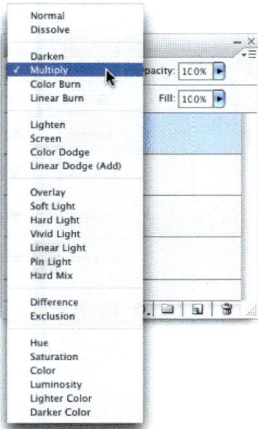

Figure 3.14 *The Blending Mode options determine how one layer's pixels blend with the layer beneath it. The Multiply option just happened to give me the effect I was after.*

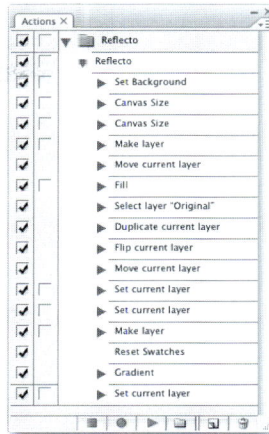

Figure 3.15 *The Reflecto action in all its glory: It's interesting to see your physical actions captured in distinct steps. Thinking in steps helps you plan automations.*

Playing Back the Action

To activate an action, select it and click the Play button at the bottom of the Actions panel (**Figure 3.16**). Note that the action you recorded in the tutorial only works with an original image the size of the one used in the tutorial. As the action plays, notice how the successive steps (or commands) are highlighted as they're carried out.

You have a number of options for playing back actions, all of which you can access via Actions panel menu > Playback Options (**Figure 3.17**). The three options that appear under Performance determine how fast an action runs. The Accelerated option (the default) plays an action without updating the file onscreen until it is completed. The Step by Step option redraws the screen

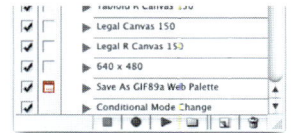

Figure 3.16 *The following buttons are lined up along the bottom of the Actions panel (from the left): Stop, Record, Play, New Set, New Action, and Delete.*

Figure 3.17 *You'll probably use the Accelerated performance option most often.*

Tip

If your actions seem to be running slowly, select the Accelerated option.

at every step, which is interesting to watch but slower. And the third option ("Pause For: [ ] seconds") allows you to set the number of seconds that an action will pause between commands. This option, like Step by Step, redraws the screen at each command. These last two options can be useful for building a self-running tutorial of sorts.

The last setting among the Playback Options—the Pause For Audio Annotation check box—is an interesting one. Audio annotations are sound files you can record using the Audio Annotation tool in Photoshop (but not Illustrator). Generally, voice annotations are used to communicate some special circumstances about the file. You can record an action command to play back an audio annotation. First, record an audio annotation (see Chapter 9 on Photoshop projects). Once you've done this, a small, nonprinting icon of a speaker will appear next to the image. As you're recording an action, double-click the icon at the point where you want it to play. If you have Pause For Audio Annotation checked, the action will pause and wait for the audio to finish before proceeding to the next command. You can create fairly sophisticated self-running tutorials and slide shows with voice-overs using this feature.

Editing Your Action

At some point you will undoubtedly need to edit your action to get it to run the way you want—for example, adding commands that weren't recordable, adapting the action for specific situations, or simply changing your mind about how you want it to perform. The following subsections demonstrate how you can adapt your actions.

ADDING COMMANDS

In the same Reflecto action you created earlier, you'll now record a command to add copyright information to the file's metadata.

1. Click the last command in the Reflecto action ("Set current layer") and then click the Record button (the circle at the bottom of the Actions panel).

   Photoshop will now begin recording again and append any new commands.

> **Tip**
>
> Activities that can't be recorded in an action include painting and drawing, setting tool options, making certain tool selections, and carrying out View and Window commands (among others). If your action missed recording a step in your task, from the Actions panel menu choose Insert Menu Item and then choose the appropriate command or option from the application pull-down menus.

2. Open the file's metadata by choosing File > File Info. In the left pane make sure that Description is selected. Now, from the Copyright Status pull-down menu, choose Copyrighted and in the Copyright Notice box type © 2007 Julie A. Wilson (**Figure 3.18**).

While you can enter any text you like, for this example I'm using the copyright information for the photographer who took the pictures that will be used in the Batch feature (explored later in this chapter).

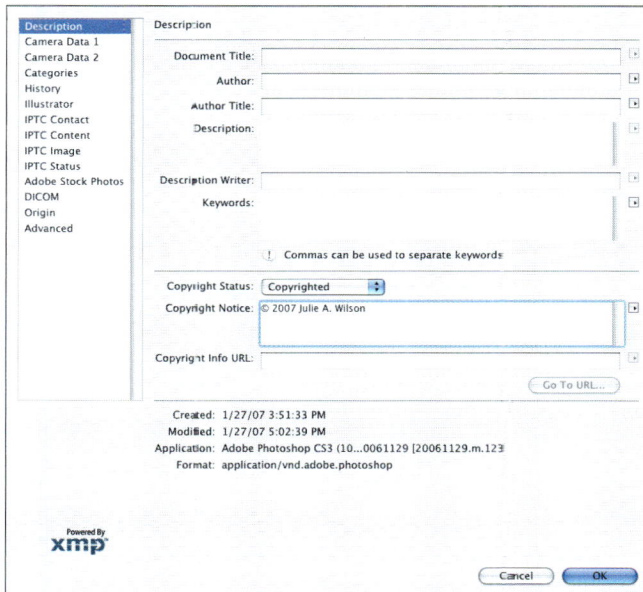

Figure 3.18 Each item in the pane on the left represents a metadata category. If you import digital photos, the Camera Data 1 and Camera Data 2 fields will display metadata recorded by the camera along with the shot.

In addition to the above, there are three other ways to add commands to an action. To add unrecorded commands, from the Actions panel menu select Insert Menu Item, to bring up a dialog box that will instruct you to select a menu item. When you select one, it's added to the dialog box.

Another way to add commands is to copy them from another action by dragging and dropping. And finally, you can duplicate a command (Actions panel > Duplicate), which you can then drag to where you want it to take place in your action workflow. After moving the command, you can double-click it to open and change its settings (if it has options).

Tip

The term *metadata*—which you'll hear from time to time in your Creative Suite work—means "data about data" and usually refers to text describing the data file in which it resides. For example, digital photo files often contain metadata describing the date they were captured, the camera they were taken with, their pixel dimensions, and more. You can view the various types of metadata that Photoshop lets you store by choosing File > File Info. Some workflow tools can act on a file based on its metadata (for example, routing a file or applying a setting).

Note

Since the Reflecto action produces layered files, you might want to add a command to flatten the image (Layers panel > Flatten Image) at the end.

Figure 3.19 To reorder commands, click and drag them, releasing the commands when the new location is highlighted with a black bar.

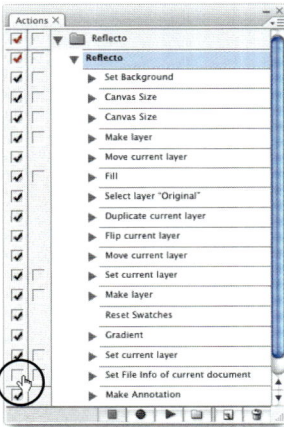

Figure 3.20 If you don't want to add copyright metadata to every image or batch of images, you could delete this command; however, it probably makes more sense to simply turn it off.

DELETING AND MOVING COMMANDS

You can delete commands from an action by selecting them and doing one of three things: choosing Delete from the Actions panel menu, dragging the command onto the Trash icon at the bottom of the Actions panel, or clicking the Trash icon. (Dragging the command onto the Trash icon is the only one of these three methods that doesn't bring up a dialog box asking if you really want to delete.) You can select more than one command to delete by holding down the Shift key for adjacent commands or the Command key for nonadjacent commands.

You can also reorder commands by clicking and dragging them to their new locations. When the divider line is highlighted in the spot where you want the command to be carried out, release the mouse button (**Figure 3.19**).

TOGGLING COMMANDS

You can turn individual commands on and off by clicking the check boxes to the left of their names. This is a great way to test your actions or to customize them for different uses. You can also turn complete actions and action sets on and off with the toggle box, though this seems to have limited uses.

Let's say that you don't want to include the copyright metadata in some images. Select the check box to the far left of the command name to deselect it (**Figure 3.20**).

INSERTING STOPS

Sometimes you'll need to halt an action and get input from the user—usually either to perform a step that can't be recorded (such as selecting part of an image or painting with the Brush tool) or to enter a value. Your Stop command can display a message to users directing them to take the required step.

Let's assume that the Reflecto action will be used on images of different sizes from our tutorial original. If you look back to the Reflecto action setup, you'll see that the canvas size was changed using percentages instead of pixels (making the action more flexible). However, the gradient can't be sized that way; it has to be drawn by hand. Thus, you will now turn off the Gradient command and insert a Stop command so that users can set custom gradients before letting the action run its course.

1. In the left column of the Actions panel deselect the toggle check box for the Gradient command.

2. Click the Reset Swatches command (directly above the Gradient command) to highlight it, and from the Actions panel menu choose Insert Stop. In the blank message window that appears, type the user instructions, in this case telling users to draw their own custom gradients (**Figure 3.21**).

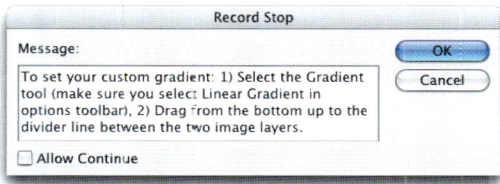

Figure 3.21 It's a good idea to provide instructions (or some kind of message) for the user when creating a Stop command.

Now, when the user plays this action, he or she will see your message dialog box and know to click the Stop button in the message window, set a gradient, and click the Play button in the Actions panel.

You can also use stops to display information about an action—for example, explaining a step's purpose. The Allow Continue check box at the bottom of the Record Stop window lets users read the message and then click Continue to let the action proceed. Take care, however, to use these "informational" stops only when absolutely necessary: Users will quickly become irritated if an action is interrupted repeatedly. And if a user has to be present to close the dialog box, the advantages of automation are mostly negated.

USING MODAL CONTROLS

Some commands have associated dialog boxes. For instance, when you record the steps you take to fill a selection with the foreground color, the command records the settings you choose. However, you can change those settings when you run the action again by double-clicking the command, which opens its associated dialog box. In this way you can customize actions for different uses without re-recording them.

To pause your action so that users can enter needed information, click the check box in the second column from the left, next to the affected command (**Figure 3.22**). This is known as the Modal Control box: When you enable modal control, a boxy-looking icon appears. (I'm not sure what the icon is supposed to look like, but it refers to a dialog box.)

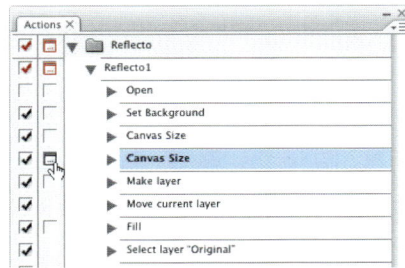

Figure 3.22 *When you check a command's Modal Control box, the action halts and the user is presented with a dialog box, where he or she can enter custom values. The user must then click the OK button to proceed.*

You'll use modal controls when a command needs to be customized for each image on which you run your action, such as when you need to use different Save settings or if you don't always merge layers when converting from RGB to CMYK. Like stops, modal controls should be used sparingly because they halt the action and await user input (which of course requires the user to be present).

To get a feel for how modal controls work, imagine that your users need to set a custom border for each image: To facilitate this, activate the modal control for the second Canvas Size command by clicking the empty box next to it.

Running Batch Actions

Running actions on individual files is a huge time-saver in and of itself; however, you can save even more time by using the Batch feature in Photoshop and Illustrator. Using the Batch feature lets you not only run an action on an entire folder of files at once, it also lets you rename the files (in the same operation).

In Photoshop you access the Batch feature by choosing File > Automate > Batch (**Figure 3.23**); in Illustrator you choose Batch from the Actions panel menu (**Figure 3.24**).

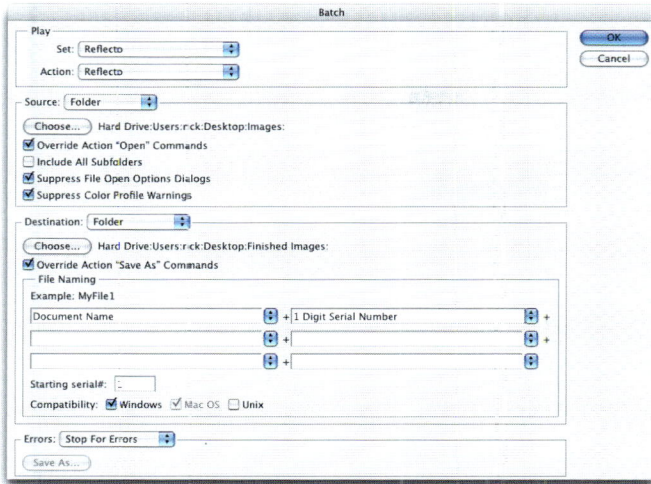

Figure 3.23 Photoshop's Batch window.

Figure 3.24 *Illustrator's Batch window doesn't have the elaborate File Naming section found in Photoshop's Batch window.*

1. Choose Actions panel menu > Start Recording (or click the Record button) to start recording again and then open any file. Click the Stop button to stop recording. The Open command will appear at the bottom of the list; click and drag it to the top, making it the first command (**Figure 3.25**).

2. Start recording again and from the File menu choose Save As and then save the file anywhere. (It doesn't matter where you save because you'll be overriding that choice in the Batch window.) Now close the file and click the Stop button.

   You are now finished with the action and ready to run a Batch.

3. Open the Batch window in Photoshop (File > Automate > Batch), and in both the Set and Action pull-down menus (at the top of the window), choose Reflecto. Set Source to Folder and click Choose to locate and select the folder that contains your batch of images. Make sure your settings match the default settings shown in Figure 3.23.

   You'll probably want to create a new folder for the processed images; also note your file-naming options here. At the bottom of the window, Batch lets you indicate whether you want it to halt when it encounters an error or continue on its merry way, making note of the problem in a log file of your choosing.

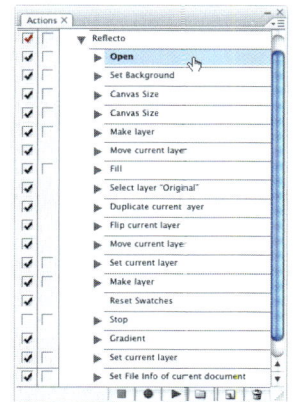

Figure 3.25 *After you record the Open command, drag it to the top of the list.*

Note

The Image Processor in Photoshop (File > Scripts > Image Processor) is another way to run actions in batch mode (see the "Mom Likes Photoshop Best" sidebar in Chapter 5). The only advantage to running an action in batch mode from here is if it would benefit from running in tandem with Image Processor's strengths in converting file formats and resizing images.

4. Click OK.

   Figure 3.26 displays the results of running the Reflecto action on six photographs of flowers.

Figure 3.26 *The results of running the Reflecto action as a batch on six images.*

Action Management

By taking advantage of the tools Photoshop and Illustrator offer for actions and action sets, you can customize the Actions panel, color-code actions, tidy up the Action panel (by only displaying the actions and sets you need), and save and distribute actions and sets to friends and coworkers.

Saving and Loading Action Sets

Since you can lose actions if Photoshop or Illustrator crashes (or if you accidentally choose Replace or Reset Actions), it's a good idea to get in the habit of saving all new actions you create. To do this, you must save the entire set containing the action; however, there's no real downside to saving a whole set at a time.

To save a new action, from the Actions panel menu choose Save Actions and then save the file wherever you wish. To load an action set, choose Load Actions from the same menu.

Tip

Take care when using the Replace Actions command—or even better, don't use it at all. When executed, this command replaces all action sets in the current document, which means you could easily lose your unsaved actions.

Sharing

Saved sets are basically text files, so you can share them with friends and colleagues. One of the great things about actions is that they're cross-platform—which means they get along well in today's mixed-platform environments.

Droplets

Droplets provide a means of saving an action in Batch mode into a small application. In fact, the Create Droplet window appears virtually identical to the Batch window (shown in Figure 3.23). You simply drag a file (or files) onto the Droplet icon to run the batch operation. You can create more than one and place them on the Desktop or anywhere, really—even in the Dock on the Mac (**Figure 3.27**). But (teeth clenched) droplets are available only in Photoshop and Acrobat, not Illustrator and certainly not InDesign.

Figure 3.27 *Drop a file or files on the droplet, and it will launch Photoshop (if it's not already open) and run your action with the batch settings.*

To create a droplet, choose File > Automate > Create Droplet (**Figure 3.28**), and the Create Droplet window will appear. The settings here will be the same as those you used to create a batch (see the Running Batch Actions section earlier in this chapter); however, you must also select a location and name for the droplet.

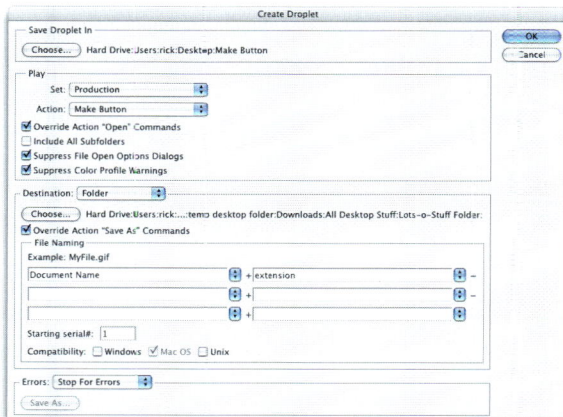

Figure 3.28 *The Create Droplet window.*

Clearing, Resetting, and Replacing Actions

Though handy, the following commands for clearing, resetting, and replacing actions can wipe out your hard work if you don't save often. Thus, you should always think twice before pressing any of these buttons.

Clearing actions (Actions panel menu > Clear All Actions) does just what it says—which means that if you haven't saved an action, it's gone. If you need to delete certain actions or sets, select them and choose Actions panel menu > Delete. You can also delete actions by dragging them to the Actions panel trash can or selecting them and clicking the trash can.

Resetting actions (Actions panel menu > Reset Actions) sets the actions in the Actions panel to the default set that came with the program—which means you stand to lose any unsaved action sets, so be very careful. Like some of the other features associated with actions, I can't imagine ever actually using this feature.

Replacing actions (Actions panel menu > Replace Actions) replaces all the current action sets in the panel with another of your choosing. This is another feature I can't really envision using; however, if you do, keep in mind that it will wipe out any unsaved action sets.

Button Mode and Color Coding

If you work with a lot of actions and need to access them quickly, Button mode might be just the thing for you. When you select Button Mode from the Actions panel menu, that panel's appearance changes into a panel of colored buttons (**Figure 3.29**). Each button represents an action and is displayed in whatever color you choose to associate with that action (select the action, then choose Actions panel menu > Action Options).

This is a great way to visually organize sets of actions. Note, however, that you have to take the Actions panel out of Button mode to do anything other than run the actions. To edit an action, deselect Button Mode in the Actions panel and return to Normal mode.

Figure 3.29 In Button mode you can visually organize actions by selecting one of eight available colors.

Advanced Actions

So far, you've learned four ways to start an action: by choosing it and clicking Play, by using the Batch feature, by dragging a file onto a droplet, and by using Photoshop's Image Processor. Now you can go beyond the basics and put actions to work with even less effort.

One way to do so is to assign your action a Function key (commonly referred to as F keys) by selecting the action, choosing Action panel > Action Options, and then choosing a Function key from the Function Key pull-down menu (**Figure 3.30**). When you now press the Function key, an action will be triggered—just as if you had pressed the Play button (as long as the Function key you chose doesn't conflict with system-assigned Function keys such as F12, which is assigned to Dashboard widgets by default on Mac OS X).

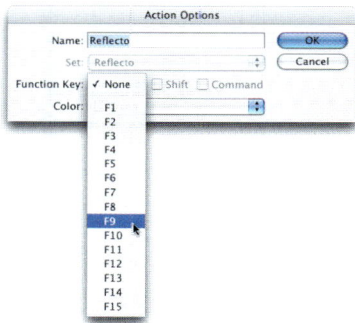

Figure 3.30 *The Action Options window is where you can set a Function key to trigger your action as well as assign a color code to your action.*

If you want to go one better with your automation, you can have Photoshop trigger an action based on events. The program's Script Events Manager (File > Scripts > Script Events Manager) can trigger scripts or actions when certain events occur, such as whenever Photoshop starts, quits, or opens a file. This option could come in handy for adding copyright information to every image opened or converting every image from RGB to CMYK. Or in a multiuser work environment, you might want Photoshop to load your chosen workspace when the application starts. The Script Events Manager comes loaded with 7 events, but more than 200 are available (they're listed in the appendix of the JavaScript Reference Guide installed with Photoshop).

Note

For in-depth information on linking scripts to actions, see the individual scripting guides that came with Photoshop (in the Scripting Guide folder) and Illustrator (Scripting > Documentation folder).

Triggering Scripts

Although you've learned a few tricks for adapting actions to Photoshop files with different characteristics—including relative values, modal controls, and inserting stops—actions are actually fairly limited in their flexibility. In addition, actions may be cross-platform, but they're not cross-application—which means you can't run a Photoshop application in Illustrator or vice versa (nor would you want to), and an action can't send instructions to any other application, such as an e-mail program or compression utility. Actions can, however, be triggered by external scripts (and vice versa).

To incorporate a script into an action, first create the script and place it in the Presets > Scripts folders for the same application as your action. The script should appear in the submenu accessed via File > Scripts. If you don't see it, you'll need to restart the application.

To add a trigger for the script to your action, highlight the command you want the script to follow, and from the Actions panel menu choose Insert Menu Item. Then choose File > Scripts and select your script. That's it.

Keep in mind that scripting is more difficult to learn and requires more setup and testing than writing actions. The upside, though, is that scripts let you handle varying conditions in a workflow and can operate across more than one application. For more detail on working with scripts, see Chapter 4.

4

Behind the Curtain

Scripting in Creative Suite

Trust that little voice in your head that says, "Wouldn't it be interesting if?" And then do it.

—*Photographer Duane Michals*

Do you remember the scene in *The Wizard of Oz* in which Toto pulls back the curtain to reveal the man/wizard operating levers behind it? As a kid, what caught my attention wasn't the revelation or the treachery of the man; it was those levers. They were the tickets to doing wonderful wizardish things. If only I knew how to move those levers, I could escape all the indignities of childhood, I thought. Pull this one, push that one, and the world would be my marionette—a seductive idea for a kid. And to tell you the truth, I didn't even care about how the levers were operated. What mattered to me was knowing that they existed and where they were. Naturally, I assumed, there was a manual tucked away somewhere.

If you could peel back the interface of a Creative Suite program, as if sweeping aside curtains, you would see little packets of instructions zipping all over the place. These packets are Creative Suite's invisible levers. When you click a button in the interface, for instance, behind the curtain a command is shot to its target. What you see on the screen of a program is its graphical user interface (GUI), which consists of the file you're working on, panels, dialog boxes, and the informational windows that are occasionally presented to the user. All of this appears onscreen for our benefit—both to collect information from us and to provide feedback about what the program is up to.

We use this GUI to communicate with the program and it with us. However, we humans—even after a couple of cups of coffee—are a relatively slow and distractible lot, so the process can be less than efficient. It involves perceiving what's onscreen, making decisions based on those perceptions, and then applying hand-eye coordination to move the mouse and press the keys. Think of the time it takes (and the dialogs you have to wade through) just to launch a program, find and open a document, locate and edit text, replace a photograph, and then save and close the document.

What if instead all you had to do was send the program a simple message stating something like the following: "Open the program; open that file; change this text; replace that picture; and then save and close"? There'd be no clicking of icons or buttons, no reading and responding to dialog boxes, no navigating the document, and no keystrokes.

Sending a program messages in this way is hundreds of times faster than manually performing the described steps. These messages can "think" and make decisions on the fly just like we do, only faster and with far more accuracy. What's more, such messages can be modular (with parts reused in other messages), and they can be sent based upon certain circumstances—meaning you don't even have to be there to trigger them.

What Is Scripting Really?

Write down the steps you take to do something—feed the cat, do the laundry, check e-mail, anything. Include every little step. Then edit your words down to a set of bare-bones statements: *Do this; make that decision; take that action.* What you're left with will look surprisingly similar to a script. Providing a kind of shorthand, or to-do list of what it takes to complete a task or series of tasks (a workflow), scripts can be used to control existing applications.

The main difference between programming and scripting is that programming is used to *create* applications, while scripting is used to *control* them. Since the Macintosh and Windows operating systems are, in fact, applications, you can use scripting to control them as well.

Now, let's revisit the hypothetical example of feeding the cat: You go to the pantry to get the cat food. *If* there isn't any, *then* you go to the store to buy some more. Otherwise, you proceed to put the food in the bowl. That's logic: If this, then that. Although other forms of logic exist, the if/then statement is the type most often used in scripting. Logic provides a means of distilling your thought processes so that you can turn your scripts into "mini-yous," applying the decisions you would make—only a lot faster and far more accurately.

> **Note**
>
> Logic allows your scripts to assess and respond to different situations. Your job is to anticipate the situations a script might encounter and write them into your scripts. Compared with the logic we apply in the "real world," scripting logic is limited in scope. But remember: Scripts live in a far simpler environment than we do. Thus, the logic applied to them doesn't need to be nearly as robust.

Why Would You Want to Script?

The phrase "to automate repetitive work" has become the mantra of the "scripterati," and I've used the phrase as much as anyone. But I've begun to think it probably causes people's eyes to glaze over. Instead, I've started comparing writing and running scripts to text messaging: Like text messaging, scripting uses its own language, is text based, and is often used to get the entity on the other end to do something (such as answer a question or complete a task). Sending someone a message in text form is often faster than talking to that person face-to-face; the same is true for scripting.

Scripting is the most fascinating of all the graphics automation tools. Opening a portal into the inner workings of the familiar graphics applications that designers know and sometimes love, scripting gives designers newfound power over their workspaces. For those of a certain bent, it also provides an entree into the exclusive clubhouse of programming. Like preparing gourmet cuisine or building a robot, scripting involves assembling parts, tinkering, experimenting, and testing.

In addition to automating soul-draining repetitive tasks, scripts can be used to:

- Perform jobs that are difficult or time-consuming to do manually, such as sorting large lists

- Set up self-running automation agents that respond to requests or react to situations

- Make multiple applications act in concert—for example, automatically editing an image in Photoshop and then placing it in a brochure layout in InDesign

- Create "watched folder" systems that trigger a script when files are added to a folder (AppleScript)

- Create automated solutions that work equally well on Macs and PCs (JavaScript)

- Add logic to automated agents

- Perform complex calculations automatically

- Serve as a stepping stone to building actual applications (AppleScript and AppleScript Studio)

- Ease the process of learning more complex programming languages
- Write custom Automator actions (AppleScript)

Although you can use scripts to perform small single tasks, that's not what they're generally used for. Since creating, testing, and maintaining scripts is a more involved process than using Creative Suite actions or general productivity tools like QuicKeys, scripts tend to be reserved for longer, more complicated workflows.

What Is Scripting Like?

Scripting represents a conversation between you and an application, its documents, and the objects inside those documents. Via the script, you ask questions, issue commands, and decide on courses of action. As objects, the application and its components respond to your questions and commands. Scripting involves asking, thinking, and telling—pretty much what humans are capable of on a good day. Although scripting may appear cryptic at first glance, when you dig a little deeper you'll find that it's actually quite human-like, replicating human actions and at least some human thinking.

When you boil it down, scripts spend a lot of time directing commands to particular objects, which they identify via their unique addresses. To understand how this works, let's consider your own mailing address, which (assuming you live in the United States) includes the following:

    Your Name
    House Number, Street
    City, State, Zip

If you were to state your mailing address in a way that made sense to a computer, it would appear as follows: `State > City > Zip > Street > House Number > Your Name`. In other words, you are in the house; the house is on a street; the street falls within a Zip code; the Zip code exists within a city; and the city is located within a state.

Now consider how a script identifies an object: A circle resides in a document, and the document itself is "in" an application. Thus, the circle's address might appear as follows: `Application > Document > Circle`. This concept is also known as *object containment:* The circle is contained within the document,

Note

You don't have to memorize object containment hierarchies. Online reference materials describing the object containment hierarchies for all of the scripting languages mentioned here are readily available. For JavaScript, use the Object Model Viewer in the ExtendScript Toolkit; for AppleScript, while in Script Editor choose File > Open Dictionary; and for VBScript, while in Visual Basic go to Tools > References and select the target application, then go to View > Object Browser and again select the target application.

and the document is contained within the application. By tracing the object containment hierarchy, you can arrive at an object's address.

Properties—which for a person might be things like height, language, hair color, and shoe size—represent another important concept in scripting. Assuming I could change the aforementioned human properties with scripting, I might phrase a command like this: *Set the height of person 1 of house 2 to 5'3"*. Or I might use the following: *Change the location of person 1 of house 2 from kitchen to garage.* The same principle can be applied to change the properties of Creative Suite objects (all objects have properties). Circles have heights and widths, fill and stroke colors, locations, and so on—all properties that you can change via scripting.

When you combine these two concepts—addresses and properties—you get what is called the *object model;* each application has its own custom object model. Much of what scripting entails, frankly, is using the object model to figure out how to talk to an object—a process that often takes the form of guessing and testing.

What Can You Script in Creative Suite?

A better question might be what *can't* you script in Creative Suite? By laying bare the inner workings of Creative Suite to scripting, Adobe has made it possible for users to control almost every aspect of its programs. For me, the question is not so much about *what to control* but rather *what I can do with that control.* In Photoshop, for example, you can write scripts for creating layers, adding type, replacing text, and running filters. In Illustrator, you can write scripts for creating and moving objects, changing colors, and saving documents in different formats. And with InDesign, you can write scripts to import type, create PDFs, change linked images, and more.

The real magic, however, comes from the workflows and projects you can facilitate via scripting. One example would be a script that allows you to open a batch of files, resize them, add a watermark to each, change their color space, and save them with different names to another directory via just one command. Take a look at your own workload, and you should be able to come up with more examples. The scripts I'm going to show you in this chapter are fairly simple, but once you get a feel for the process, you'll be able to build more complex scripts and even workflows.

When developing scripts, it's often helpful to evaluate their return on investment: If, down the line, you can save more time by using the script than it took to write and test it, your scripting efforts represent a sensible investment. If that's not the case, however, you should consider another form of automation, such as using Creative Suite actions. I can't say I've always followed this reasonable rule though. Learning and experimenting are hard things to put a value to, so keep it in mind but don't let it hinder you unduly.

Scripting Benefits

By using scripting with Creative Suite, you can reap the following benefits:

- **Speed.** In my own informal testing, I've watched scripts complete tasks hundreds of times faster than a human could complete the same tasks.

- **Accuracy.** What if we made a mistake in the previous bullet point? What if we typed an *i* instead of an *o*? To catch mistakes in text, we generally have to read what we've typed, perceive the error, and then reenter the text to correct it—not a time-consuming task for a single document. Apply this same process to tens or hundreds of documents, however, and you begin to see how scripting can help.

- **Lowered costs.** Increased speed and accuracy equal an improved bottom line. You're not only saving in labor and reprinting costs, you're also fostering happier, more productive, potentially healthier employees, and you're able to redirect resources from graphics production to higher-value work such as brand development and graphic design.

- **Design and brand consistency.** Thanks to both faulty operator decisions and inadvertent errors, a certain amount of inconsistency is inherent in any manually produced work. Scripting, in contrast, ensures consistency, making sure that things are done the way you want them to be.

- **Multiplier effect.** With scripting you can be in two or more places at once, as well as do two or more times the work.

- **Logic.** By applying the logic you've written into them, scripts can react to situations and make decisions on the fly—consistently and with lightning speed. Logic also gives scripts the flexibility to react to unanticipated situations.

A Bit of Tough Love

Now that I've outlined the benefits of scripting, I'm going to reveal what few scripting evangelists are willing to divulge—namely, that scripting can be one of the most infuriating and confusing tasks you'll ever wrestle with … and you won't always win. But in the right hands, scripting is a beautiful thing—even an art form. In writing scripts you will practice some of the same processes as those in design or music or literature. Simplicity, form following function, flow, and balance. There are ways to turn a phrase, lead the eye, make interpretations. In short, a script can have grace.

I may be overstating the case, but if all you want to see is a boring, geeky tool, that's what you'll see. Do yourself a favor: Check your preconceptions at the door and keep your brain open as we explore what scripting has to offer.

Three Scripting Languages

Creative Suite is somewhat singular in that it supports not one but three scripting languages: AppleScript, JavaScript, and VBScript. Why go to all the trouble when most programs only support one? To its credit, Adobe has done its best to meet the needs of the entire creative community by providing multiple avenues into scripting its programs.

AppleScript

Made by Apple (who else?) and only capable of running on Macs, Apple-Script's claim to fame is its similarity to the English language—which should make it easier to learn than other scripting languages. Like all marketing claims, however, this one should be taken with a healthy dose of skepticism. Like English, AppleScript also can be convoluted, offers many ways of saying the same thing, and at times makes absolutely no sense (at least to me).

On the plus side, a wealth of AppleScript learning resources and free scripts for Creative Suite are available. What's more, if a Macintosh graphics program supports scripting, it probably supports AppleScript. Plus, you can use Apple-Script to control multiple applications simultaneously; it is a relatively easy scripting language to start learning; and nonprogrammers will find it easier to get the gist of what AppleScript is saying and doing than with the other scripting options.

JavaScript

Hailing from the Web side of the tracks, JavaScript is often used to create dynamic, interactive Web pages—and it was dynamic and interactive long before Flash was born. Although its name suggests a relationship with the Java programming language (and Sun Microsystems licenses both), JavaScript and Java actually have little in common. JavaScript is the only one of the three languages we're looking at that works on both Macs and PCs, and that feature alone makes it very attractive.

In addition to producing great free instructional PDFs for all three scripting languages, Adobe publishes the Creative Suite JavaScript reference in book form. And with Creative Suite 3, Adobe has even included a robust script editor for JavaScript. There are also plenty of free JavaScripts on the Web for Creative Suite, and its relatively strong user base means that you have a built-in support group.

Like Microsoft and its JScript brand of JavaScript, Adobe has implemented its own version of JavaScript, called ExtendScript. It is basically JavaScript that's been "extended" to add a few additional features and it works across the board with all Creative Suite applications.

On the minus side, ExtendScript can only control one application per script (unless you're using the ExtendScript Toolkit; see the sidebar on page 55). JavaScript can be confusing to the nonprogrammer because it may look too "programmy." And most of the JavaScript learning resources you'll find are focused on building Web pages and making interactive forms in Adobe Acrobat. In fact, you'd be hard pressed to find learning resources other than Adobe's on topics other than writing JavaScripts for Web pages or Acrobat. That is a serious limitation at times.

VBScript

If you know the Visual Basic programming language, you'll pick up the Windows-only VBScript easily, because it was derived from Visual Basic. I suspect that most people who script Creative Suite with VBScript either already know it from another context or are Visual Basic programmers. There are practically no VBScript learning resources or free scripts for Creative Suite and, as with JavaScript, you can only control one application at a time with VBScript.

> **Tip**
>
> You can trigger JavaScripts from within AppleScript and VBScript, making it easy to take advantage of prewritten JavaScripts.

MOM LIKES PHOTOSHOP BEST

Photoshop has gotten more than its fair share of scripting privileges, with three useful tools (and some extra features in ExtendScript) that should really be available in the other Creative Suite applications as well.

Script Events Manager

Photoshop contains a little-known tool called the Script Events Manager for automatically triggering JavaScripts—and Actions—based on Photoshop events, such as creating a new document, starting the application, or exporting a document. The Script Events Manager comes loaded with seven predefined events. But if you look in the appendix of the JavaScript Reference Guide.pdf manual that comes with Photoshop, you'll find a list of more than 200 events that you can access.

To use this tool, choose File > Scripts > Script Events Manager (**Figure 4.1**). This utility is an event-based triggering mechanism. Instead of running a script from an editor or double-clicking the script file, the Script Events Manager keeps an eye peeled, and when the event you specified occurs, it automatically takes your script (or action) by the shoulder and puts it in the game.

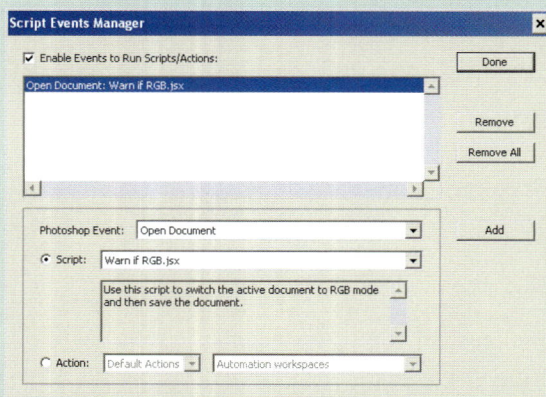

Figure 4.1 *Photoshop's Script Events Manager lets you set scripts or actions to run when a specified event occurs, such as opening a Photoshop document or starting the application.*

Scripting Listener Plug-In

The free Scripting Listener plug-in "listens" to everything you do in Photoshop and writes a log or text file in JavaScript (Mac) or JavaScript and VBScript (Windows). The code it writes, while usable, is hardly easy to read for the beginner. Even though you might not be able to completely understand the code, it is a great way to quickly "write" a script for a process without a lot of good prewritten resources. For instance, scripting filters is not documented very well, and the code that the Scripting Listener plug-in writes will show you how it's done.

To activate the Listener, find the plug-in called ScriptingListener.plugin, located in the folder Adobe Photoshop CS3 > Scripting Guide > Utilities and drag it into the folder Adobe Photoshop CS3 > Plug-Ins > Automate (**Figure 4.2**). Restart Photoshop, and you'll see the ScriptingListener.log on your desktop (if you're using Mac OS X) or at the root of your C: drive (if you're using Windows). Do something in Photoshop (for example, open a new file) and then double-click the log file, copy the text you find there, paste it into a script editor, and see what happens when you run it. Since the code is so hard to read, you might want to copy and paste the code for one action at a time so that you can keep the script organized.

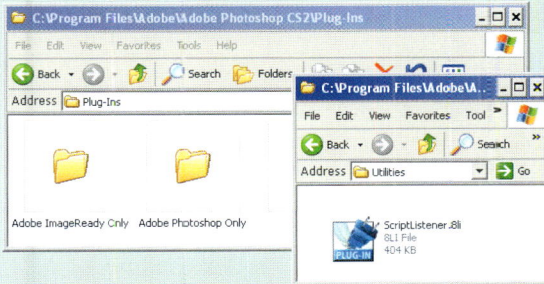

Figure 4.2 To install the Scripting Listener, drag the plug-in into the folder Adobe Photoshop CS3 > Plug-Ins > Automate, and restart Photoshop.

A final note: When you're not using the Scripting Listener plug-in, drag it back into the Utilities folder and restart Photoshop. If you don't, it will keep writing code for every little thing you do, eventually generating such a large file that it will slow down Photoshop.

Image Processor

Although not a scripting resource per se, the Image Processor is actually a prebuilt JavaScript and is available under the File > Scripts menu. It's like the Batch feature (available under File > Automate > Batch) except that you don't have to use an Action if you don't want to. Image Processor provides a quick way to:

- Convert open files (or a folder of files) to one or all of the JPEG, PSD, or TIFF formats
- Resize images according to specific pixel dimensions
- Embed color profiles
- Convert a folder of images to sRGB and save them all for the Web
- Process a folder of camera raw files using the same settings
- Add copyright metadata

You can also include an action by clicking Run Action in the Preferences section at the bottom. Note that actions are run prior to any file resizing (if selected). If you need your action to run after resizing (such as applying the Sharpening filter to a resized image) you should download a modified Image Processor script from www.russellbrown.com/tips_tech.html.

Scripting the User Interface

When using ExtendScript for Photoshop you have access to many new elements for building dialog boxes. These include static text, icon buttons, images, check boxes, radio buttons, progress bars, sliders, list boxes, and drop-down pop-up lists. For an example of the types of interfaces you can build for Photoshop, open the Image Processor (File > Scripts > Image Processor), which itself is an ExtendScript.

Which Scripting Language Should You Choose?

Here are my guidelines for choosing a Creative Suite scripting language:

- If you spent all of your parents' money on a liberal arts education, you'll probably be most comfortable with AppleScript.

- If you need your scripts to work on both Windows and Mac machines, go with JavaScript.

- If you're familiar with Visual Basic, shake hands with VBScript.

The scripting language you choose will likely depend more on preexisting factors and personal tendencies than any rational criteria. I chose AppleScript because it came free on my Mac, and I was in a culture that supported AppleScript. It was covered in the design magazines I already read, people I knew were dabbling in it, and programs I used to make my living were AppleScript-able. Now that I've been using AppleScript for awhile, I can use it to write Automator actions and full-blown Macintosh applications with AppleScript Studio—but these capabilities are just gravy.

If you are the type who's into rational decisions—and you're starting from scratch—JavaScript is probably the best all-around choice because it's cross-platform; lots of free scripts are available for it; and its strong online culture means that you might be able to get answers to your JavaScript questions at 3 a.m. With JavaScript, you can also program forms in Acrobat and add interactivity to Web pages; plus, you get a nice free JavaScript editor in the box with Creative Suite, called the ExtendScript Toolkit.

I've chosen AppleScript for the simple tutorial later in this chapter because it tends to be easier for newbies to follow, and those familiar with either of the other languages shouldn't have any problem translating.

Scripting Editors

Scripts are text files—which means that (at least in theory) you can write them in any old text editor. Scripting editors, in contrast, supply some tools that you'll soon find you can't live without.

A decent script editor should do three things:

1. **Provide color-coding and indenting.** This makes the script much easier to read (**Figure 4.3**).

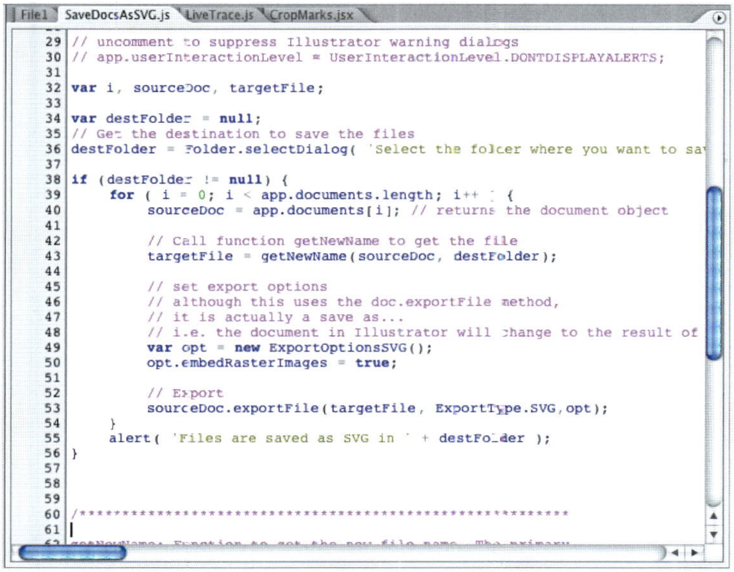

Figure 4.3 *Color coding and indenting in the ExtendScript Toolkit. Both serve to visually organize the script.*

2. **Check syntax.** Each scripting language follows its own syntax, or grammatical structure. The editor should check that syntax and warn you when you've run afoul of the law.

3. **Run the script.** You should be able to run a script in a scripting editor by clicking a single button, as you can with Apple's Script Editor. Windows, in contrast, doesn't include a scripting editor. Without a third-party editor, in Windows you have to write your script in Notepad and then save the file with the correct extension (.js or .vbs). To run your script, you have to navigate to the file and double-click it. To debug the script, you have no option but to go back and forth until it finally runs successfully (or you die of old age).

AppleScript

Apple provides a free scripting editor called Script Editor with every Mac. Not only does it fulfill all of my requirements for script editors, it's perfect for beginners. Because some applications are "recordable" in AppleScript, you can record yourself manually performing tasks in a program, and they will be written out as AppleScript code in the editor—similar to recording Actions

> **Note**
>
> Apple also provides a free application development tool for AppleScript called AppleScript Studio. With it, you can develop full-blown Macintosh applications.

Tip

Script Debugger provides the same powerful debugging features (breakpoints, pausing, a view of changing values as the script runs, and more) as the ExtendScript Toolkit.

in Creative Suite or recording a macro in Microsoft Office. Before you get too excited, though, you should understand that few applications have been written to take advantage of this feature.

Two other AppleScript editors to consider are Satimage's Smile (available free at www.satimage.fr/software/en/index.html) and Late Night Software's Script Debugger (free demo, $199, available at www.latenightsw.com).

JavaScript/ExtendScript

If you own Creative Suite, you're in luck because you also own Adobe's ExtendScript Toolkit, an "extended" implementation of JavaScript. The ExtendScript Toolkit works with both ExtendScripts and good old JavaScripts. It meets all of my basic script editor requirements, plus throws in some features typically found only in editors you pay good money for (see "The ExtendScript Toolkit"). These extra features generally fall into the category of helping you figure out what you've done wrong. Debugging is the process of tracking down and identifying errors other than syntax errors, incorrect math, and generally harebrained commands.

Note

You can trigger scripts from within any of the three Creative Suite graphics applications. In Photoshop and Illustrator, go to File > Scripts and select a script that appears there. Any JavaScript that includes the .js or .jsx extension and is saved in the /Presets/Scripts folder will appear in that menu. InDesign is a little different. Put either JavaScripts or AppleScripts (Mac only) in the same folder (/Presets/Scripts) but access them in InDesign via the Window > Automation > Scripts panel (**Figure 4.4**).

Figure 4.4 *The Scripts panel menu and the panel itself in InDesign. Any AppleScript (Mac only) or JavaScript/ExtendScript in the Adobe InDesign CS2 > Presets > Scripts folder will appear in this panel.*

THE EXTENDSCRIPT TOOLKIT

Free script editors tend to be stripped-down affairs. But the free ExtendScript Toolkit (**Figure 4.5**) provides some extras that can help you track down errors—typically a frustrating and futile process if you don't have a debugging tool. For the beginner, the process of deduction usually goes something like this:

1. Does the error I get give me any clues? (Probably not.)
2. From what happened or didn't happen, can I locate the error in the script? (Maybe.)
3. Try changing something and run the script again.
4. Repeat ad nauseam.

Debugging tools give you a leg up on all this. Scripts run very fast; there are usually lots of things happening; and it's truly hard to keep up. ExtendScript Toolkit eases this process by letting you add break points that stop the action so you can check out what's going on in the script at that point (simply click once on the line number). When the script stops at a break point, you can look in the Data Browser to see the current values assigned to all variables—a good source of clues for solving your mystery.

Other debugging tools include the Call Stack, for tracking function calls (a function is a chunk of reusable code or module that is "called" or triggered from within the body of the script); buttons to "step" through a script one line at a time; and the JavaScript Console, a cool little tool that lets you type in a piece of code and test it immediately by pressing the Return key. With it you can test as you go when you're building a large, multipart script.

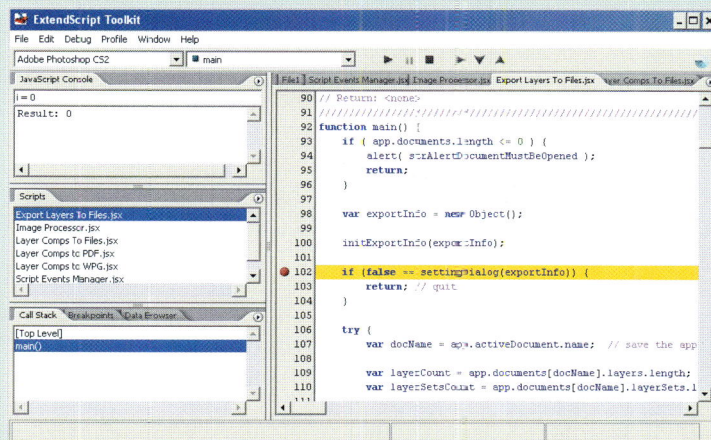

Figure 4.5 *The ExtendScript Toolkit interface in Windows XP. You can drag or close any tab. Here the Data Browser, Call Stack, and Breakpoints tabs are stacked together in the lower left window.*

VBScript

As mentioned earlier, the Windows operating system does not provide a free scripting editor. Instead, you must type your script in a text editor like Notepad, save it with the .vbs file name extension, and then double-click the file itself to run the script.

Some scripting VBScript editors to consider are Adersoft's VbsEdit ($49, available at www.vbsedit.com) and Modelworks' SitePad Pro (starting at $129.95, available at www.modelworks.com).

The Obligatory "Hello World" Tutorial

Tradition dictates that the first project you attempt with a new computer language be the "Hello World" project (look up the history on http://en.wikipedia.org). The project usually entails creating a small program to write "Hello World" onscreen. Not very exciting maybe, but tradition is tradition. Thus, our first project will be to draw, with the aid of AppleScript, a circle in Illustrator (the world) with a blue fill and no stroke. Our script will then write the word *hello* centered in the circle with a white fill.

To begin the tutorial, carefully type the following script in Script Editor:

```
tell application "Adobe Illustrator"
    activate
    make new document with properties {height:792, width:612, ruler¬
    origin:{0.0, 0.0}}

    make new ellipse in document 1 with properties {position:{256.0,¬
    446.0}, width:100.0, height:100.0, fill color:{class:CMYK color¬
    info, cyan:84.0, magenta:63.0, yellow:0.0, black:0.0}, stroked:false}

    set theText to make new text frame in document 1 with properties¬
    {kind:point text, contents:"hello", position:{306.0, 396.0}}

    set properties of text of theText to {fill color:{class:CMYK color¬
    info, cyan:0, magenta:0, yellow:0, black:0}, text font:text font¬
    "Myriad-Roman", size:32, justification:center}
end tell
```

Click the Run button (if Illustrator isn't already open, Script Editor will automatically open it for you). You should see the Hello World circle and text as shown in **Figure 4.6**.

Tip

AppleScript uses the convention of adding the continuation character (¬) to show that a line of code continues on to the next line. Lines are arbitrarily broken in print because of space constraints. So when typing in an AppleScript simply ignore the continuation characters or treat them as spaces.

After you've typed the text in Script Editor, click the Compile button (which resembles a hammer). This causes the editor to check the script's syntax to ensure that it's consistent with the AppleScript language. If you get an error message, make sure you typed it in exactly as shown.

Creating a New Page

Take a look at the preceding script and see if you can make some sense of it. The line `tell application "Adobe Illustrator"` directs the script to Illustrator. It's a way of saying, "Take this note to Illustrator and have it do the things that follow." The last line of the script is `end tell` which closes what's called the *tell block*. Because an AppleScript can change which application it's referring to mid-script, application tell blocks provide a means of indicating where the instructions for a particular program are contained.

The second line (`activate`) brings Illustrator to the front so that you can watch the show.

The third line starts with `make new document`—which is precisely what the script does. Documents have properties, and this specifies its height and width in pixels (AppleScript's default). Since the Macintosh has 72 pixels per inch, we can see that this creates a page that is 11 inches tall (792 pixels divided by 72 pixels per inch) and 8.5 inches wide (612 pixels divided by 72)—or a letter-size page. The `ruler origin {0.0, 0.0}` portion of the script sets the horizontal ruler to start in the top left corner and the vertical ruler to start in the lower left corner—important because all commands will use this origin to set or return positioning properties.

Building the Circle

As you've already learned, all objects have properties. In this case, the ellipse, or circle, is drawn using five characteristics, or properties. The first property is its position (`256.0`, `446.0`), which is its x,y coordinates on the page expressed in pixels. (You could substitute inches for pixels by typing `3.5 inches`, `6.2 inches`.) Our circle will be drawn 256 pixels (3.5 inches) from the left edge of the page and 446 pixels (6.2 inches) down from the top of the page.

The second and third properties we'll use to draw our circle are its width (`100.0`) and height (`100.0`). Again, these measurements are expressed in pixels

Figure 4.6 *The output of your Hello World script.*

Tip

Save your script before making any changes to it, and the editor will check the script's syntax before saving the file.

and will result in a circle about 1.4 inches in diameter (100 pixels divided by 72). If we wanted an ellipse, we'd only have to specify two measurements.

The fourth property of our circle is its fill color, which we build by specifying its CMYK mix (though we could also use an RGB mix or even a swatch color).

The fifth and final property is the stroke. Known as a Boolean data type, the stroke can only be one of two values: If its value is "true," our circle will have a stroke; if it's "false," it won't. So `stroked:false` means no stroke.

There are many other properties you can set, and if you don't specify a property, AppleScript will use Illustrator's defaults. For instance, one of the circle's properties is "fill overprint." Again, it's a Boolean data type, and the default is false. Since the circle is not on top of another object, the default of no overprint is fine—and we don't need to specify it.

Adding the Text

Let's look at the line that starts with `set theText`. "theText" is a variable name I created so that I could refer to the text by that name in the next line. Variables are nothing more than placeholders—like the *x*'s and *y*'s in your high school algebra class—used to store values that change over time. We use variables all the time in our daily lives—take, for example, the expression "my car." You may have many cars over the years ; "my car" simply serves as the label (or *variable name*) for the vehicle that's sitting in your driveway right now.

> **Note**
>
> Position is not actually a property of a text frame. Text frames inherit properties (including position) from their parent class, called the "page item" class. This is another example of the object model. Not only are classes contained within other classes, they also inherit certain properties from their parent class and have certain properties of their own.

In **Figure 4.7**, the variable text shows up in green thanks to color-coding (you can change the color in Script Editor's Preferences), which helps you quickly understand a script's structure. In this example I've also used blue to indicate language and application keywords, and black for operators and values.

A *text frame* is Illustrator's scripting term for any text created using the Text tool. The three types (or "kinds") of text frames are point (text anchored by a single point), area (text within an object), and path (text attached to a path). We can see that the three properties specified in this script are kind (`point text`), contents (`"hello"`), and position (`306.0, 396.0`).

We now want to set the fill color, font, size, and justification of the word *hello*. These are not properties of a text frame but of the text contained within the frame. Thus, in the next line (starting with `set properties`), we set those properties for the `text of theText`. This may seem weird, but remember that everything is contained within something else, and certain objects have certain properties. The fill color is set the same way it was for the circle. The font thing is a little interesting because `text font:text font` looks like a mistake but it's not. The first "text font" is the property and the second "text font" is the class of the value. Size and justification are self-explanatory.

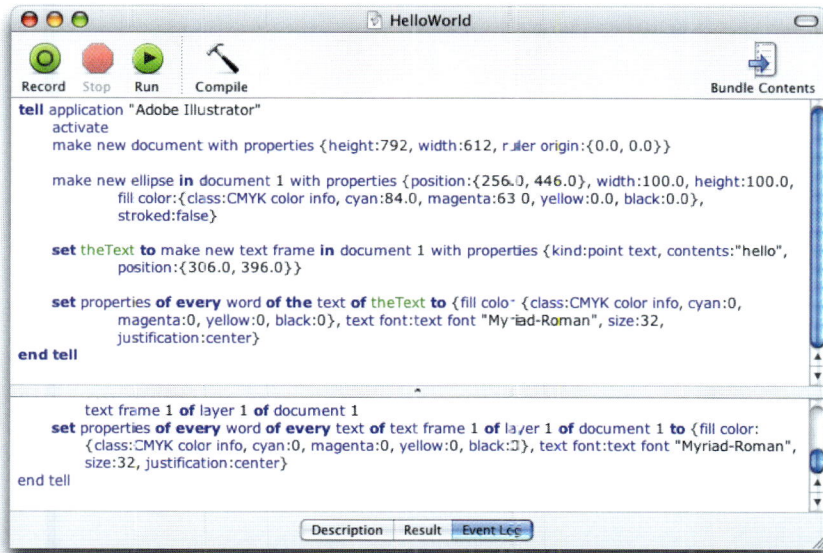

Figure 4.7 *The Hello World AppleScript in Script Editor. The events that result from running the script are shown in the lower pane because the Event Log button has been selected. The bar separating the two panes is draggable to adjust the size of or hide either window.*

During the early stages of scripting, you'll spend some (OK, a lot) of your time trying to figure out how to address objects (containment) and what properties you can change. This is where using (read: *stealing*) someone else's scripts (with that person's explicit or implied consent, of course) can come in handy. If you can find a script that does approximately what you want, it's often easier to adapt code that someone else has written than to write your own from scratch. Not only do you save yourself time and grief, it's a great way to learn.

Playing with Your Script

Now it's time to make a copy of your script (copying and pasting it into a new window) and start moving and changing things—in short, play. Some of the

Note

You can't change every property of an object. While most properties are changeable, some are "read only" and are usually set by the application.

most important lessons we learned as children were acquired through play. And playing is a great way to learn scripting, too. For instance, what would happen if you were to change the ellipse bounds? Would its shape change? And what if you were to change the contents of the text frame to, say, your name? Or if you were to change the font and color? What would happen if you were to change the text frame position, add other text frames, or change the "stroked" property to "true"? Try to get into the mode of experimentation. If you screw up, your script won't work, but nothing will catch fire. Just as you would do when editing an image, make a copy so that you can't destroy all your previous work (in this case, typing in all that code).

Here's something cool: In Illustrator select just the circle and then go back to Script Editor and type the following in a new window:

```
tell application "Adobe Illustrator"
  get properties of selection
end tell
```

Click the Result button (in the middle at the bottom of the window), and you'll get back a wealth of information about our little circle (**Figure 4.8**).

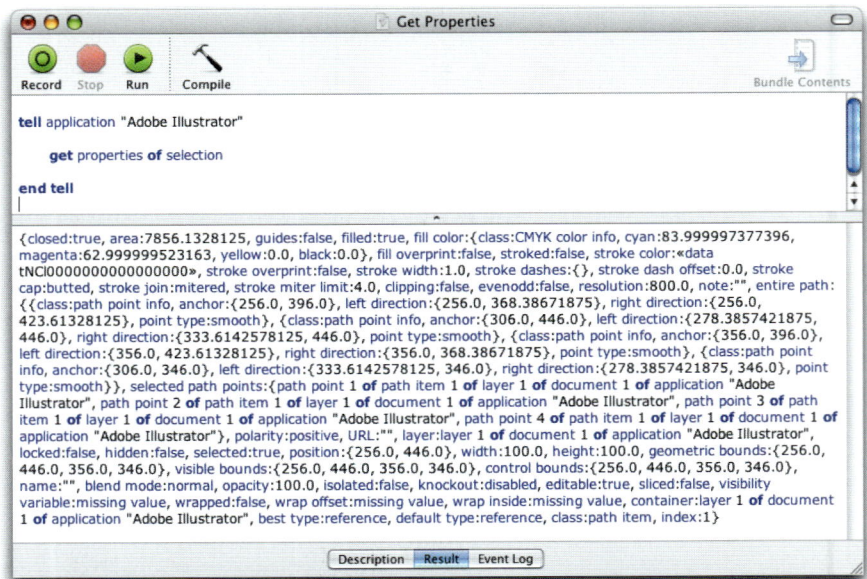

Figure 4.8 *After running this script, the bottom pane will display information that Illustrator records for your circle. If the bottom window is hidden, drag the horizontal bar (with the dot in the center of it) up to reveal the Result text.*

You'll get an idea of what Illustrator tracks for every object and what you potentially have access to. Unfortunately, you can't modify the Result window's tangle of text in Script Editor to make it more readable. Still, it's worth taking some time to wade through it, seeing if you can use any of the information there to change the circle. For instance, toward the bottom of the window you'll see that the name property has a value of nothing (name:""). Let's go ahead and name our circle Gaia, which means "living planet." To do that, return to Script Editor, create a new script window, and type the following (with the circle still selected in Illustrator):

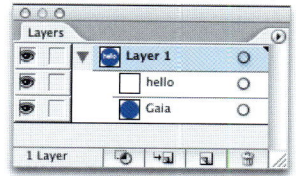

Figure 4.9 *The circle is now named Gaia, as shown in the Layers panel. In future scripts you can refer to it by name.*

```
tell application "Adobe Illustrator"
   set name of selection to "Gaia"
end tell
```

Click the Run button in Script Editor, then go to the Layers panel in Illustrator and expand Layer 1 to see Gaia in the lineup (**Figure 4.9**). Note that Illustrator automatically gave the text frame a name matching its contents—"hello."

If you run the "get properties of selection" script again (with the circle selected in Illustrator), you'll see that the value for the name property is now, in fact, Gaia. In future scripts you can refer to our little planet by its name—which means you could write and run something like the following (the circle doesn't need to be selected now since you're referring to it by name):

```
tell application "Adobe Illustrator"
   set the opacity of path item "Gaia" of document 1 to 50.0
end tell
```

This sets the circle's transparency to 50 percent. Just to confuse you, in the Illustrator application this property is called transparency. But when scripting Illustrator you have to refer to it as *opacity*. It seems Adobe used the scripting word *transparency* already as a GIF property and had to call it something else for path items.

Now, let's change the text as follows:

```
tell application "Adobe Illustrator"
   set contents of text frame 1 in document 1 to "bye"
end tell
```

For our last trick, let's do something more interesting. Although I'm sure I'm not the first to discover it, I've found that scripting lets you animate objects in

Tip

I've tried to stick to Apple's Script Editor program for this tutorial because it's free and not as intimidating to the first-time scripter as some other editors. After you get the hang of scripting, you should at least look at the free demos of more robust editors such as Script Debugger. In Script Debugger, for instance, the Result window is not only much easier to read but you can change values there and have them sent or to the target program. Features like this make scripting easier to learn.

the host program (in our case, Illustrator). The following script will fade the circle Gaia from white (or zero opacity) to full blue (100 percent opacity). You can also make objects fade in or out and move incrementally (as if sliding), and you can incrementally change text (to make it look as if someone were typing it manually). Here's the fade-in script:

```
tell application "Adobe Illustrator"
    activate
    repeat with i from 0 to 100
        set opacity of path item "Gaia" of document 1 to i
        redraw
    end repeat
end tell
```

The preceding script introduces the concept of loops, which are useful for controlling the flow of scripts. Loops generally repeat a task until a condition is met, usually changing something incrementally with each pass. In this case, the stop, or end, condition occurs when the variable i equals 100. (For no particular reason, the letter *i* is commonly used in AppleScript for loops. I could have just as easily used the letter *g* or *z*, or a variable name like LoopCounter.) In AppleScript, a loop starts with repeat and ends, appropriately enough, with end repeat. The part that says with i from 0 to 100 means that it will loop 100 times (actually 101 times, since we're starting with 0 instead of 1).

For the first go-round, i has a value of 0; the second time it's 1; and so on. At the end of the set opacity line, we see the variable i again. In our example, i is doing double duty, acting as both a counter for the loop and as the opacity percentage for the circle. If we didn't use variables, we would have to write 101 set opacity lines in the script, which would look something like the following:

```
set opacity of path item "Gaia" of document 1 to 0
set opacity of path item "Gaia" of document 1 to 1
set opacity of path item "Gaia" of document 1 to 2
```

and so on up through 100.

If we decided that we wanted to change the progression of opacity and had, in fact, written 101 lines of code, we'd have to go back and rewrite the whole thing. Since the script uses a variable, however, all I would have to do to change it would be to alter the values. For instance, if I wanted the circle to fade out rather than in, all I'd have to do is change one line, which would look like this:

```
tell application "Adobe Illustrator"
    activate
    repeat with i from 100 to 0 by -1
        set opacity of path item "Gaia" of document 1 to i
        redraw
    end repeat
end tell
```

You'll notice that I added by −1, which tells the script to count backwards by 1. I didn't have to write by 1 in the first script because AppleScript defaults to the value of 1 when counting loops. If the animation fades out too slowly for your tastes, try setting the count to −2 or −5 and see what happens. Can you make it fade in faster?

Note

Illustrator sometimes has difficulty updating the view when you change something with scripts. The redraw command in the script forces it to refresh the screen on every pass of the loop.

Tip

If you click the Event Log button at the bottom of the AppleScript window before running the script, you can actually watch as Apple-Script writes those very lines internally to get the job done (**Figure 4.10**).

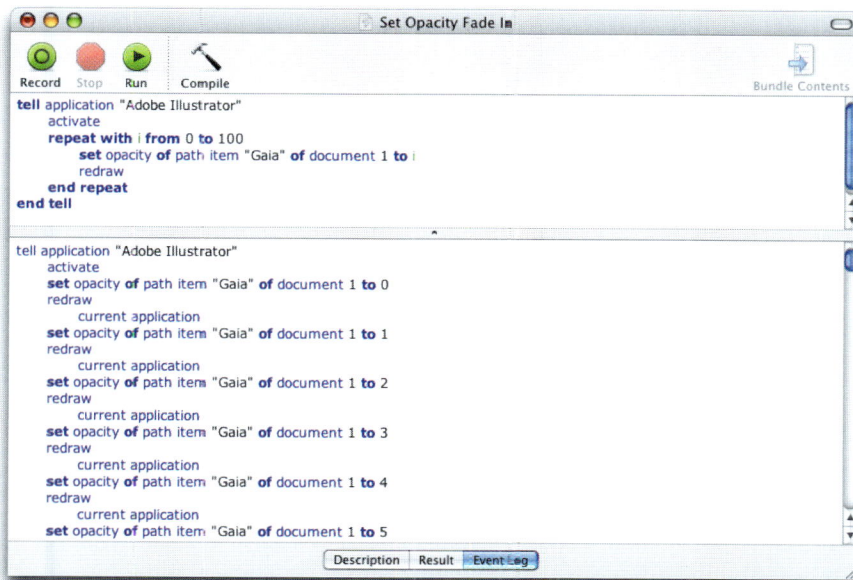

Figure 4.10 *The log for the fade-in script (note the Event Log button selected at the bottom). The Event Log provides a written record of what happens while the script is running, showing all the events the script generates. These logs are invaluable for troubleshooting.*

Give It a Go

I'm no scripting expert, and you don't have to be one either. We don't need to be Jedi masters to say we script. Start out slowly; try some simple scripts; and see what you can do. If your interests or needs take you further, more power to you.

Here are three things you can do to learn more:

- **Rip off any script not nailed down.** No kidding. First look on the Creative Suite Resources and Extras discs for some starter scripts. Then look on the Web. Read some of the articles that occasionally pop up in magazines, and buy a book or two (see the Resources appendix for some suggestions). Copy and paste with a vengeance. Adobe's scripting reference documents, which should have come with your software but are also available online, are actually very good sources of information and scripts. Check out the Web sites listed in the next paragraph for additional scripts.

- **Ask for help.** Web sites, such as http://macscripter.net, javascript.internet .com, and http://visualbasicscript.com, have forums where you can post your questions. People are generally nice and want to help, but don't let the occasional insensitive reply bother you (nobody knows it all, even those who act as if they do). Read the frequently asked questions section first and then skim the posts to make sure your question hasn't already been answered; then be specific in what you're asking and mindful of people's time.

- **Play.** There are very few times in adult life when playing is encouraged, so take advantage of this one. Mess around with scripts. Try to do something weird or even wrong. Treat scripting as if it will give you clues to a mystery. If this does that, then what will this other thing do? Every time you solve a mystery, you get closer to understanding what scripting can do. Try out some scripts for applications you like other than Creative Suite, like iTunes.

One last piece of advice: As people help you and you learn more, try to give back to the community by helping others who aren't as far along as you are. The real teaching and learning comes from the interaction of people helping each other.

5
Robot with a Pipe

Mac's Automator

Ants are more like the parts of an animal than entities on their own. The circuits are so intimately interwoven that the anthill meets all the essential criteria of an organism.

—*From* Lives of a Cell *(Lewis Thomas)*

With the exception of the Actions included in Photoshop and Illustrator, Automator (which comes with Mac OS X) is the easiest-to-learn automation tool available today. Using its prewritten modules, you can quickly assemble an automated workflow—in fact, it's a bit like playing with Tinker Toys or Lincoln Logs. But there will inevitably be occasions when the task you want to accomplish isn't covered by any of the prewritten modules, so I'll show you how to build your own as well, using free tools from Apple along with some AppleScript. After completing this chapter's tutorial, you'll be able to repurpose your home-grown action by changing its interface and replacing the Apple-Script, thus adapting it for other uses and applications.

Imagine that you have a toy box filled with hundreds of tiny robots, each of which can complete one small, focused task. Imagine further that you can snap the little robots together to form a larger robot. The order in which you snap them together determines the order in which the robots carry out their tasks. Each little robot passes information to the next, as in a bucket line; thus, the work flows sequentially—from first task to last, or from the big robot's head to the big robot's toes.

This is essentially how Automator works—though in Automator, the little robots are called *actions* (not to be confused with actions in Creative Suite), and the big robot is called a *workflow*. Automator's chain of actions forms a kind of assembly line in which tasks are completed at every station in order to yield a final product at the end of the line.

Single Automator actions may seem insignificant, laughable even, in what they can accomplish. But like a single ant, an action's power grows

Note

Here's a geeky bit of trivia: Automator's mascot is a robot holding a pipe, and its name is Otto, which sounds like *auto* … get it? The pipe Otto is holding is a reference to the Unix operating system's pipe operation, which connects separate commands into a single larger one. The operation is symbolized by the vertical bar, or "pipe character."

exponentially when combined with other actions. To push the ant metaphor even further, consider the following: Ants exchange information and are so intensely social that they die if left alone. Similarly, Automator actions are practically useless by themselves. As a group, however, they come to resemble an organism whose parts touch, convey information, and contribute to a common goal.

Although small in scope, Automator actions do what they do very well: All you have to do is drag the self-contained actions into the conga line of the workflow. Actions generally let you fine-tune what they do by making selections in their interfaces, such as choosing a folder or entering text via a dialog box. And workflows have a rudimentary debugging feature: Actions will snap together only if one has been programmed to accept data from the other.

Automator in Action

If you've never opened Automator before, the interface may seem confusing on first glance (**Figure 5.1**). Not to worry: The following should serve as a guided tour. In Automator, actions are associated with specific applications—

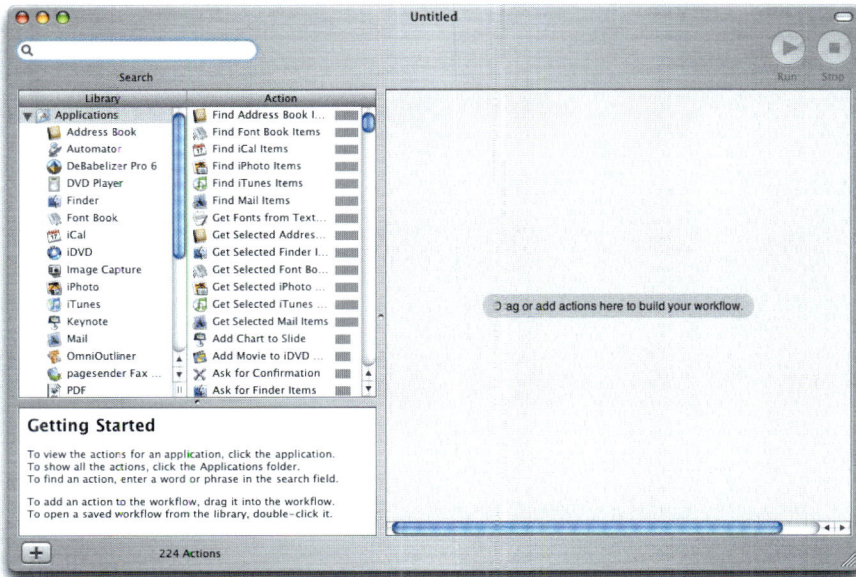

Figure 5.1 *Automator's window is made up of three panes and a Search field.*

usually just one. However, an action can work with more than one application or no application at all. The Library column lists applications that have associated actions (**Figure 5.2**). You can see that the Finder (highlighted in blue), which is an application, has associated actions in the Action column, installed and ready to go. If you single-click an action, a short description appears in the small pane in the lower-left corner of Automator (**Figure 5.3**)—helpful with actions whose names aren't very descriptive.

Notice that since the Get Specified Finder Items action is highlighted in the Action column, you can read its details in the lower-left corner of the

Figure 5.2 *Automator's Library column shows all applications that have associated actions installed.*

Figure 5.3 *Actions sometimes have cryptic names, making it hard to understand what they do. However, if you highlight an action's name, its description appears at the lower left, which should help. The pane can also display the types of input required and the output produced by the action.*

Automator window. If you don't see the action you need, you can enter a word or phrase in the Search Actions field in the top-left region of the Automator window (**Figure 5.4**). Automator searches by action names and their text descriptions. Once you choose a particular action, click and drag it from the Action column into the Workflow pane on the right.

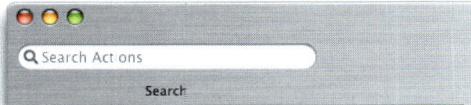

Figure 5.4 *Automator's search locates actions by name, keyword, category, or phrase.*

You can always reorder actions by dragging them around (or by clicking their numbers and using the Move menu item). In this way you build and tweak workflows step by step and action by action.

A short workflow consisting of two actions is shown in the Workflow pane in **Figure 5.5**. The first action (called Get Specified Finder Items) serves as a hopper where you choose the documents you want to have the rest of the workflow act on. After I dragged Get Specified Finder Items into place, I chose the InDesign documents I wanted my workflow to affect by clicking the plus sign in the lower-left corner of the Action's frame and then browsing for them, but I could also have dragged and dropped them from the Finder. As you can

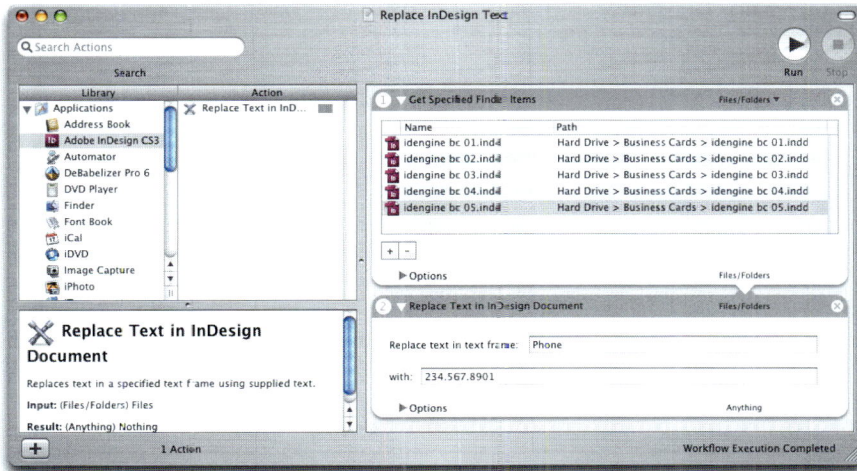

Figure 5.5 *Two Automator actions are visible in this Workflow pane, both of which are ready to run. You will build the second action shown here.*

idengine

identity design & implementation
400 cutter drive
camp hill, pa 17012

susan weeks
ceo
123.456.7890
ext. 123

Figure 5.6 *The phone number in this example file (123.456.7890) will be automatically replaced in the tutorial action.* ©iStockphoto.com/Tyler Stalman

see, I'm using five documents for this tutorial; however, I could just as easily have chosen 10, 50, or 100 documents. The first action was written by Apple and included with Automator; I wrote the second one, which I'll show you how to build.

This first action demonstrates the flexibility of Automator workflows. Although simple, workflows are customizable via dialog boxes that let users choose settings, or files, for the action to operate on. If an action contains a user interface, in its lower left you'll see a triangle and the word *Options*. Click the triangle, and you'll see a Show Action When Run check box. When the workflow runs, that action presents the user with a small dialog box where he or she can customize the action. Keep in mind that doing so will temporarily stop the workflow, and a user must be present to choose the settings, which makes the workflow less than totally automated.

The second action—called Replace Text in InDesign Document—finds a text frame in each of the chosen files and replaces the contents with new text. As this action runs, two dialog boxes pop up: In one, the user must input the name of the text frame (which is how Automator finds the frame); in the other, the user enters the new text. The overall workflow lets you easily change the phone number in five InDesign business card documents (**Figure 5.6**).

Each action displays a small In Progress icon in its lower-left corner as it runs. When a green check mark pops up in its place, you know that the action has been completed (**Figure 5.7**). A red X appears if the action fails. You can also follow an action's operation via the information bar in the lower-right corner of Automator itself as the workflow runs. Look at where the actions in the workflow snap together: As long as one action passes the correct kind of data to the next, the actions will snap together as shown, white tab to gray tab. If not, the tabs won't link and the data types will be displayed in red to show you that Automator is not amused (**Figure 5.8**).

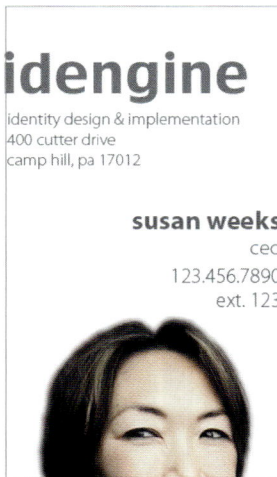

The Power of Workflows

Although the above-described workflow may seem a bit dull, think about what it does: I was able to drag together a complex task with two applications (the Finder and InDesign) and two steps in under a minute. And I could easily

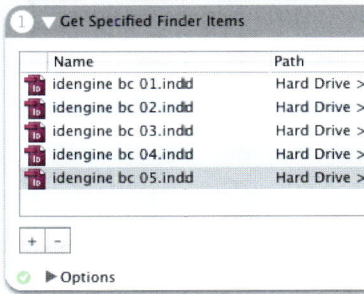

Figure 5.7 *When a green check mark appears in the lower-left corner of an action's window, this means that the action has run without errors.*

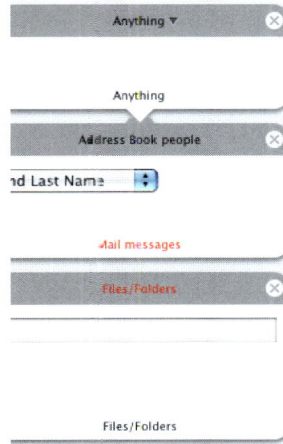

Figure 5.8 *The top two actions snap together because their input and output data types are compatible. The bottom two aren't compatible, so they don't snap together.*

have expanded it to include more applications, actions, and documents. The only other way to build such a powerful cross-application agent would be to use scripting, which is much more time- and labor-intensive (see Chapter 4, "Behind the Curtain: Scripting in Creative Suite").

Once you've constructed a workflow that does exactly what you want, you can save it in one of three ways: as a workflow, which is the default (**Figure 5.9**); as an application; or as a plug-in. When you double-click a workflow in the Finder, it opens in Automator, where you can edit it. Saving the workflow as an application makes it a droplet; you can drag the files or folders you want to affect onto the droplet's icon to launch the workflow. Droplets are just as editable as any other Automator workflow: You just drag the droplet icon onto the Automator icon, which causes it to open in its original form.

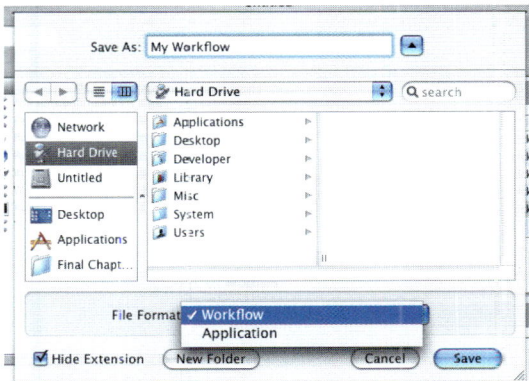

Figure 5.9 *Saving a workflow in the Workflow file format.*

The third way of saving a workflow (as a plug-in) provides the most interesting options. For a quick way to launch workflows in specific applications or situations, you can save a workflow as any of the following six types of plug-ins (**Figure 5.10**):

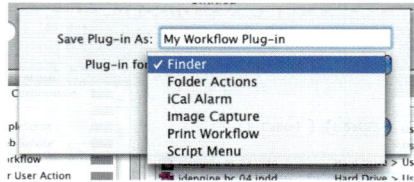

Figure 5.10 The six ways to save a workflow as a plug-in.

- **Folder Actions plug-in.** Lets you choose items to be fed to the first action in a workflow when you put them into a designated folder.

- **iCal Alarm plug-in.** Lets you trigger a workflow based on date or time.

- **Finder plug-in.** Lets you right-click or Control-click a file in the Finder to see an action name and launch it to act on your chosen file (**Figure 5.11**).

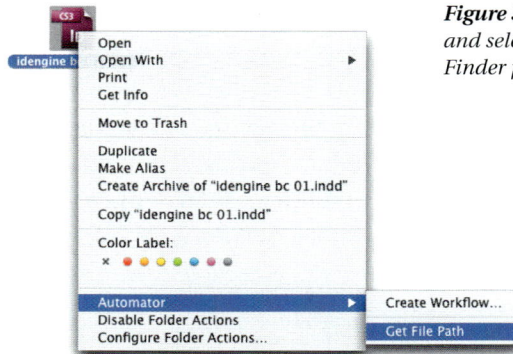

Figure 5.11 Control-clicking a file and selecting a workflow saved as a Finder plug-in.

- **Image Capture plug-in.** The action triggers a connected digital camera to take a photograph, and the resulting file is fed into the workflow.

- **Print Workflow plug-in.** Lets you save a document as a PDF and feed it to the first action in a workflow from the PDF pull-down menu in any Print dialog box.

- **Script Menu plug-in.** Lets you launch a workflow from the Script pull-down menu, which usually appears in the Mac's menu bar, to the left of the date (**Figure 5.12**).

Tip

If you don't see the Script icon in the menu bar, open AppleScript Utility (in the Applications folder) and select "Show Script Menu in menu bar."

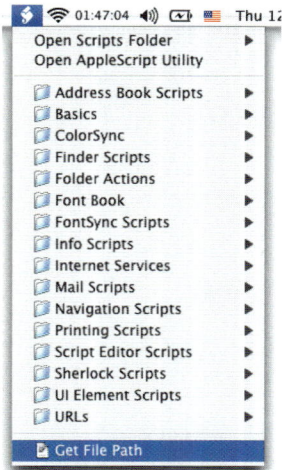

Figure 5.12 Selecting a workflow that has been saved as a Script Menu plug-in.

Caveat Emptor

I should mention right away that there are a few drawbacks to using Automator. Unlike scripts, workflows do not contain intelligence—that is, Automator actions typically don't make decisions; they only follow instructions. And each action is only "aware" of the action on top of it, so you can't have an action down the line react to one nearer the beginning. In general, there's no capability to repeat an action until a condition is met (known as *looping*). If you need more brainpower than Automator can deliver, you'll want to consider using scripting via one of the languages described in Chapter 4.

Automator's other big limitation is that actions have to be prewritten—which can make it feel like a solution in search of a problem. It's great that Automator can pull all of the linked images off a Web site and use them to create a new album in iPhoto, but if that's not what you want to do, then it's of no use to you. Theoretically, if you have a large enough collection of actions, you can string together a workflow for almost any situation. However, if what you want to do is not in the action cards, you have two options: Gather up your toys and head home, or roll up your sleeves and write your own.

Workflow Strategies

Automator workflows aren't complex: One action executes at a time, in sequence, until the workflow is complete. This means that all you need to do is break down the workflow you wish to automate into small, distinct tasks, and then build it back up in Automator. To get a handle on what your workflow consists of, try sketching it out before you start building (**Figure 5.13**).

> **Note**
>
> A new version of Automator is slated to be released with Mac OS X 10.5 in October 2007, with some additional capabilities. Few details were available when we went to press, but Apple has announced that Automator 2.0 will be able to record your manual actions in almost any application (much like QuicKeys, described in Chapter 7). Apple also announced that the new version will be able to use variables to store values and use them throughout a workflow. Don't take this as the final word, though: Apple says these features are subject to change.

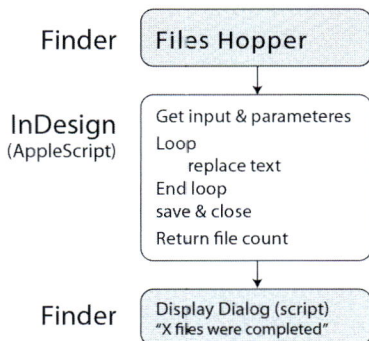

Figure 5.13 It often helps to plan any kind of automation before you start building. Here, an action has been casually diagrammed in Illustrator. You can use flowcharting software or scrawl it on the back of a napkin—whatever works for you.

And rather than try to build a long workflow all in a single go, build it in steps. Test each step as you go, and then add more. This makes it easy to pinpoint issues and results in a more stable workflow, since it will have been tested from the ground up.

Since you can spend a substantial amount of time trying to figure out if what you want to do is covered by pre-existing actions, you'll want to familiarize yourself with what's available and possible. Your workhorse actions will be located in the Finder and System libraries (for file handling and system-level tasks), Spotlight (for locating files), Automator (for workflow tools), Safari (for Internet tools), and Mail (for communications). For additional actions, check the application folders and Web sites for your other Mac applications (since software makers sometimes develop actions for their products), and look in this book's appendix for a list of additional Internet resources for adding to your collection of actions.

By playing around with the Apple-provided actions for each of its Mac OS X applications (like iTunes and iPhoto), you can figure out which prewritten ones will do the trick for you. Again, some actions' titles are far from self-explanatory, so read their information in the lower-left portion of the Automator window. And finally, since it can be maddening to gather 95 percent of the actions you need only to be sunk by that last unavailable 5 percent, you may want to add action writing to your toolbox of skills. Although one of Automator's strengths is the quickness with which it can assemble a workflow, there will inevitably be days when you need to slow down and write the missing-link action yourself.

Tutorial

Time to regroup. After poking around a little, I learned that you can write the guts of your own action using AppleScript—and, hey, I know a little Apple-Script, so I dug a little deeper to find out how hard it would be. Actions are actually small programs, and the (free) tools Apple provides simply wrap an action shell around the bit of custom code you've written. The upshot is that most of what you would normally have to write is written for you. Word to the wise: What you learn here can apply to writing big-boy Mac programs in the Apple development tool AppleScript Studio (also free).

Note

This tutorial demonstrates how to build a simple Automator action shell and insert a small amount of AppleScript code to provide its functionality. You can swap the tutorial Apple-Script code with your own, tweak the action interface, and easily build other actions for InDesign (or other applications).

Keep in mind, however, that if the problem you're trying to solve isn't likely to crop up again, it's not worth your time to write Automator actions to solve it. Instead, look at the macro-like action feature that Adobe has built into Photoshop and Illustrator: Adobe has written quite a few actions for these programs, and they're even easier to work with than Automator.

In the following pages you're going to learn to build an action to replace the text in specific text fields in InDesign documents. Specifically, you'll build the action's simple user interface—which will contain two text fields, one specifying which text frame in InDesign should be modified and another for entering the text that goes in that frame—and combine it with other Automator actions (since you can reuse and combine actions). The action you create in this tutorial serves as an example of how Automator can be used in a graphics workflow to quickly correct multiple documents.

Beyond that, the general concept is that by naming document objects, you position yourself to be able to use automation to build (using templates), update, and correct production files—a small effort on the front end that can save you a great deal of time in the long run. As you go through this tutorial, remember that the information you glean here can be adapted to other Creative Suite tasks—usually by just changing the interface and the AppleScript code—so begin thinking about how you can adapt the action you create here for other purposes.

Getting Started

I'm going to warn you straight off that what you're about to see will be intimidating. The programs that you'll use for our tutorial typically build much bigger programs than actions and have lots of buttons, levers, and sparking wires—most of which you can simply ignore. While building the Replace Text in InDesign Document action, you'll be presented with lots of distractions—most of which you can simply ignore. If you remain focused on the steps on the following pages, you won't get lost; in fact, you'll find it's not even that difficult after you've built the first one.

As mentioned previously, Automator actions are simply small programs: They have interfaces; they accept input; they operate on some data; they produce output—and because they're so small, they're pretty easy to assemble. I've distilled the process into the following four steps:

1. **Build the interface.** The first part of this task—which involves simply dragging and dropping the interface elements into place—is fun. The second part, quite frankly, is tedious and involves associating each interface element with a variable so that it's accessible via the AppleScript.

2. **Configure the action.** This step consists primarily of mundane but necessary activities like giving the action a description, specifying what kind of data it will take, and so on.

3. **Supply the code.** This is the AppleScript portion of your action. Although I explained how to write AppleScripts in Chapter 4, you can probably avoid the task altogether, since a Web search is likely to turn up a free AppleScript that does what you want. From there, it's just a matter of retrofitting the AppleScript to work in an action, which I'll show you how to do.

4. **Test and build.** Accept that it will probably take a couple of tries to get your action to run correctly. View those problems as learning opportunities: Hokey as it sounds, you can learn more by tracking down the source of a problem than by doing it right the first time. In other words, be grateful for your mistakes: They'll teach you far better than any book.

You'll use two programs for this tutorial, both of which are free: The first is the ominously named Xcode, which you can use to develop full-blown applications for the Mac—for free (amazing). For this project you'll use only a small part of Xcode and tiptoe past the rest. The other program is the straightforwardly named Interface Builder. While both of these programs are included on your Mac OS X installation discs, they're likely to be outdated if you've installed any system updates. You can download the current versions from http://developer.apple.com/tools/download/ (you'll have to join Apple Developer Connection, but it's free and easy).

Time to synchronize your watches: You'll kick off the project in Xcode, hop to Interface Builder to—*wait for it*—build the interface, and then return to Xcode to write the AppleScript and adjust some dials. Finally, you'll jump into Automator for testing.

Open Xcode, and from the File menu choose New Project. Now, double-click AppleScript Automator Action (**Figure 5.14**). In the dialog box that appears, give the project the name Replace Text in InDesign Document. Decide where you want to put it, and click the Finish button. The next window that appears is one of those where you'll have to simply ignore a lot of stuff you won't be using (**Figure 5.15**). First off, make sure that the first group (Replace Text in InDesign Document) in the left pane under Groups & Files is selected, and then ignore this pane for the rest of the project. Second, ignore everything in the right pane except for the following three items: InfoPlist.strings (English), main.applescript, and main.nib (English). Double-click main.nib (English), and the application Interface Builder will open.

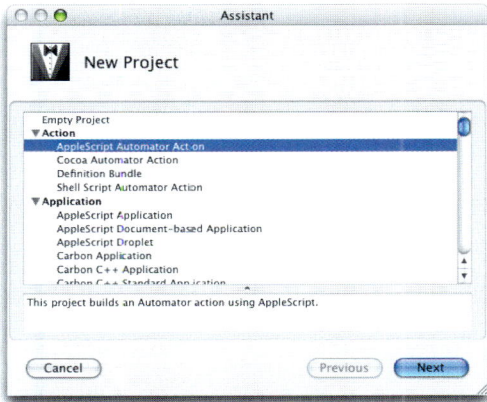

Figure 5.14 *Xcode's New Project window gives you an idea of what other kinds of projects it can build. Automator actions use only a small part of Xcode.*

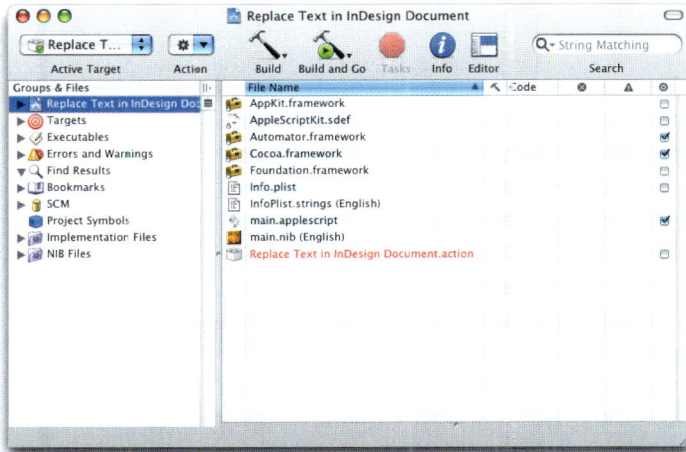

Figure 5.15 *The complexity of Xcode's main windows can be intimidating. Stay focused on what is necessary to build actions and, for now, ignore the rest.*

Building the Interface

When Interface Builder opens, you'll see three windows (**Figure 5.16**). If you don't see all three windows, choose Tools > Palettes > Show Palettes. You will drag objects from the Palette window (the one on the right titled Cocoa-Text) into the View window. You can think of the View window as a canvas on which you assemble the elements of your user interface. The icons placed across the top of the Palette window provide access to various types of interface elements, though we'll only be using one, Cocoa-Text, which is accessible by clicking the button that looks like it says *Text* twice. The other interface elements you might use for actions are the controls, and they're accessible by clicking the icon to the left of the Cocoa-Text icon, called Cocoa-Controls. This palette contains buttons, sliders, and radio buttons (among other screen elements). Although the other groups of elements are used primarily for building full Macintosh applications, there's no harm in clicking around to investigate—who knows, you may eventually step up to building full Macintosh programs.

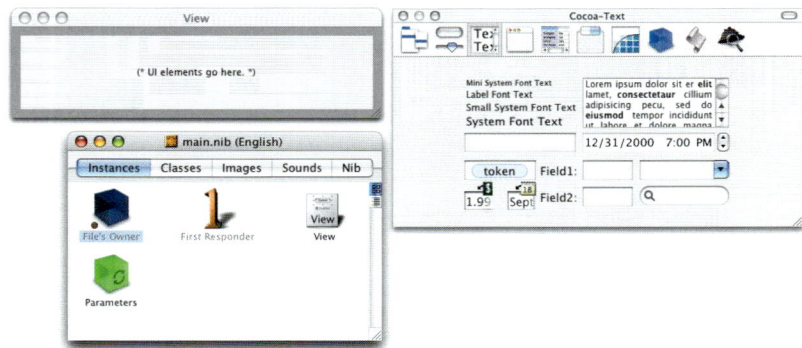

Figure 5.16 *Interface Builder's application interface consists mostly of these three floating windows, plus the Inspector.*

ASSEMBLING THE ELEMENTS

To assemble the elements of your user interface:

1. To tidy up, first select and delete the (* UI elements go here. *) text in the View window.

2. From the Cocoa-Text palette, drag the line "Small System Font Text" into the View window, double-click it to make it editable, and change its text to read Replace text in text frame: For now, you can place this text box

anywhere in the View window. (If some of the text disappears because the box is too small, choose Layout > Size to Fit.)

3. Grab the empty box that's located under System Font Text in the Palette window, and drag it into the View window (**Figure 5.17**). In your action, this empty box will be a field into which users can enter text.

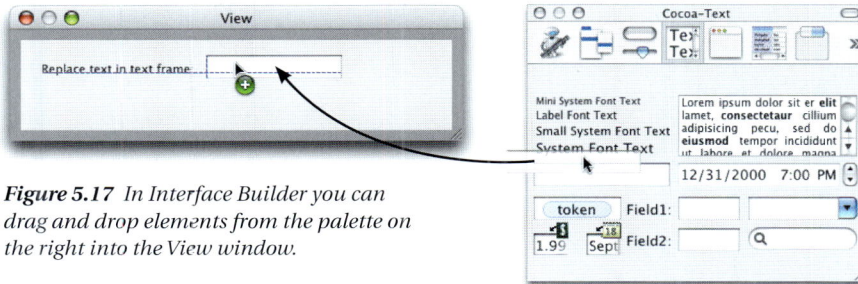

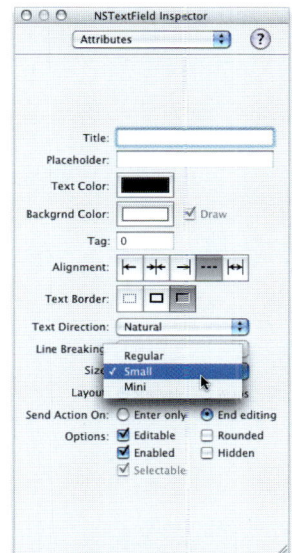

Figure 5.17 *In Interface Builder you can drag and drop elements from the palette on the right into the View window.*

4. If you select the box after it's placed in the View window, handles (blue dots) will appear, which you can use to resize it.

5. Repeat Steps 2 through 4 to make a second label that says "with" and a second data entry field, then arrange them so your window resembles **Figure 5.18** (though don't kill yourself trying to get it to match exactly). To give the user more space for text entry, you'll probably need to make the View window wider and stretch the two text fields.

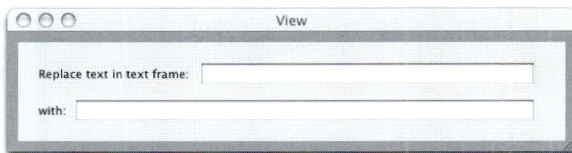

Figure 5.18 *When building the action's interface, try to match what you see in this View window.*

To conserve screen real estate, Automator uses interface elements (text, boxes, and so on) that are smaller than those that appear in most Mac applications. For instance, you may have noticed that you used the Small System Font Text rather than the System Font Text. To make sure you're using smaller text-entry boxes, select a text field in the View window and go to Tools > Show Inspector. Make sure Attributes is selected in the Inspector's top pop-up menu (**Figure 5.19**), then from the Size list choose Small. Select the other text field in the View window and select Small Size for it as well.

Figure 5.19 *Since Automator actions are small, they use smaller interface elements than most Macintosh applications do.*

BINDING

Now, it's time to assign names to the two text fields. Called binding, this process can be confusing. Just keep in mind that you're simply assigning, or binding, names (and some properties) to the two text fields in the interface.

1. Go back to the View window and select the top text field (next to "Replace text in text frame").

2. In the Inspector window, choose Bindings from the pop-up menu at the top. Click the disclosure triangle (the little arrow) next to the word *value*.

3. In the "Bind to" pop-up menu, choose Parameters (NSObjectController), and in the Model Key Path pop-up menu, type the name TextFrame (as shown in **Figure 5.20**). Press the Return key, and the name will bind to the text field. The check box next to Bind at the top right of the Inspector window should now be checked, confirming that the binding was successful.

4. Repeat Steps 1 through 3 for the other text field in the View window and name it WithText. Again, be sure to press Return to verify the binding. Now choose File > Save to save your work on the interface.

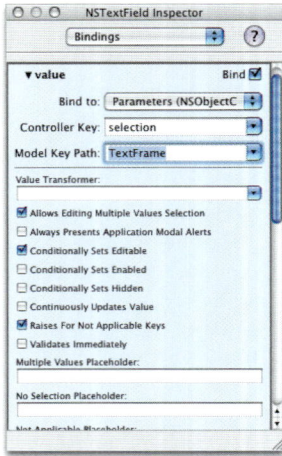

Figure 5.20 *After entering the text field's name in the Model Key Path field, be sure to press the Return key to bind the name to the interface element. After doing so, make sure the Bind box is checked.*

Configuring the Action

Although Actions can have quite a few settings, we're only going to set the bare minimum for this tutorial.

1. Go back to Xcode and select Project > Edit Active Target 'Replace Text in InDesign Document' (**Figure 5.21**). Make sure the Properties tab is selected, and General is selected in the Collection pop-up menu.

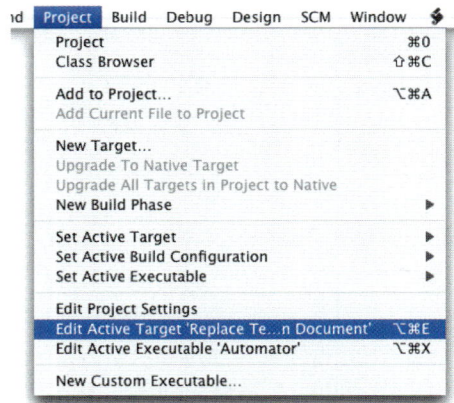

Figure 5.21 *Selecting Edit Active Target 'Replace Text in InDesign Document' is not the most intuitive thing you'll ever do. This is where you configure actions.*

2. Double-click the text in the Value column to highlight it and type the following: For Action name, type `Replace Text in InDesign Document`; for Application, type `Adobe InDesign CS3` (it might already have been typed for you); for Category, enter `Utility`; and for Icon name, type `Action`. Make sure the "Can show when run" box is checked and the "Can show selected items when run" box is unchecked (**Figure 5.22**).

This is also the window where you can set the input and output. *Input* describes the type of data the action can accept from another action, and *output* describes the type of data the action will produce. These two settings determine whether actions can snap together in Automator.

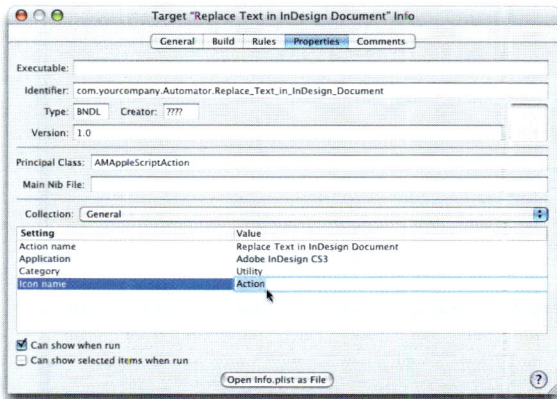

Figure 5.22 Double-click in the fields under Value to highlight and change them. Make sure you type everything in exactly as shown, or the action may not work as expected.

3. From the Collection drop-down menu, choose Input and click the plus sign in the lower-left corner. Double-click whatever strange text appears to highlight it, then type `public.item`, which means the action will accept files and folders (**Figure 5.23**). We'll leave Output at its default value.

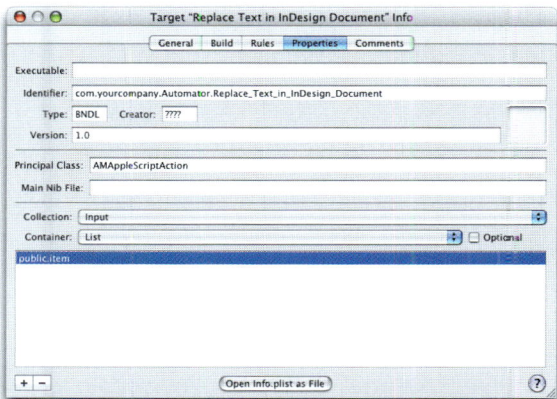

Figure 5.23 Setting the input to public.item means the action can take files and folders as input.

Tip

The input and output categories are called Type Identifiers. The full list is available at http://developer. apple.com/documentation/ AppleApplications/Conceptual/ AutomatorConcepts/ Articles/AutomatorPropRef. html. Scroll to the bottom to see the table.

4. You now need to specify the default value types for the data entered in the two text fields. *Value types* describe what kind of data is expected in that field. Called data types, they can include string, integer, Boolean, and real. From the Collection pop-up menu, choose Parameters, then click the plus sign, double-click the Name field to highlight it, and type TextFrame. Click and hold in the Type field to make sure "string" is selected. Rinse and repeat for WithText, and it all should look like **Figure 5.24**.

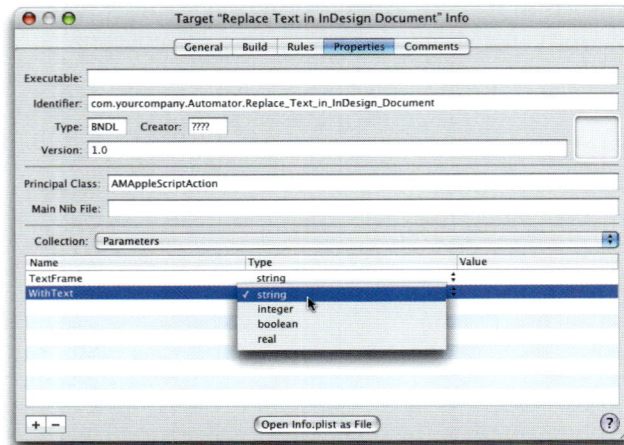

Figure 5.24 *Setting a text field's type to "string" means that it will only accept text as user input and will, in fact, try to convert anything else entered into text.*

5. Close this window and return to Xcode's main window (**Figure 5.25**). We're now going to enter the descriptive text that will appear in the lower-left corner of the Automator window. In the Xcode main window, double-click InfoPlist.strings (English) and then scroll down to find the line of text that reads /* AMDescription localized strings */ and drag and select all the lines from the one that starts AMDAlert = down to (but not including) the one that starts AMDSummary =. Delete the selected lines (**Figure 5.26**). On the AMDSummary = line, replace all the text inside the quotes with a description of the action. Type Replaces text in specified InDesign text frame. (as shown in **Figure 5.27**). Make sure to leave the quotation marks in place.

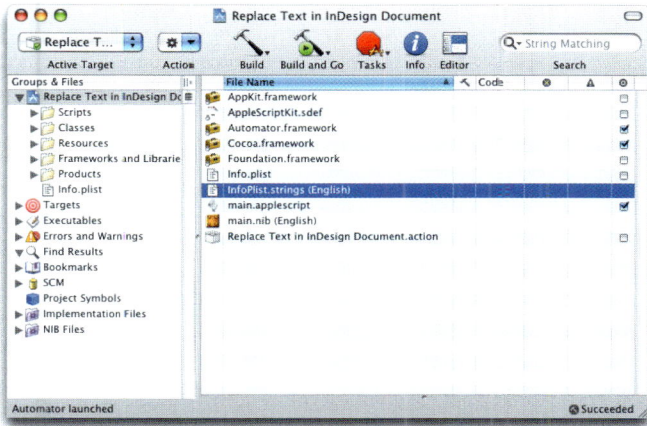

Figure 5.25 *InfoPlist.strings (English) contains, among other items, the action's description that appears in the lower-left corner of the Automator window.*

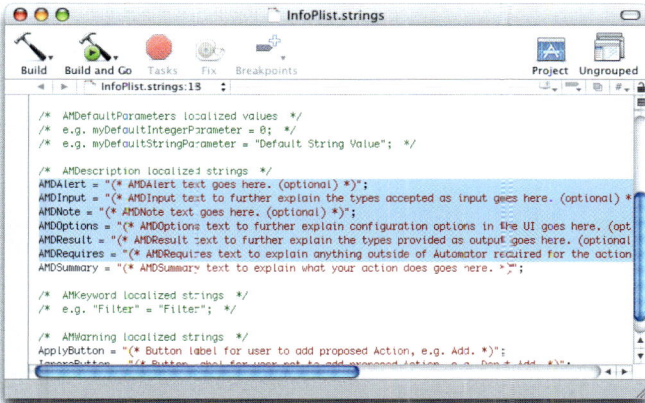

Figure 5.26 *For this tutorial only, you're deleting most of what appears in InfoPlist. strings (English). When creating a real action, fill in all applicable fields to provide better feedback to the user.*

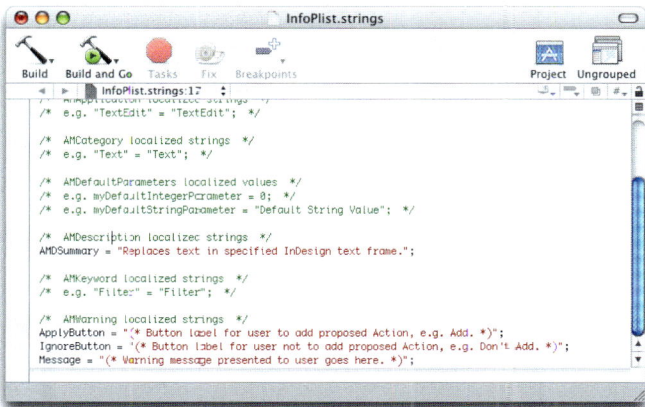

Figure 5.27 *The AMDSummary contains the descriptive text that appears in Automator.*

Writing the Code

Close the InfoPlist.strings (English) window and go back to the main Xcode window, where you will need to double-click main.applescript and replace whatever is there with the following AppleScript:

```
on run {input, parameters}
    set the Text_Frame_Name to |TextFrame| of parameters
    set the With_Text to |WithText| of parameters
    repeat with i from 1 to (count of items of input)
        set ItemOne to (item i of input)
        set theDoc to POSIX file ItemOne
        tell application "Adobe InDesign CS3"
           try
              open theDoc
              set contents of text frame Text_Frame_Name of document 1¬
              to With_Text
              save document 1 to theDoc
              close document 1
           end try
        end tell
    end repeat
    set input to i
    return input
end run
```

Save the AppleScript by choosing File > Save (or by pressing Command-S) and the script will compile (**Figure 5.28**).

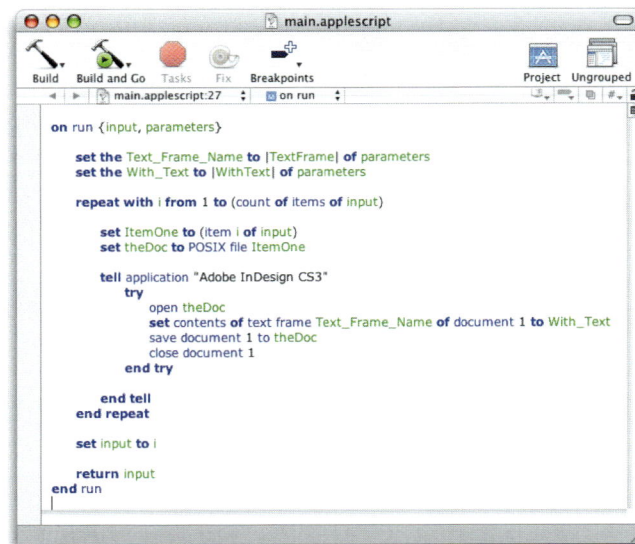

Figure 5.28 *The entire tutorial AppleScript.*

Here's what your newly created script does: It grabs the data from the first action in the workflow (input—in this case, a list of file paths), sorts and assigns the data from the interface (parameters—these are the two text fields the user will fill in), and then uses those variables in the AppleScript code in the middle. At the end, the action passes along the number of files processed to the next action in line.

The segment of the script that says on run {input, parameters} is accepting the data passed to it from the previous action. The input variable stores this data. (Variables serve as placeholders.) In this case, the previous action passes along a list of file locations, all of which are contained in the one placeholder, or variable, input. The parameters variable stores the text the user typed into the two text fields in the action's interface.

The next two lines grab and store the text the user entered in the action's interface:

```
set the Text_Frame_Name to |TextFrame| of parameters
set the With_Text to |WithText| of parameters
```

The parameters variable contains all of the data entered in the interface—in this case, the name of the InDesign text frame, |TextFrame|, and the replacement text, |WithText|. All you're doing here is separating the two and storing them in separate variables (Text_Frame and With_Text).

The next line sets up a loop: repeat with i from 1 to (count of items of input) It will go through the loop once for however many files there are. The variable *i* is a counter. It starts at 1 and ends at the count of input items. The loop starts with the repeat line and ends farther down with the end repeat line.

The next two lines:

```
set ItemOne to (item i of input)
set theDoc to POSIX file ItemOne
```

define which document the script will be working with this time through the loop. The first of the two lines instructs the action to grab the first file path from the variable input, which contains a list of files passed to this action. Because the variable *i* will be set to 1 on the first pass though the loop, this line is saying, "Get Item 1 from the list of all file paths stored in the variable input and store that one file path in the variable ItemOne."

Note

The following description applies only to this particular script. But even though AppleScript may be fairly foreign to you, you should be able to pick through it and see what the different parts are doing. As you start scripting (whether with AppleScript, JavaScript, or VBScript), it's helpful to pick up a script someone else has written and modify it to suit your needs (or just to see what you can get it to do). The more you borrow and rewrite, the more you'll learn.

But now, you've got a little problem. That file path will look something like the following: Hard Drive:Users:rick:Desktop:InDesign Docs:Document 1.indd. The colon delimiters tell me that this is a Macintosh-type path—but InDesign hates colons. For that reason, the second line converts the Macintosh-type path to what is known as a POSIX path—meaning it replaces the colons with forward slashes, transforming it to look like the following: Hard Drive/Users/rick/Desktop/InDesign Docs/Document 1.indd.

The next three lines:

```
tell application "Adobe InDesign CS3"
try
   open theDoc
```

direct this part of the script to InDesign, where it will open the first document. The second line (try) opens what's called a *try block,* an AppleScript error-handling feature that ensures the process won't halt if it encounters an error. For instance, if the current document did not contain a text field with the script label Phone, the try statement would go on to the next document without stopping and displaying some sort of error message.

The next line:

```
set contents of text frame Text_Frame_Name of document 1 to¬
With_Text
```

finally gets to the meat of the action. This basically states, "Replace whatever text is in the target text frame (whose name is now stored in the variable Text_Frame_Name) with whatever text is stored in the variable With_Text." Remember that whatever text the user typed was passed to this script in the parameters variable; we pulled out just the replacement text and stored it in the With_Text variable.

Two more lines save and close the document:

```
save document 1 to theDoc
   close document 1
```

Three more lines:

```
      end try
   end tell
end repeat
```

close the `try`, `tell application`, and `repeat` blocks. In AppleScript, `tell` and `repeat` lines (among others) have to be closed with an end line.

The next line is interesting:

```
set input to i
```

You're assigning the value of *i* to the variable `input`, which is used to pass along data to the next action in line. To illustrate this concept, you'll pass along the value of *i*, which will be the number of times the script goes through the loop. In other words, how many files were completed. The next line:

```
return input
```

is where it actually passes values to the next action. You could have passed along anything else you have access to in this action, such as the name of the text frame or the replacement text.

Testing Your Action

Close the AppleScript window, and in the Xcode main window click the Build and Go button (**Figure 5.29**). This builds a temporary action and opens it in another instance of Automator with an empty Workflow pane for testing. (Just to clarify: By "another instance," I mean that an additional Automator icon will appear in the Dock, and if you run the Activity Monitor application, you'll see two Automator applications running.)

Figure 5.29 *The Build and Go button builds the Xcode project and opens it in Automator.*

To test this new action, I've created five representative InDesign business card documents, each with a text frame named Phone (**Figure 5.30**). I can imagine having 10 or 50 or 100 cards in which the phone number has changed, and the Replace Text in InDesign Document action and workflow could update them all in no time. You can set up a similar (or simpler) InDesign file to test the action you built. To name an InDesign text frame, select it with the Selection tool (the solid arrow), choose Window > Automation > Script Label, and type Phone (**Figure 5.31**).

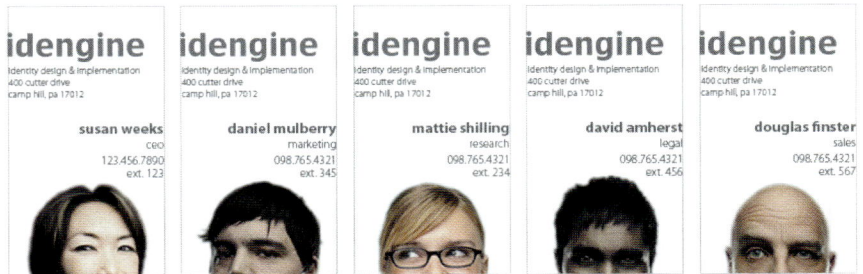

Figure 5.30 *The five tutorial files.* ©iStockphoto.com/Tyler Stalman

Figure 5.31 *Applying a Script Label to an object in InDesign is similar to naming an object in Illustrator and Photoshop using the Layers palette.*
©iStockphoto.com/Tyler Stalman

For the test, return to the new instance of Automator. In the Library column, choose Finder from the Application folder and drag the Get Specified Finder Items action into the workflow pane (**Figure 5.32**). You can add the five InDesign test files in one of three ways:

- You can click the plus button in the lower-left corner of the action and select the five files in the dialog box (Shift-click to select all five at once).

- You can drag the five files from the Finder into the action.

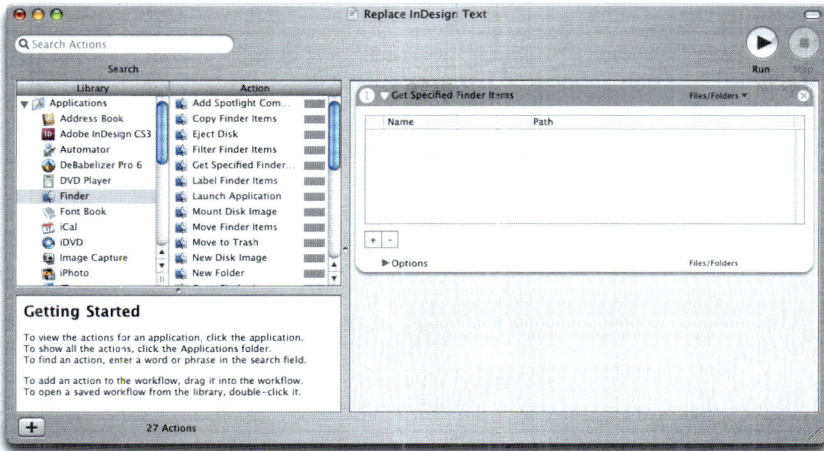

Figure 5.32 *How the Get Specified Finder Items action looks before files are loaded.*

■ Or you can simply drag the files from the Finder into the empty workflow pane, and Automator will automatically create the Get Specified Finder Items action and add the five files to it (**Figure 5.33**)—a trick that comes in handy when you have to test your action multiple times.

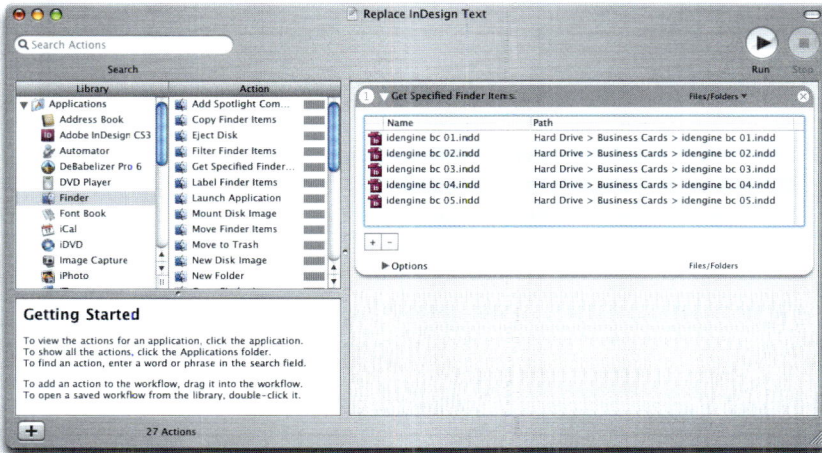

Figure 5.33 *The five business card files have now been loaded into the first action.*

Once you've added the InDesign files, go back to the Library column and open the Applications folder, then select Adobe InDesign CS3 and drag the Replace Text in InDesign Document action into the workflow pane; place it underneath the Get Specified Finder Items action (**Figure 5.34**). Now, type Phone in the "Replace text in text frame" text field and type 234.567.8901 in the "with" text field (**Figure 5.35**). Click the big Run button in the top-right corner of Automator to test the workflow.

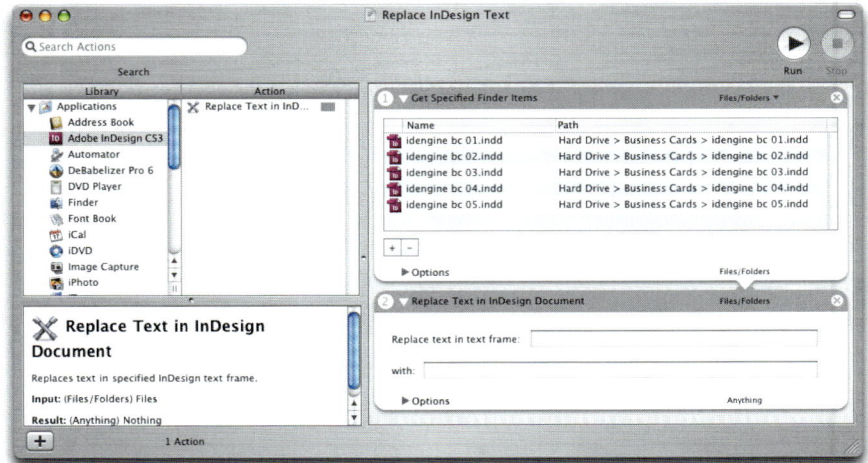

Figure 5.34 *The two actions snap together in the Workflow pane.*

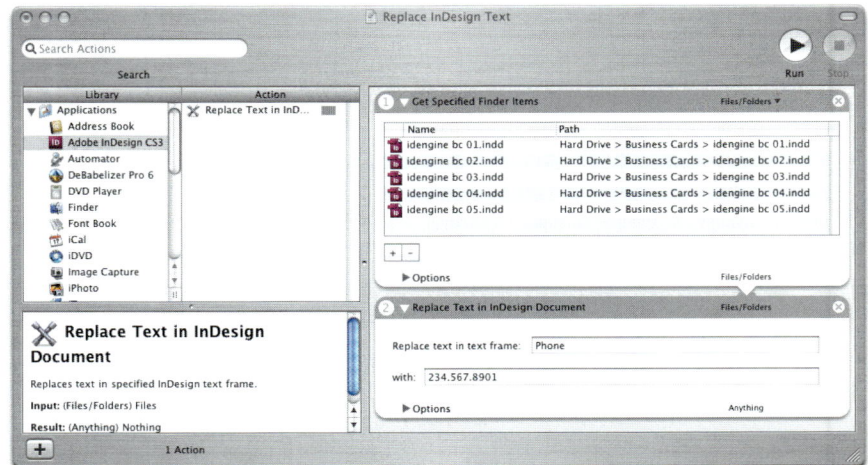

Figure 5.35 *With the files chosen and text entered, the workflow is ready to run.*

If everything is correct, the workflow will run without a hitch, and little green check marks will appear in the bottom-left corner of each action. If everything is *not* correct, you now enter into the troubleshooting phase. Don't despair: Troubleshooting is how you learn. It's like trying to figure out who committed the murder in a mystery novel. When something goes wrong with your project, you gather clues. Figuring out where the process stopped might tell you where the offending line of code is. And error messages—though notoriously cryptic—can also sometimes help (though at times you'll only find them vexing).

More often than not, the error will be in the AppleScript. If something is mistyped, the code won't compile and it won't let you create the action. Thus, the first thing you should do is check your input. If there are no problems with it, look for clues at the point where the process halted. Does InDesign open the files correctly? Is it able to find the Phone text field? Does it insert the correct replacement text? And so on. The place where the process grinds to a halt is where you'll find the problem.

You can also run into problems if the text fields aren't bound properly—resulting in an error when you try to build the action or a failure to correctly pass the data through the `parameters` variable. Do you get an AppleScript error that starts out something like "Can't get lTextFramel of…"? Although this error appears in AppleScript, its source is likely a typo in Xcode, since the AppleScript is simply telling you it can't grab that data from the TextFrame. Make sure that the interface element names match exactly everywhere you type them—in Xcode, Interface Builder, and AppleScript. (This goes for upper- and lower-case letters and spaces, too.)

If you don't find any clues that point to a solution, go back over everything and double-check it against the code printed here. There are also a couple of troubleshooting tricks you can try to pinpoint the problem. One is to put a `display dialog` line in different places in the AppleScript. For instance, type `display dialog theDoc` after the line that says `set theDoc to POSIX file ItemOne`. This will display a dialog at that point in the script, showing you the file path to `theDoc`, which will be the current document. You'll be able to check that it is the correct file path and that it's in POSIX format (with forward slashes instead of colons).

The second trick is to add the View Results action (in the Automator Library) after an action to check what it is passing along to the next action. You could add it after the Get Specified Finder Items action to see in what form the file paths are being passed to your action (**Figure 5.36**).

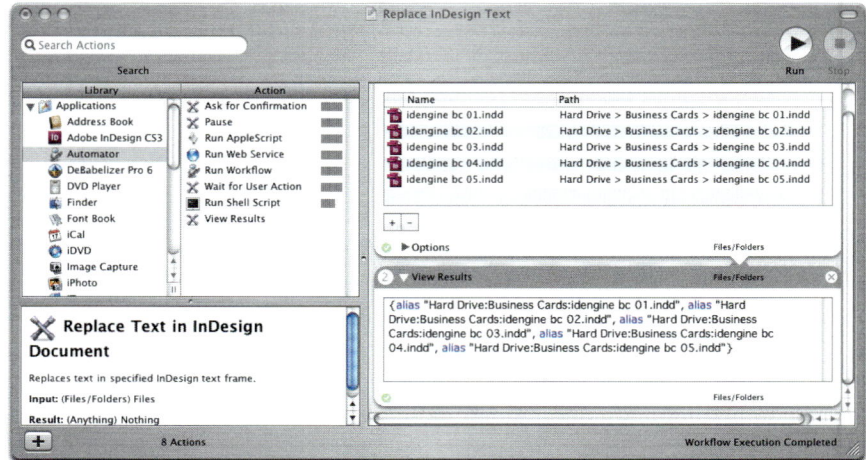

Figure 5.36 *A quick troubleshooting tool is the View Results action, which you can use to verify what an action is passing to the next in line.*

Remember the line in your AppleScript that says `set input to i` followed by the line `return input`? The first line sets the variable `input` to the value of the variable *i* (which in our tutorial is 5 since we ran five files through our action), while the second line passes this value on to the next action. You can verify this by dragging the View Results action (in the Automator Library) underneath your action, running the workflow, and then verifying that your action passed on the number 5.

As one small example of what you could do with the number of files that were run through this workflow, delete the View Results action and replace it with the Run AppleScript action (also in the Automator Library) under your action. Select the entire line that reads (`* Your script goes here *`) and replace it with the following:

`display dialog (input as string) & " files were successfully completed."` (**Figure 5.37**). The whole script now reads as follows:

```
on run {input, parameters}
   display dialog (input as string) & " files were successfully¬
   completed."
   return input
end run
```

Run the workflow and you should see the dialog window as shown in
Figure 5.38.

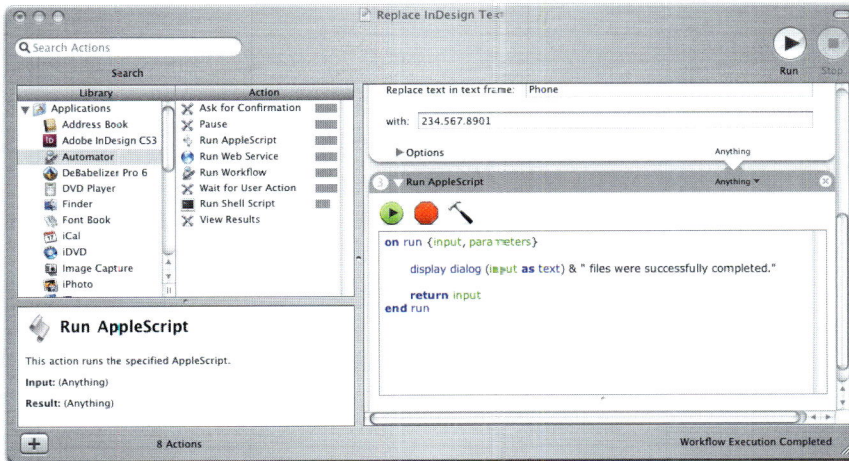

Figure 5.37 *By grabbing the data passed from the previous action and running it through a Run AppleScript action, you can display a process completion confirmation.*

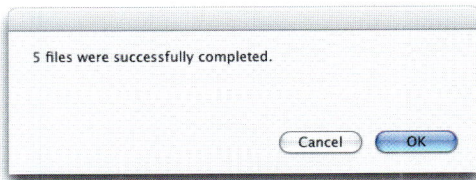

Figure 5.38 *This dialog box gives you a quick visual confirmation of how many files were processed.*

The Final Build

Assuming everything is running fine with your action, it's now time to do the final build to produce an official Automator action. (The first two steps get the project ready for the build.)

1. In the Xcode main window, choose Build > Clean all targets.

2. Choose Project > Set Active Build Configuration > Release.

3. Choose Build > Build.

4. In Xcode's main pane, Control-click Replace Text in InDesign Document. action. From the contextual menu choose Reveal in Finder (**Figure 5.39**).

5. Replace Text in InDesign Document.action will now appear in the Finder: Drag it into the Library > Automator folder (**Figure 5.40**).

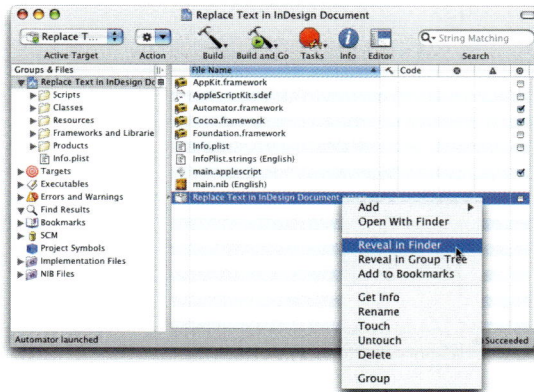

Figure 5.39 Using the contextual menu (Control-click) shows you the location of the action file.

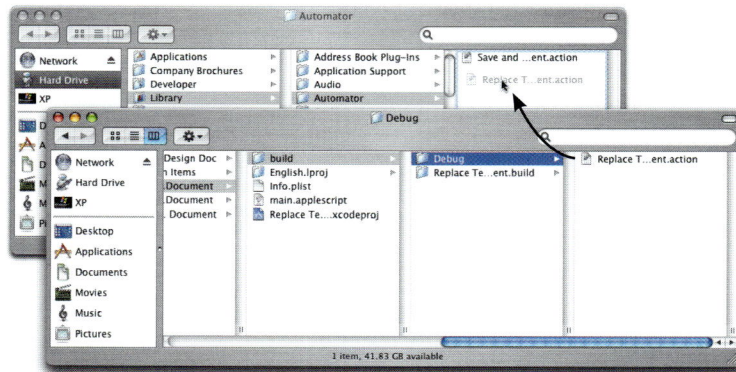

Figure 5.40 *Once you've dragged the action's build file into the Library > Automator folder, quit and restart Automator to have the action appear in InDesign's library.*

6. Restart Automator.

Upon restarting Automator, your action should appear in the Adobe InDesign CS3 Library.

Now think about what you could do with this action. With some fairly minimal AppleScript retooling, you could get it to work with Illustrator or Photoshop. You could also rewrite it so that it created documents from a template, such as letterhead or business cards, instead of just editing existing documents. You can probably imagine plenty of ways this could streamline your work.

6

From One, Many

Data-Driven Publishing with Creative Suite

Isn't life a series of images that change as they repeat themselves?

—*Andy Warhol*

Travel back in time with me to June 2004 and imagine that you're one of *Reason* magazine's 40,000 subscribers. You get your monthly issue, and on the cover you see an aerial photograph of your neighborhood—with your house circled in red (**Figure 6.1**). And that's not all: Inside is a customized editor's page peppered with stats from your community, a street map of your mailing address, customized ads (that incorporate your street address), and your Congress member's name and voting record.

Now, let's deconstruct the moment you began flipping through that magazine. You were probably thinking something like the following: Magazines are mass-produced, so typically the only thing distinguishing one copy of an issue from another is the mailing label (which is actually produced by a form of data-driven publishing, or DDP). Since magazines generally concern themselves with just about anything but you, and high-quality printing isn't economical for single copies (remember, you're back in 2004), just how did *Reason* get that neighborhood picture and street map?

For a moment, you forget your surroundings and become completely focused on and open to the thing in front of you. That *Reason* magazine cover epitomizes the stop-you-in-your-tracks power of data-driven publishing—a potent combination of data, graphics, and high-speed quality printing. The magazine is also unsettling in its Big Brother implications—but that too illustrates the power of DDP, and was very much a part of the statement the issue was trying to make with its personalized cover and contents. The great graphical DDP advances brought about in part by features in Creative Suite mean that anyone who works in this field needs to be conscious of privacy issues and vigilant about avoiding even the appearance of breaching customers' privacy. For instance, *Reason*'s subscribers freely gave their information to

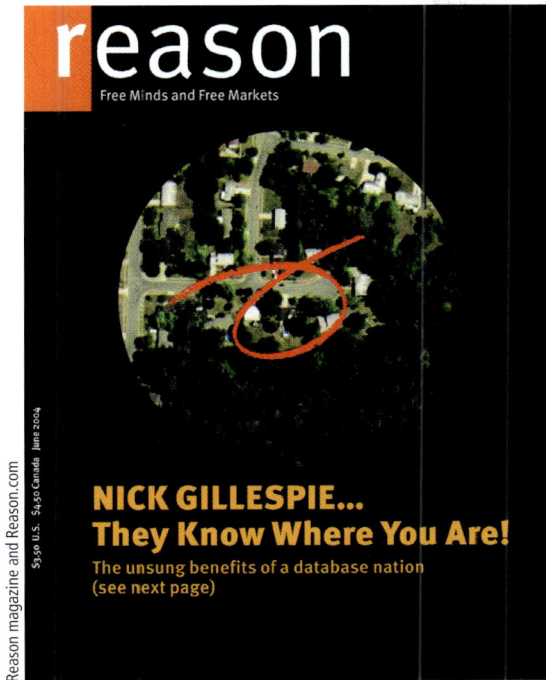

Reason magazine and Reason.com

Figure 6.1 *A representative cover of* Reason *magazine's June 2004 issue. If you were a subscriber, the aerial photo would have been of your neighborhood with your house circled in red.*

the magazine (as we all do), but they didn't expect it to be translated into the product they held in their hands.

But what if the recipient found the issue intriguing or exciting (as some *Reason* readers most likely did)? What if that magazine engaged subscribers, excited their imaginations, or gave them customized information they could actually use? DDP is nothing if not targeted marketing: It means you don't have to blast your message to the masses and *hope* it sticks with enough of them.

Although today's media-savvy consumers may be more cynical about personalized communications than they were in the past (making them harder to reach via standard DDP), Creative Suite's DDP features help you grab and hold their attention by enabling you to create more interesting customized graphic messages. And keep in mind that DDP is not just for direct-mail pieces: As you will see in the following sections, you can employ it to create production files for a wide range of products, including packaging, ads, business cards, contact sheets, and more.

Data-Driven Publishing

Data-driven publishing technology—also known as *variable-data publishing, data merge,* and *dynamic publishing*—describes an efficient way of producing many variations of a document by changing out specific text and images.

Producing multiple variations of a project by hand isn't a new task for any graphic designer—but producing hundreds or thousands of slightly different documents is a whole different ballgame from creating a half-dozen comps or revisions. Take the standard business card: Across a company they look pretty similar, with the exception of personal data like names, phone numbers, e-mail addresses, and so on. If you had to type in the data for 100 of these, you'd shoot yourself. You'd be hunched over the keyboard, looking at some photocopied sheet of everyone's information, building file after file after file after file. Your mind would wander. You'd begin to wonder where your life went off track, and sooner rather than later, you'd screw up 10 files by looking at the wrong line.

DDP automates processes like the one described above and—as long as your data source has the correct information—it doesn't mess up by putting Jean Smith's phone number on John Doe's card. If you were to use DDP to produce the same business card described above, the basic card layout would contain all the information common to every card, such as the company logo and address, filled in (this is known as a *parent file*) and *data fields* for the information that changes from card to card (the *variables*). A parent file with variables is called a *template,* and that photocopied sheet with everyone's info is now a text file called a *content file.* The program plugs each set of personal info into the template and produces a file for each (these are known as *child files* or *children*). In other words, *Template + content = output.*

To give you an idea of how useful this type of automation can be, I built a 10,000-business-card DDP test project in Illustrator, and the program cranked them out at a rate of about *1,700 files per hour.* Granted, business cards are relatively small (in terms of file size), but that rate is at least 100 times faster than a human—even an experienced operator working at full tilt—could produce without a single mistake. Of course, not every project will result in such dramatic time savings, but you get the idea.

A Little History

Data-driven publishing has been around a long time. If you're old enough, you may remember when Publishers Clearing House started sending out its famous mailers. They varied in style, but an individual's name was always prominently featured in the best-quality dot-matrix printing available. That was the visual hook, and what a hook it was. Until then, most people had only seen their names printed like that on certificates commemorating special moments in their lives.

DDP has also been available to individuals for quite some time. Microsoft Word's Mail Merge feature, for example, brought the Avery 33-up mailing label project to the masses. You simply set up your template and imported data from a spreadsheet, and all the labels for that month's newsletter mailing would be set up to print in one pass. If you think about it, it was a critical piece of the desktop publishing revolution. My first Word mailing-label project actually used a dot-matrix printer and a one-up roll of self-adhesive labels, but those 33-up sheets weren't far behind—and of course printing them all at once was the revolutionary part.

Data-Driven Benefits

The economic advantages of DDP don't end with improved response rates. Since they target narrower niches, DDP mailings tend to be smaller than other mailings and thus consume less paper, ink, and fuel. The result is reduced costs all around. And, frankly, DDP pisses off fewer people than traditional direct junk mail. At its best, DDP can be an elegant form of communications that may even bring a little wonder into the world—not a bad use of technology.

DDP in Creative Suite

Photoshop, Illustrator, and InDesign all employ their own versions of DDP. All handle text and linked images, and both Photoshop and Illustrator also provide users with the option of showing or hiding elements (known as *visibility*). That, however, is where the feature consistency ends: Photoshop and Illustrator offer tools for creating data sets within the application, while InDesign doesn't. Photoshop and InDesign import simple tab- or comma-delimited text files, while Illustrator requires XML-format data sets. Illustrator exports data sets, whereas the other two don't (**Table 6.1**). Finally, Illustrator has a

TABLE 6.1   Data-Driven Publishing Across Creative Suite

	Photoshop	Illustrator	InDesign
Feature Name in Program	Data-Driven Graphics	Data-Driven Graphics	Data Merge
Variable Types Handled	Text	Text	Text
	Linked Image	Linked Image	Linked Image
	Visibility	Visibility	
		Graph	
Creates Data Sets Internally?	Yes	Yes	No
Imports Data Sets?	Yes (in tab- or comma-delimited text format)	Yes (in XML format)	Yes (in tab- or comma-delimited text format)
Exports Data Sets?	No	Yes (in XML format)	No

great but little-known capability to generate data-driven graphs, in which each iteration can have a different design and orientation.

It's not easy to pick a favorite, but of these three programs, InDesign offers the most robust DDP. It points toward where I hope Adobe plans to take Creative Suite's DDP across the board: error reporting for text-frame overflow and missing images; maintaining links to external data files; and flexible text handling, with the capability to handle *inline variable text* (variable text that doesn't need its own frame).

The Clock Project

In this project, I've placed a logo on a clock face; however, it will be a variable that sits behind the clock's hands and their shadows. I also placed a variable trademark line running along the right side of the image.

Take a look at a sample of the results (**Figure 6.2**), and you'll see that there are two variables in this image: The first is the logo (in this sample, the Adobe Photoshop logo), and the second is the trademark line running up the right-hand side (**Figure 6.3**). One of the keys to designing a successful DDP image is to make it look utterly real: The casual viewer should never think that the logo wasn't in the original photograph, or that it could be replaced with another logo.

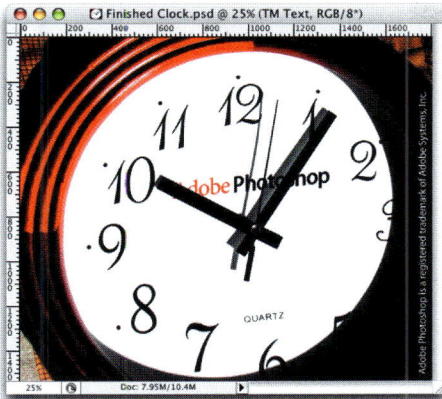

Figure 6.2 *A sample of the output, or child file: The Photoshop logo and the legal text on the right are both variables.*

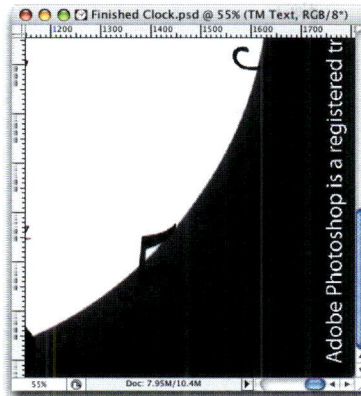

Figure 6.3 *A close-up of the variable text on the right side.*

Building the Template

1. To begin building my clock face, I opened an image of a clock in Photoshop and named its single layer Clock Face.

2. I then opened a logo file that I'd previously skewed to fit the perspective of the clock face, copied and pasted it into the clock file, and named the layer Variable Logo.

3. After positioning the logo, I gave its layer a blending mode of Multiply, to make it appear behind the clock hands and beneath their shadows (**Figure 6.4**).

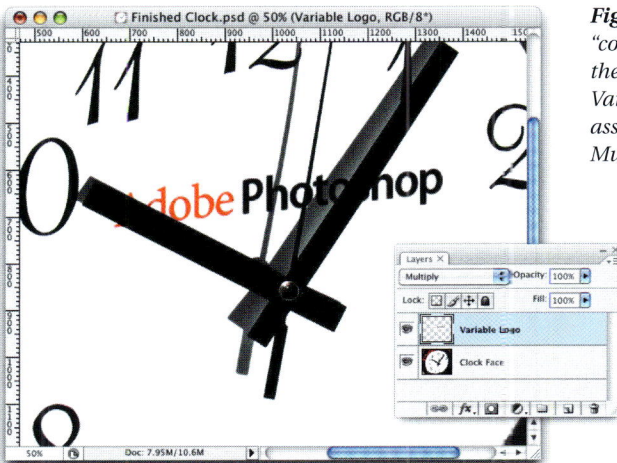

Figure 6.4 *Close-up of the "convincing shadow" and the layer order. Note that the Variable Logo layer has been assigned a blending mode of Multiply.*

4. Next, I added a text layer and named it TM Text. With the text still selected, I rotated it 90 degrees counterclockwise and positioned it in the lower-right corner (**Figure 6.5**). In this project, the text will be replaced with trademark copy from an external text file.

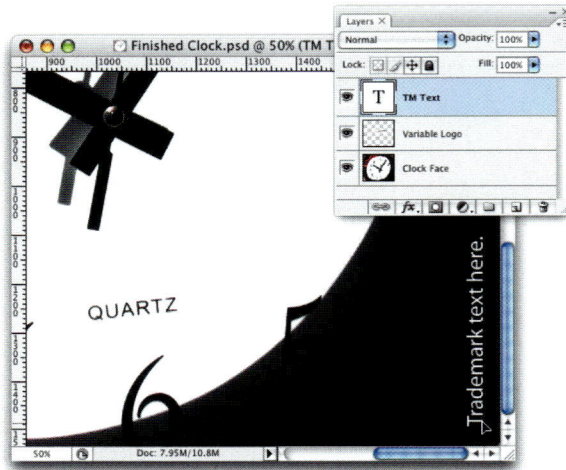

Figure 6.5 *The placeholder trademark text, placed in the lower right corner.*

Creating the Variables

1. To make two of the layers in my template into variables, I chose Image > Variables > Define. This brought up the Variables dialog box: From its Layer pull-down menu (which lists all layers in a document), I chose Variable Logo. Since I planned to replace all the pixels in this layer, I checked the Pixel Replacement box. I then gave this variable the name Logo in the Name field and left the Method pull-down at the default choice, Fit (**Figure 6.6**).

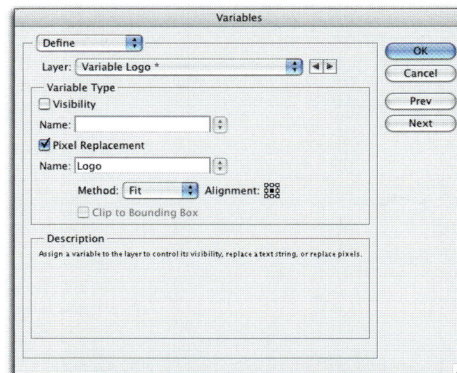

Figure 6.6 *You define a file's variables in the Variables dialog box: Simply pick the layer from the pull-down menu and make your selections.*

Note that there are four choices for Method: Fit, which fits the image in the bounding box while maintaining proportions; Fill, which fills the bounding box while maintaining proportions; As Is, which inserts the replacement image while maintaining its size; and Conform, which fills the bounding box but doesn't maintain the original proportions. For both Fill and As Is, the Clip to Bounding Box check box is available, which allows you to mask any part of the image that extends beyond the bounding box.

Note

To avoid trouble, start variable names with a letter and don't use spaces or nonalphanumeric characters.

2. Next, from the Layer pull-down menu I selected the TM Text layer. You'll notice that because this layer contains text, the Pixel Replacement option has changed to Text Replacement. I checked that box and named the variable TMtext. Note that for both of these layers (in addition to their other variables), I could have chosen to make their visibility variable by checking Visibility in the Variable Type area. Each layer can thus have as many as two variables assigned to it.

Creating Variable Logo Files

Using the test logo that I'd skewed to the clock face, I determined the correct skew angle to match the perspective of the clock. After getting the angle, I recorded a quick action for a –7 percent skew, and then ran it as a batch action on three logos (**Figure 6.7**).

Creating the External Data Sets File

A data set consists of a group of variables and the data used to populate them. You can create data sets within Photoshop by manually populating the variables and saving the resulting data set (for this project, that means replacing the image on the Variable Logo layer with another image and typing new text in the TM Text layer). To save the data set, choose Image > Variables > Data Sets and click the New Data Set button (**Figure 6.8**). Repeat this process

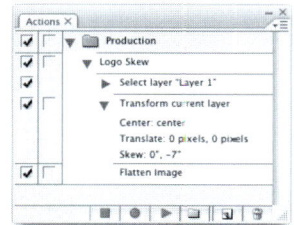

Figure 6.7 I set up a batch action to skew my logo files –7 percent to match the perspective of the clock face.

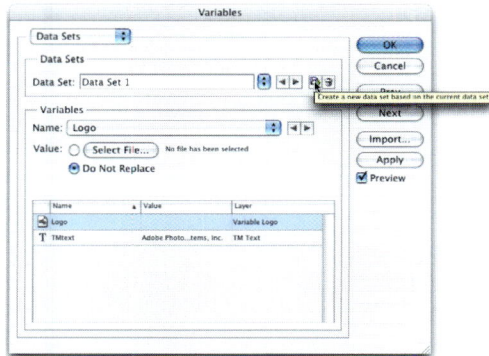

Figure 6.8 Click the disk icon to save a data set that captures the current content.

(replacing the variable content and saving the data set) for as many iterations of your image as you need.

A far more common scenario, however, would be to import a text file containing the data sets. A file of external data sets usually comes out of a spreadsheet or database as a text file, but you can also build one by typing the data in almost any text editor. Photoshop will import either a tab- or comma-delimited text file.

1. For this project I used my favorite text editor to type the data in a text document. I set up the file like a spreadsheet, with columns, rows, headers, and tabs separating the columns (**Figure 6.9**).

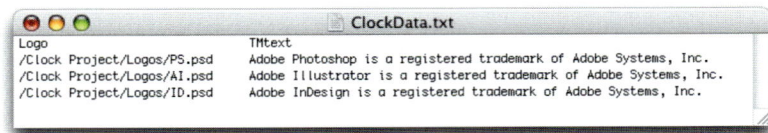

Figure 6.9 The content text file containing pointers to the variable graphics and the actual variable text. Each row is one data set.

2. The first line of the text file must contain the variable names. It doesn't matter what order the "columns" of variable data are in as long as the variable names on the first line (the "column headers") exactly match the variable names in the Photoshop file. I decided to put the Pixel Replacement variable data first, so I typed Logo (precisely matching the variable name I assigned in Photoshop). I then pressed the Tab key and typed TMtext for the name of the text variable.

3. On the second line of the text file (beneath Logo), I typed the path to the Adobe Photoshop logo file. Note that data set files *point* to images via their file paths rather than containing the actual images. To quickly find a document's file path on a Mac, open Terminal (Applications > Utilities > Terminal) and drag the file from its location into the Terminal window. You'll immediately see the path name, which you can then copy and paste into the content file. To locate a document's file path in Windows, choose Start > Run and then drag the file into the Run field. The file path will appear, and you can then copy and paste it into the text file. After pasting the file path, I pressed the Tab key and entered the trademark line for the Photoshop logo.

4. I repeated the same steps for the last two data sets and saved the data sets file as ClockData.txt.

Importing the Data Sets File

For the next task, I had to return to Photoshop, where I imported the external data sets file by choosing Image > Variables > Data Sets and clicking the Import button on the right side of the dialog box that appeared. I then navigated to the ClockData.txt file and clicked OK. (Adobe has crammed a lot into this dialog box, so it's a little hard to make out what's going on sometimes.) Photoshop matches up the data under each of the headers in the content file with the same-named variables. If you click the Preview check box, you can flip through the data sets and watch the image and text change in the template file. You can do this by clicking the Back and Forward arrows in the Data Sets area or by choosing them from the Data Set drop-down menu. When I had verified that my data sets were correct, I clicked the OK button.

Outputting the Child Files

1. To build the final files, from the File menu I chose Export > Data Sets as Files. Then, in the Save Options area, I chose the destination folder by clicking the Select Folder button and navigating to the folder I'd set up for my final images (called Clock Pics).

2. In the File Naming portion of this dialog box, I used the pull-down menus to tell Photoshop how to construct the filenames for the child files (**Figure 6.10**). Notice the Name Example at the top of the File Naming area.

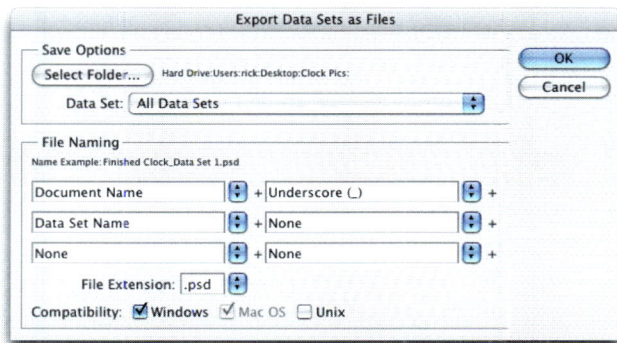

<table>
<tr><td colspan="2">**Export Data Sets as Files**</td></tr>
<tr><td>**Save Options**
Select Folder...   Hard Drive:Users:rick:Desktop:Clock Pics:
Data Set: All Data Sets

File Naming
Name Example: Finished Clock_Data Set 1.psd
Document Name + Underscore (_) +
Data Set Name + None +
None + None +
File Extension: .psd
Compatibility: ☑ Windows ☑ Mac OS ☐ Unix</td><td>OK
Cancel</td></tr>
</table>

Figure 6.10 *You select the destination folder for your finished files in the upper area of the Export Data Sets as Files dialog box. In the bottom area you determine how your child files will be named. Click OK, and you're off to the races.*

Tip

The headers in the content text file (in this case, Logo and TMtext) must exactly match the variable names set up in the template, or Photoshop won't be able to match them up when importing the content file.

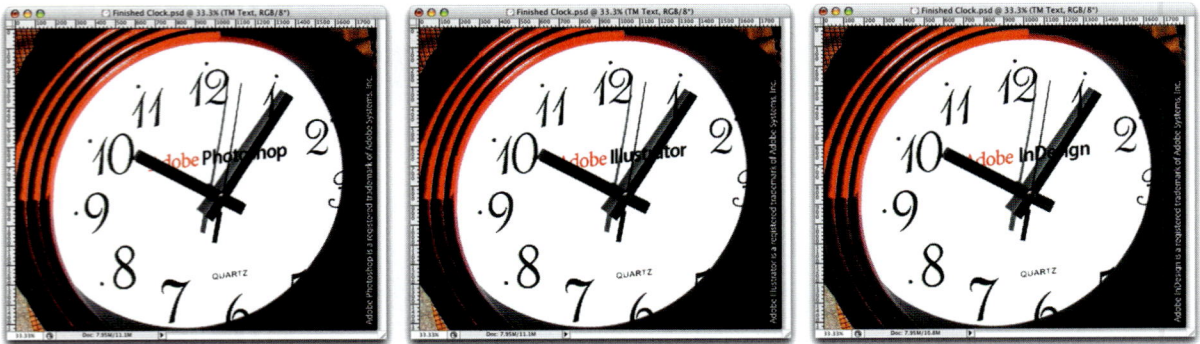

Figure 6.11 Like human children, these files inherit some traits from their parent but contain enough variables to make them unique.

3. When I'd set up everything the way I wanted, I clicked OK, and the files were built and saved in the destination folder (**Figure 6.11**). Ta da.

The Future

Despite its usefulness, the future of data-driven publishing remains cloudy. An underutilized technology—due either to its obscurity or poor usability—it hasn't seen much technological progress lately.

In the meantime, just as progress in data-driven print technologies was stalling, the Internet revolution ushered in an era of communicating with very small and focused audiences—via advertising on customized e-greeting cards and e-invitations and personalized e-mail (much of it unwanted, aka *spam*). Both happily and unhappily, this microcasting trend exposed us all to a wealth of personalized imagery and messages—so we've grown, at least partly, sickened by it. As a result, we now look at personalized marketing materials with a great deal more skepticism and wariness. Long gone are the wide-eyed and heady days of the Publishers Clearing House envelope.

But remember that DDP can be used for more than just personalized marketing communications. There will always be a demand for elegantly designed, respectful personalized marketing materials targeted to audiences that have opted in (either implicitly or explicitly) for the experience.

As for the evolution of the technology, I think DDP tools could be fine-tuned to make tying external data to variables much easier—InDesign's drag-and-drop method of data merging represents a step in the right direction. Now that Adobe's suites are one, big, happy standardized family, it also wouldn't hurt to expand and standardize DDP tools across the product lines.

7

Mixed Bag of Tricks

Auxiliary Tools

At each increase of knowledge, as well as on the contrivance of every new tool, human labour becomes abridged.

—*Charles Babbage*

The more tools you have at your disposal, the better equipped you'll be to adapt to constantly changing production needs. In this guided tour of my favorite auxiliary tools, I'll explain what each tool does best and point out some of the most common problems they can be deployed to solve.

The three categories of tools covered here—multipurpose automation tools, data-cleaning tools, and triggering tools—generally play a supporting role to the other tools covered in this book (though there's some overlap in capabilities). Multipurpose automation tools, as their name implies, cover multiple areas of automation and can be used to automate system-level tasks, Creative Suite applications, and other software. Data-cleaning tools also do precisely what their name implies—clean up and edit text and numbers. Triggering tools start or run automations based on time or state.

Multipurpose Automation Tools

In your Creative Suite design work, you'll inevitably run into situations where your main automation tools (actions, scripting, Automator, data-driven publishing, and server-based applications) are either unable to perform a task or don't do it well. The multipurpose automation tools described here offer ways to automate operating system–level tasks and fill in some of those automation gaps, including (but not limited to) those included in components of Creative Suite. In fact, you'll probably use these multipurpose tools at the operating system level and with applications other than Creative Suite. However, one of them (QuicKeys) can automate any Creative Suite application.

QuicKeys

About a decade ago I began working with QuicKeys ($79.95, free 30-day demo, www.cesoft.com, Windows/Mac), and it was a big part of what hooked me on graphics automation. Using QuicKeys revealed to me how many boring, repetitive tasks lurked in my job—and helped me start rooting them out. I think it's perfect for anyone new to automation and for graphics production environments.

QuicKeys is macro software, which means it records your mouse movements and keystrokes and plays them back on demand. You can also manually build automations in QuicKeys, one step at a time. Usually you trigger a macro with a key combination of your specification (**Figure 7.1**).

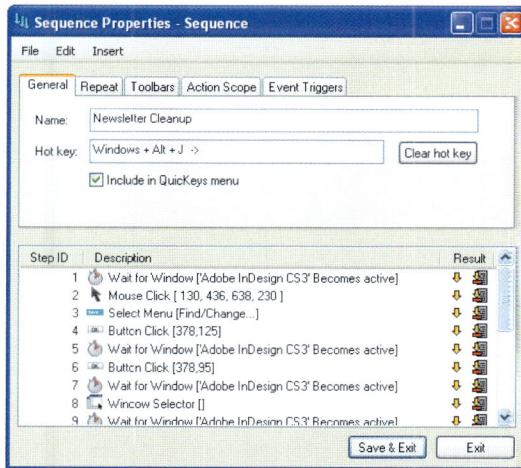

Figure 7.1 *QuicKeys records and lets you edit multistep tasks, which you can assign to a key combination.*

I used QuicKeys in a graphics production environment to assign key combinations to tasks in Illustrator and Photoshop (this was in the days before InDesign)—but I also used it to name disks, mount servers, and change printers. There seemed to be no computer operation it couldn't automate. Back then, applications assigned fewer keyboard shortcuts, making QuicKeys invaluable. And QuicKeys' support for application-specific sets meant I could avoid conflicts if I chose to reuse key combinations. I built up dozens of QuicKeys to control processes in the Finder and in my applications. The hardest thing about QuicKeys was remembering all the keystrokes.

In recent years, scripting and Adobe actions have largely eclipsed QuicKeys for graphics production—and automation experts tend to look down on macro recorders like QuicKeys for their lack of sophistication—but QuicKeys has actually grown more sophisticated over the years. These days, it can handle if/then statements (which QuicKeys calls Decisions) as well as looping (the ability to repeat a process until a condition is met). It also offers lots of ways to trigger your macros, including timers and toolbars. QuicKeys can also trigger scripts and Automator workflows. It's the Swiss Army Knife of general automation tools.

QuicKeys remains a great tool because it brings keystroke assignment to almost any application, including the operating system. Given its ease of use and functionality, I've never found anything to replace it.

Proxi

Proxi is my new favorite program (http://proxi.griffintechnology.com, free, Mac only). An interesting piece of software, it was ostensibly written to automate the hardware products of Griffin Technology; however, it can also automate the Mac OS, some of Apple's applications (including iTunes, iChat, and Mail), other programs, and some non-Griffin hardware such as the Apple Remote.

Proxi resembles Automator in both interface and function (**Figure 7.2**); however, it differs in two important respects: It includes an automated trigger system that Automator lacks, and it's geared to system and application events (while Automator is focused more on file processing). With Proxi, you build a

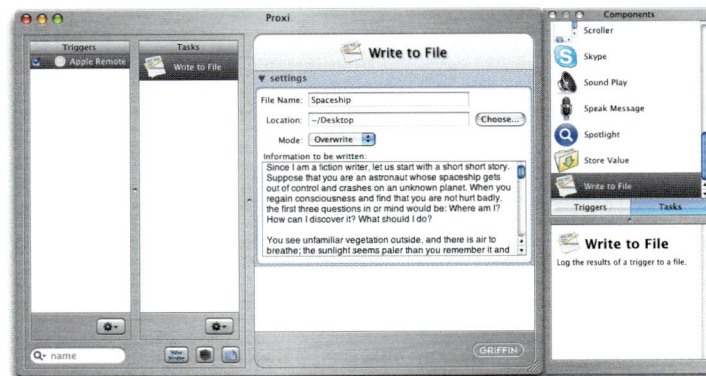

Figure 7.2 *Proxi has an Automator-like three-panel interface (plus the Components menu on the right).*

set of tasks (like Automator's workflow) called a Blueprint and assign a trigger to it. Triggers can be time- or event-based and include filters to include or exclude conditions when the trigger fires.

Proxi is a work in progress—and as such, it's hard to tell where it's headed—but it has a playfulness that I love (check out Bubbles and the different kinds of screen messages), making it a great introduction to automation. And it's also solid enough to do serious automation work.

Data-Cleaning Tools

You're probably all too familiar with the need to clean up source material before you can get down to designing. If you work in publishing, you've probably spent far too many hours styling long blocks of text or picking hard returns out of copy that some bonehead e-mailed to you. And you've probably come up with a few work-arounds out of self-defense. This section examines each of the applications commonly used to clean up data, showing you some new tricks for turning garbage into clean copy fast. Good strategies for automating data cleanup are essential once you start producing custom communications from external data sources (as described in the next part of the book).

Text Editors

Depending on the kind of work you do, text is possibly the most common type of supporting file you'll receive. When choosing a text editor, look for one that allows you to save multiple text edits into one automated operation. Even though each will save you time, being able to batch multiple edits will save you *blocks* of time. Go slowly, however, trying one here and one there. When you feel confident in each, string them together into a single automation.

CLEANUP TASKS

Find and Replace. Most users of Microsoft Word and other text editors are familiar with find/replace capabilities: You simply type in the text you want to find and the text you want to replace it with, and then press OK. Find/replace then either steps through the document occurrence by occurrence or all at one go. Word also offers more advanced features, which you can access by clicking the More button in the Find and Replace window (**Figure 7.3**). Word lets you search and replace using wildcards (symbols that stand for letters or words) and regular expressions (patterns of text), giving you a great deal of added text-cleanup power. You could, for instance, strip out all HTML tags by typing \<*\> in the "Find what" field and nothing in the "Replace with" field. The first slash instructs Word to search for the following character, not interpret it as a command. The less-than sign is the first part of an HTML tag. The asterisk is a wildcard for any text, and \> is the end of the HTML tag (again, the slash tells Word to search for the following character). This search string will find every HTML tag with opening and closing brackets, regardless of what's between them. Word can also search and replace by text style.

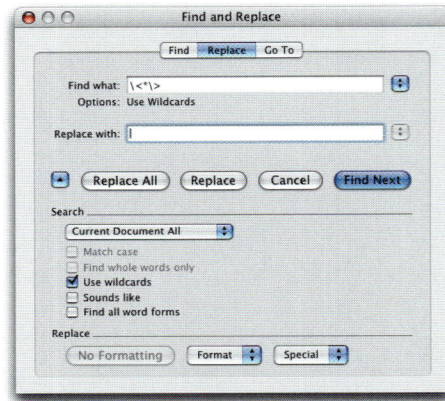

Figure 7.3 Clicking the More button (next to the Replace All button) provides access to Word's advanced search features. Make sure the "Use wildcards" check box is selected before using.

Gremlins and Line Feeds. Text files can contain superfluous formatting information (such as fonts and colors), multiple spaces, nonprinting characters called gremlins, line numbers, and line feeds—all of which you will need to get rid of. Some of these can be taken care of with the trusty find and replace. But some of this junk is a bit trickier to eradicate. Gremlins, for example, can take the form of many different characters and character combinations, which makes them hard to ferret out. Line numbers are somewhat difficult as well. For example, do you search for every instance of *1* plus a tab and replace it with nothing (effectively deleting it)? And how do you strip out *2*, *3*, and so on without searching for each in turn (spending more time than you would just deleting them by hand)? Some applications provide tools specifically for thorny problems like gremlins and line numbers.

Find/replace features and special tools, however, only go so far. Some complex formatting cleanup jobs require still more powerful tools. For example, you might want to reformat all the phone numbers in a file, replacing parentheses around the area code with a hyphen between the area code and number. Regular find and replace just doesn't cut it (though Word's find/replace can handle some of this). Enter grep, originally a program for the Unix operating system with a text-only interface, which can identify patterns (also known as *regular expressions)* in text files.

Not only does grep allow you to identify a search pattern, it also lets you replace that pattern with another. Searching for incorrectly formatted phone numbers and changing the formatting is the kind of problem grep is made for.

InDesign includes some robust grep capabilities, which you can access from the Find/Change dialog box (click the GREP tab at the top). You can type in the grep characters manually or access them by clicking the @ menus next to the "Find what" and "Change to" fields (**Figure 7.4**).

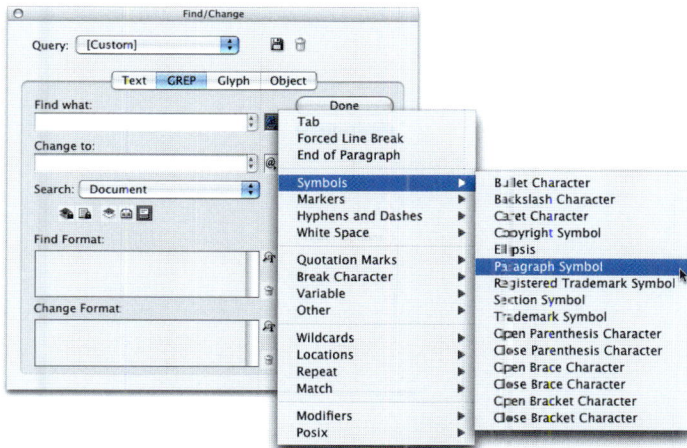

Figure 7.4 *The GREP tab of InDesign's Find/Change dialog box includes preset grep characters that you can access via the @ menus next to the "Find what" and "Change to" fields.*

InDesign Tags. When importing text into InDesign, you can have it apply preset character and paragraph styles based on *tags*, which are simply text characters you add to precede (and sometimes follow) the text you want styled. To automatically apply InDesign tags to text files, the particular text must be made identifiable—a tricky and sometimes even impossible task.

If you want to tag headlines with the Headline paragraph style, exactly how do you do it? If you're lucky, headlines in the text file may be preceded by two returns (also known as *line feeds, newlines,* or—back in the day—*carriage returns*). If this is the case, you can set up an edit to add the tags to every line that follows two returns. This, however, is a hit-and-miss process that depends on how the text file has been built (not something you control). If you study the file carefully, though, you'll probably be able to spot patterns that let you efficiently insert tags.

To get an idea of how this works, open an InDesign document, select the text, and export it as tagged text (choose File > Export and from the pull-down menu choose Adobe InDesign Tagged Text). Now open this file in a text editor (**Figure 7.5**). You can change the paragraph styles by changing the text tags and importing the text back into InDesign.

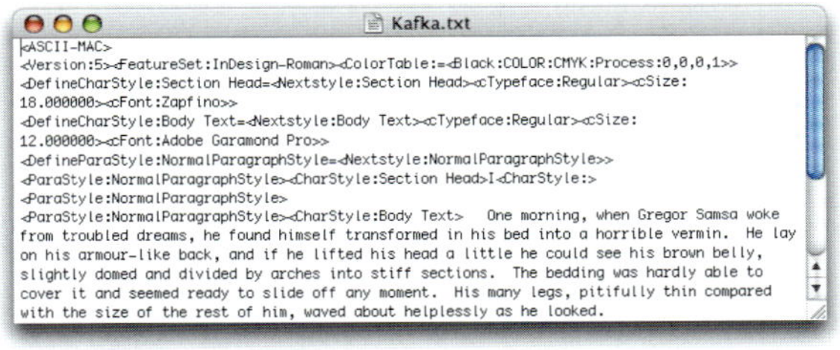

Figure 7.5 A file containing both InDesign paragraph styles and text.

TEXT EDITING SOFTWARE

There are a billion or so text editors, many of them free, but to get serious text-editing functions you might need to spend some money. On the Windows side, if your employer hasn't already made the choice for you, consider the aforementioned Microsoft Word. It's compatible with most files you'll receive simply because most people use it. Also check out UltraEdit (www. ultraedit.com, $49.95), which includes grep features and is JavaScriptable. For the Mac, check out BBEdit (www.barebones.com, $125), which is a favorite among programmers for its Clippings (for saving and reusing text), built-in HTML editor, and Text Factories (providing a means to save and apply multiple text manipulations); it's also scriptable. BareBones offers a free, scaled-down editor for the Mac called TextWrangler (www.barebones.com/products/textwrangler)—which if you're not a programmer may be plenty for your needs. Don't forget that Word is still available for the Mac. And if you're adventurous, go to www.gnu.org/software/grep and download the free grep editor offered by the Free Software Foundation.

Spreadsheets

Data may sometimes reach you in the form of a spreadsheet file (**Figure 7.6**). In spreadsheets, data is stored in cells (which form rows and columns) that can be moved, sorted, calculated, and manipulated in a host of other ways. Spreadsheets are thought of primarily as tools for crunching numbers, but they can also be used to store non-numeric lists (that is, text) and recordlike data.

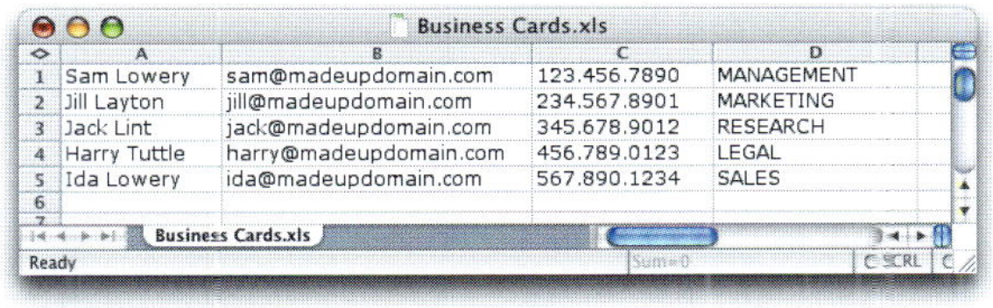

Figure 7.6 *An Excel spreadsheet.*

Although spreadsheets let you massage your data by sorting or filtering it, moving blocks of it around, and running find-and-replace operations on it, they don't have as many text-editing tools as some text editors. Still, many people prefer to view and edit their data in tabular form. In addition to data manipulation, spreadsheets also provide a great way to store data to feed Creative Suite templates via scripting. Microsoft Excel is the undisputed spreadsheet application leader, and it's available for both Windows and Mac. That ubiquity means almost everyone can open and view Excel files, which can be reason enough to use it. However, its price (more than $200) can be prohibitive for casual users. If that's the case for you, check out Calc, which is part of the OpenOffice suite of applications (www.OpenOffice.org)—free software that runs on both Windows and Mac (as well as other platforms). And Google has also released a free online spreadsheet in its Google Docs & Spreadsheets application (www.google.com/google-d-s/intl/en/tour1.html).

Databases

Databases organize your data by field and record (**Figure 7.7**), making it easy to edit and export that data as a batch. You can think of databases as spreadsheets in which you view one column (or row) of data at a time (unless you're working in a table view, which looks a lot like a spreadsheet). Think of my usual example of 100 business cards: In a spreadsheet, you would see the data for all the cards on one page. In a database, it would be like flipping through the cards, seeing one person's data at a time.

Figure 7.7 *A database record in FileMaker for Windows.*

Databases have even more limited text-editing tools than spreadsheets. If you're given project data in database form, you'll probably want to export the data and edit it in either a spreadsheet or text editor. Like spreadsheets, however, databases are very useful for storing and accessing data that you'll use for a scripted data-driven publishing automation in Creative Suite.

The most commonly used desktop databases are Microsoft Access (on Windows) and FileMaker Pro (on Windows and Mac). FileMaker Pro has a decent, easy-to-use proprietary scripting feature, but it can also store and run AppleScripts internally. Access will run you about $200, while FileMaker Pro is $300—a bit steep for occasional use. Try the Base application in the Open-Office suite (www.OpenOffice.org) as a free alternative.

Triggering Tools

A trigger is anything that starts an automation. Usually that means double-clicking something, but there are many ways to trigger a process, many of which can be automated. With some exceptions, most of the main graphics automation tools (scripting, actions, and so on) don't contain triggering capabilities—which means that you'll need to turn to these helper tools if you want to trigger an agent automatically.

The three types of triggers are time, event, and condition. A time trigger is as simple as setting an alarm or a timer; however, something has to watch the clock. If this isn't system-level software, then it's usually a program that's open and running all the time. The second type is an event, something that can be defined and watched. An event is any sudden change of state, such as when an application is opened or closed, when a file suddenly exists or doesn't, or when a window appears. The third type of trigger is a change in a characteristic or property of an object—known as a *condition*. Examples of conditions are when a number reaches a certain value or when an object changes color. To be honest, though, graphics automation triggering software doesn't deal much in conditions.

All of the tools discussed here use some or all of these triggering types. All have graphical interfaces that make setting up a trigger easy and painless.

> **Note**
>
> Photoshop includes a Script Events Manager that can watch as many as 200 Photoshop events.

Macintosh Software

The Macintosh operating system's calendar program (iCal) can trigger AppleScripts based on time and date (**Figure 7.8**). All you need to do is set a date and time (and if you want it to repeat) and tell it which script to trigger.

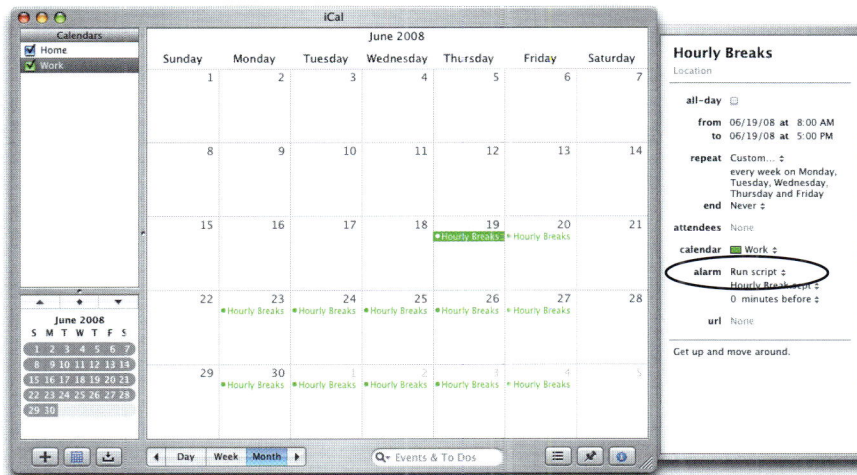

Figure 7.8 In iCal's Event pane (on the right), you can set a date and time to trigger an AppleScript: In the "alarm" menu, choose "Run script." Be sure to select "0 minutes before" for the warning time.

An application called iDo (www.sophisticated.com, $24.95) works similarly but adds a few interesting features. With it, you can pass parameters to AppleScripts (**Figure 7.9**). You can even have different iDo "events" (time-based triggers) trigger scripts with one or more variables. Say your script runs a backup: You could use iDo events to trigger a script to run a partial backup on most days and a full backup on Sunday nights (which just happens to be a good night to run a backup). In addition to time-based triggers, iDo will also respond when the system has been idle (no user activity) for a preset number of minutes. iDo can also run in the background, which means you don't have to have the application open all the time (the same goes for iCal) and you can assign triggers to keystrokes.

Figure 7.9 *An iDo event passing the Morning parameter to an AppleScript.*

Proxi—which I described earlier in the chapter—is also noteworthy here because it can be triggered based on date and time. It can also respond to triggers such as battery conditions, new stories on Digg.com, iChat user status changes, changes in network status, and even voice commands. And it's free!

Windows Software

Windows XP includes the free Windows Task Scheduler (**Figure 7.10**), which not only triggers tasks based on time but can also (in the Windows Vista version) respond to system state changes. And Task Scheduler is scriptable using VBScript. Aimed at IT professionals such as system administrators, Task Scheduler can also wake the computer to run a task and send notifications via e-mail.

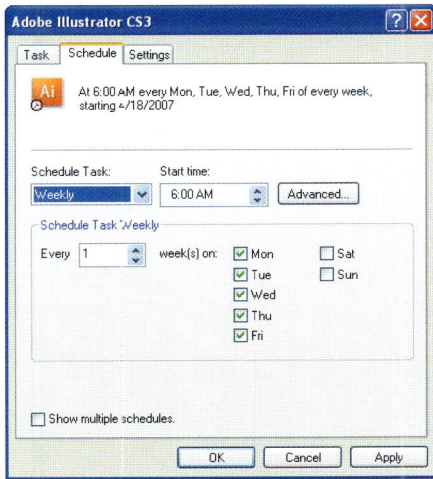

Figure 7.10 Windows Task Scheduler, set to open Illustrator every weekday at 6 a.m. for one week.

There is not much middle ground in Windows between Task Scheduler (which is included in the price of the operating system) and a big system administration application like AutoMate (www.networkautomation.com, starting at $995). Vista's Task Scheduler is going in the right direction to fill that gap.

E-Mail Rules

Most e-mail programs have a rules feature, which detects data in incoming e-mails (such as recipient, subject line text, or date received) and handles the message according to settings you've chosen. The most common type of e-mail rule detects spam and either deletes it or moves it to a spam folder.

The rules in Apple's Mail application can trigger AppleScripts (**Figure 7.11**). When you think about it, e-mail is an interesting way to start an automation process, since it can deliver data files and images to you from anywhere,

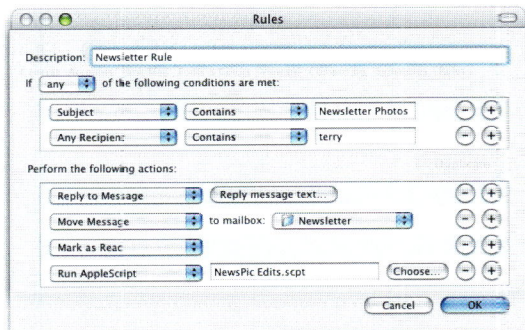

Figure 7.11 An Apple Mail rule showing two criteria and four actions, including running an AppleScript.

and those files and images can be automatically processed. You could, for instance, have your client e-mail you a zipped file containing images for a monthly newsletter. The condition to be met could be that the e-mail must come from a particular person and contain agreed-upon standardized text in the subject line (such as "images"). The rule determines whether the conditions have been met, and if they have triggers a script that detaches the zipped file, decompresses it, runs a Photoshop Batch action on the images, renames them by appending the month to the filename, and saves them in a new folder.

E-mail rules can also send messages themselves; coupled with scripting, you'd be surprised at how personalized these e-mails can be. For example, you could reply to the client who sent you the newsletter files with a message confirming receipt of the files and the number you received. (See Project 3 in Chapter 10, and the newsletter project in Chapter 12 for examples of how rules can be used in an automated workflow.)

Watched Folders

On the Mac you can "attach" an AppleScript (see Chapter 5) to a folder, which then watches the attached folder for certain events (such as when a file is added or removed or a folder is opened or closed) (**Figure 7.12**). This creates a "watched folder." Folder Actions are often triggered manually—for example, by dragging a file into it—but they can also be used for folders that are populated by other processes such as when e-mail attachments are automatically detached and placed in a certain folder.

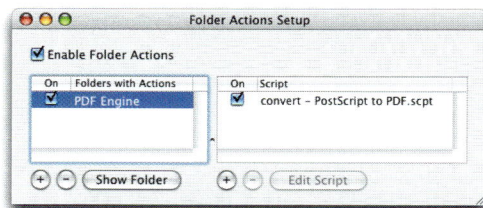

Figure 7.12 On the Mac you can attach AppleScripts to folders, creating watched folders. Here, a folder named PDF Engine has a script named "convert—PostScript to PDF.scpt" attached to it. When a PostScript file is placed into the PDF Engine folder, the attached AppleScript automatically creates a PDF from it.

8

Automatic for the People

Server-Based Applications

Now, if you frequent Weaver D's Delicious Fine Foods, you'll
know I'm automatic. Everything about me is automatic.
When you walk through the front door, you know you'll
get some good food like you're supposed to, food that's
automatic for the people."

—Dexter Weaver, describing his restaurant in Athens, Georgia

Most of the time graphics automation agents quietly churn out the work you've given them, and they don't need you looking over their shoulders, thank you very much. And since they can run unattended, it can be helpful to move them off your production computer so that they don't interfere with the other projects you're working on. You might be part of a workgroup that's all doing the same thing, and you might all want to offload automation projects to an unattended computer. Members of the group could send work to the central computer, monitor its progress from their own computers, and then be notified when their projects have been completed. That's the basic concept of server-based applications—kind of a hub-and-spoke affair.

You might also need to make your projects available to (or modifiable by) people outside your office—either remote workgroup members or clients. Via a Web interface, those people could log in and work from anywhere in the world (or anywhere your security policies allow), whether they're generating one-off customized documents or offloading work.

What's a Server?

When I hear the word *server*, I think of brightly lit, over-air-conditioned rooms filled with row upon row of rack-mounted computers all humming away, lights a-blinking. Although this is not an inaccurate picture, it's not a complete picture either: Server hardware can be almost any computer of almost any size or shape. In 1999 Vaughan Pratt, a computer science professor at Stanford, built a Web server about the size of a matchbox that ran a pared-down version of the Linux operating system and served 5,000 visitors in its first three days of operation (**Figure 8.1**). As long as the computer can be

Figure 8.1 *Vaughan Pratt's Matchbox Webserver next to an antique Russian matchbox.*

hooked to a network or the Internet and run the server software, it's a server. Depending on the context, when people say "server" they may be referring to the hardware, the software, or a combination of the two.

Clients and Servers

An arrangement of multiple client computers feeding work to a centralized server is known as *client-server architecture*, and you probably experience this type of architecture every day when you access the Internet. Your Web browser is the client, and the software and hardware that deliver the Web pages make up the server. Although there are many types of servers (including file servers and print servers), we're only interested in one type—*application servers,* which run automation applications.

At their core, server-based applications aren't much different from their single-user counterparts. For instance, Adobe InDesign Server is built on the same core and has all the same basic features as the InDesign version you use; it just includes some extra muscle. Because jobs are thrown at it all day, from all directions, server-based software requires some additional capabilities to survive. For starters, this kind of software must act as a kind of maître d', determining which jobs get run when, and where they go—or in tech-speak, *queuing* and *routing* jobs. A server-based application also needs security features to prevent unauthorized access and document tampering. And as mentioned earlier, it might need an interface that lets authorized users talk to it from any platform, anywhere. Finally, server software must be able to run on some kind of server operating system (such as Windows Server or Mac OS X Server). A server-based application may also have additional capabilities and work with other server software

Server-Based Graphics and You

We're talking about the graphics automation big time here, since server applications can run anywhere from about $4,000 to $60,000. On top of that, there are costs for the hardware, a robust network, IT support and administration, and training. If you run the design department of a big company with large volumes of work and tight deadlines, these costs represent an investment that will pay off in higher productivity. If you're an individual graphic designer, however, these costs are out of the question. As an individual, you're likely to experience server-based graphics production only as a user; however, it's helpful to understand what server-based applications are and what they can do. And you might be able to create your own server-based graphics system on a small scale. In the Roll Your Own section at the end of this chapter, I've included some hints about how small workgroups might benefit from server-based graphics without making a huge investment in hardware and software.

Playing with the Big Toys

If and when you find yourself designing a server-based graphics system for a large workgroup or a far-flung enterprise, you almost certainly won't be doing it by yourself. Since these systems are big and expensive, people with "chief" in their titles will likely be approving budgets, and lots of people will have a stake in how the system works. Even if you're specifying a fairly modest system, you'll probably need the services of a consultant who specializes in server-based graphics. When you're sitting in those planning meetings, keep the needs of your graphics workflow foremost in your mind; provide objective and detailed usability feedback to the system builders; and don't sweat the technological details.

The Applications

Since this book is about automating Creative Suite, I've focused on the handful of server-based applications that work directly with Photoshop, Illustrator, and InDesign files. I've also included some that import Creative Suite file formats such as scalable vector graphics (SVG) and PDF. This list, though not exhaustive, represents a fairly thorough survey of what's currently on the market.

For Photoshop: Automated Imagery

DEBABELIZER

Graphic artists have long used DeBabelizer Pro (available from www.equilibrium.com) to automate optimizing, manipulating, resizing, converting, and adding watermarks to raster images (it also works on animations and digital video). While it used to run most Photoshop filters, now it mostly runs blur and sharpen filters.

It's easy to set up scripts in DeBabelizer by either dragging and dropping tasks from the menus or recording your steps. DeBabelizer scripts can contain loops and conditionals, making them capable of complex, flexible automations. Although you can accomplish the same kinds of automations by combining Photoshop actions with scripting DeBabelizer pulls it all together in one place, making it easier to use and more powerful—but it's another $550 beyond what you paid for Photoshop.

The Pro version automatically recognizes and communicates with DeBabelizer Server if the server version is installed on the network. You can use the client to build and send automation jobs to one or multiple servers (if installed) and monitor them all from your client desktop. Despite its power, DeBabelizer remains a study in client-server ease of use (see sidebar on next page).

ADOBE GRAPHICS SERVER

Adobe Graphics Server (AGS)—which has been around for quite a while—is used mostly for resizing and converting raster images, producing data-driven raster images (typically for Web sites), and creating data-driven SVG files with a focus on charts and graphs. Although SVG is a promising file format, it hasn't really caught on in general use, so files generally need to be converted to a more common format after production. Aside from being a server, AGS doesn't have any special capabilities that the single-user Creative Suite applications lack, but its specialties are color-mode conversion, image manipulation, file-format conversion, and data-driven publishing (of Photoshop files). It differs from DeBabelizer in two respects: It can customize PSD (Photoshop Document) files using text and pixel replacement (that is, graphic elements can be associated with variables), and it can dynamically change Illustrator files (charts and graphs in particular) that have been saved in the SVG format.

> **Note**
>
> AGS can only import SVG files saved from Illustrator (known as AISVG files). It does not import any other flavor of SVG.

SETTING UP A SERVER JOB IN THREE EASY STEPS

Setting up a DeBabelizer Server job is easy, consisting of just three steps, and it beautifully illustrates the basic concepts of offloading workflows to a server.

1. Drag a bunch of image files into the Global Batches window (**Figure 8.2**). This is the source, which I've named Monthly Newsletter.

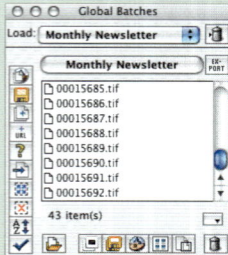

Figure 8.2 *To create a group of source files (known as a global batch) in DeBabelizer, drag the files into this window. You can save these groups to load later for use in either the client or the server.*

2. Build a set of manipulations that you want to apply to the source files (**Figure 8.3**). In DeBabelizer you can use pull-down menus to select the steps that make up the workflow. In this example the image resolution will be set to 300 dpi, the contrast and saturation adjusted, a selection made, and the image trimmed to that selection. I named this Newsletter Workflow.

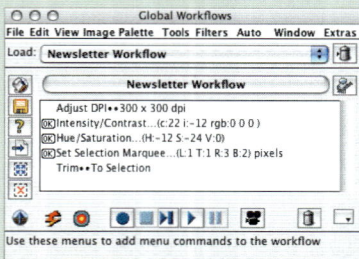

Figure 8.3 *Like the global batches, DeBabelizer Server workflows can be saved and loaded for later use.*

3. In this step you'll create the server job. The four pull-down menus allow you to indicate which source files you want to use, which workflow you want to run, what

destination you want the finished files saved to, and which server will run the job. Click the Submit button to start the job (**Figure 8.4**).

Figure 8.4 *The "job list" window is where DeBabelizer Server jobs are assembled and sent.*

In the Job Status window, you get almost-real-time feedback from the server (**Figure 8.5**), including notification of how your jobs are progressing, and you can monitor multiple jobs. (If multiple jobs are running, they will all appear in this window.) Although you build, send, and monitor DeBabelizer jobs from your desktop computer (the client), they can be sent to run anywhere on the network—on either Mac or PC hardware.

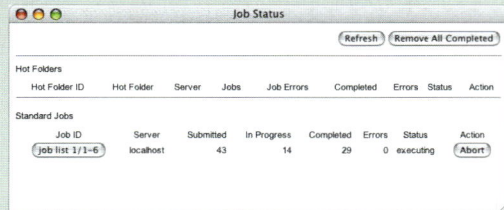

Figure 8.5 *The Job Status window shows you what's happening to your jobs on the server. Here, 29 of 43 files have been processed with no errors. If you have more than one job under way (even on different servers), you'll see them listed here. The server is called "localhost" here because it's actually installed on my desktop machine.*

You can try both the client and server versions of DeBabelizer for free, and you don't even need a server: DeBabelizer Server runs on regular ole' Windows and Mac OS X. You'll have to talk to someone from Equilibrium (DeBabelizer's developer) to get the server demo, but it's a great *and free* way to get an idea of how server software works.

Although it can read EPS (Encapsulated PostScript) and PDF files (from Illustrator and InDesign), it rasterizes any vector data. AGS reads and maintains the layers and text of PSD files.

AGS can read and write metadata (data about the file stored in the file itself) and is often incorporated into asset-management applications and workflow management tools.

For Illustrator: Packaging

Esko Graphics (formerly Barco) develops production and automation software that tightly integrates with Adobe products. The company's packaging production plug-ins for Illustrator and Photoshop, called DeskPack, and its prepress product, PackEdge (used for label distortions and trapping), are standards in the packaging industry.

Although there is no server version of Illustrator and currently no server-based application that imports or generates Illustrator files, Esko's BackStage comes closest to filling that need. The server-based BackStage and client BackStage Pilot work with PDFs saved out of Illustrator (**Figure 8.6**). BackStage includes many modules that give it additional capabilities, including Design-Wizard, a more robust version of Illustrator's own data-driven publishing feature. It ties the design content in a PDF with a database file to produce multiple versions. In addition to handling text and images (as Illustrator does), DesignWizard can edit colors and bar codes.

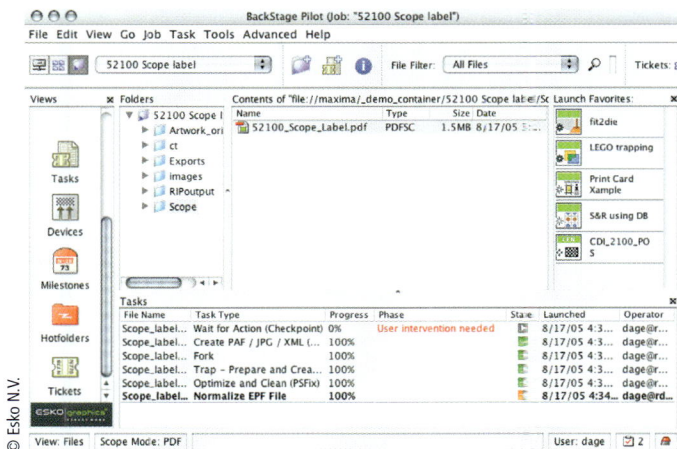

Figure 8.6 The BackStage Pilot interface. The tasks that make up the workflow are listed at the bottom.

Other BackStage modules provide capabilities for trapping, automatic job report building, 3D file generation (using the company's ArtiosCAD application), file transfer, rules-based file checking, and step-and-repeat image generation.

For InDesign: Automated Composition

InDesign is the only Creative Suite application that has its own server version. InDesign Server uses the same code as the desktop version of InDesign but adds some server features. You can script it, use all the features of the single-user version, and output files in all of the formats you're familiar with in InDesign.

InDesign Server has no graphical interface—that is, it's "headless" (**Figure 8.7**). Instead, the user interface is usually provided by a larger publishing system (often a custom-designed one) of which InDesign Server is a module. These systems typically provide data-driven publishing (multiple, varying files derived from one template), automated publishing (single, personalized files derived from a template), or large-scale collaborative publishing (such as at magazines and newspapers).

Figure 8.7 The image on the left is the InDesign Server logo (which is the only graphic you'll see in this application). Notice that InDesign Server runs "headless," which means it has no graphical interface.

InDesign Server is not a fully functional page-composition application. It doesn't manage overset text (text that's too long for its box) and cannot move and resize objects on a page based on white space.

Rolling Your Own Server System

A server doesn't have to be anything more than an extra computer dedicated to running automations—and with the advent of cheaper, more powerful computers as well as operating systems with easy-to-use file sharing, it's become much more feasible to set up a server on the cheap. All you really need is a network or Internet connection, file sharing enabled, and software to handle the incoming jobs. Instead of a server-based application, you could install a single-user version of Creative Suite to do the actual production chores.

To automate sending jobs to the server, you would need to write some scripts triggering Creative Suite's actions and batch features. On the Mac you could use Folder Actions to trigger automations. In workflows where most or all of the files reside on the server, you could improvise a kind of client using the Web-page and e-mail rule setup described in Chapter 12.

This type of system does have limitations. For instance, what if two or more people were to send jobs to the server at the same time? Without some kind of queue, the software would probably crash. And unless you write some software specifically for the task, the system won't include error-checking (which tells the software how to handle errors), which would also lead to crashes. You begin to see why server-based applications are so valuable.

Although the term *server* has traditionally meant some sort of network or Internet connection, you could even do without that. An individual or group could manually load jobs onto the "server" using a sort of sneakernet (a time-honored file-transfer technique). While loading and launching files by hand isn't ideal automation, it works, and it sidesteps the need for a file queue, error-handling, and job-launching scripts.

> **Note**
>
> All users of Creative Suite must be covered by Adobe software licenses. If an unlicensed user were to employ this system, it would violate the end user license agreement: Don't say I didn't warn you!

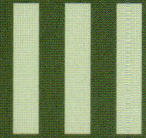

III
Projects

These four chapters are where you'll see the concepts and tools of graphics automation put to work. The projects here are all designed around the scenario that you own a graphic design studio, and you have a client known as the Star & Fey Seed Co. Star & Fey started out as a high-end seed catalog company but now has dozens of retail stores. The company has asked you to design and produce a campaign to increase awareness of the cafés in some of their retail spaces, encouraging repeat visits to the stores and boosting customer visit time.

You may never have an assignment identical to any of these projects, but you should be able to adapt their strategies and techniques. Experiment with the project files, and then look for ways you can adapt the techniques in your own work. Swipe the ideas, actions, and scripts—and hack them to make them your own.

9
Thinking in Pictures

The Photoshop Projects

That which is static and repetitive is boring.
That which is dynamic and random is confusing.
In between lies art.

—*John A. Locke*

Photoshop serves as fertile ground for graphics automation, providing unparalleled tools for producing photo-realistic images, and containing more automation tools than any of the other applications in Creative Suite. You will also find more free automation agents for Photoshop on the Web.

The Projects

As mentioned earlier, our scenario is that you run a graphic design firm whose client—Star & Fey Seed Co., a gardening retail and nursery business with in-store coffee shops—is betting its future on using customized marketing to connect to and retain customers.

Even though your firm is a design studio, you do an increasing amount of production work to provide more services to your design clients. Your clients feel more comfortable with the one-stop shopping, and you get an additional revenue stream—one that makes production work even more profitable and frees your employees up to design. The following are some Photoshop automation projects you could perform for your customers.

Project 1: Metadata

The premise for this project is that someone, ideally the photographer, enters the name of the subject of the photograph (in this case, a flower name) in Photoshop's Description field (**Figure 9.1**). Not only does this help in image file searches but since you can access text via scripting, it can also serve as a database of sorts for accessing the text of the flower's name.

Description: Lotus

Figure 9.1

This project involves adding black bars to the bottom of your flower photographs, inserting the name of each flower (in white text) in those bars, and saving them as JPEGs for use on a Web site (**Figure 9.2**). Since the flower names are contained in the files' metadata, you don't need to rekey the text by hand. Not only does this reduce human error, it provides a way to automate the process.

Because these photos arrive a few at a time, you need a quick way to process smatterings of files on an ongoing basis. On the Mac you can attach an AppleScript to a folder that's triggered when a folder state changes (for example, by adding files to or deleting files from the folder). Using these "folder actions," you can set up a "watched" folder. As you receive the files, you can drag them into the folder, triggering the automation agents so that the process automatically runs. On Windows you can manually run a script on a folder of images or set up a time-based script trigger using Task Scheduler.

Another interesting feature of this project is that the script triggers two actions within Photoshop for part of this process. By combining automation methods, you're taking advantage of their different strengths. You could achieve the same ends with scripting, but actions can be much faster and easier to create and generally require less troubleshooting to get up and running.

Here's the full script; I'll explain how it works as we go along:

```
on adding folder items to ThisFolder after receiving AddedItems

    tell application "Adobe Photoshop CS3"
        activate

        repeat with i from 1 to (count of items of AddedItems)

            set FilePath to item i of AddedItems as string
            open file FilePath
            set FlowerName to caption of info of document 1

            do action "MetaAction" from "MetaSet"

            set TextLayer to make new art layer of document 1 with¬
            properties {kind:text layer}
            set contents of text object of TextLayer to FlowerName
            set position of text object of TextLayer to {1 as inches,¬
            2.375 as inches}
```

Figure 9.2

```
        set justification of text object of TextLayer to center
        set stroke color of text object of TextLayer to {class:RGB¬
        color, red:255, green:255, blue:255}
        set font of text object of TextLayer to "MyriadPro-Regular"
        set size of text object of TextLayer to 15
        set antialias method of text object of TextLayer to sharp

        do action "MetaSave" from "MetaSet"

    end repeat
  end tell
end adding folder items to
```

Once you see that most of the code in the middle simply specifies how the text should look, you'll realize that the script isn't that complicated. Now let's break it down and build it back up in pieces.

SETTING UP THE FOLDER ACTION WRAPPER

The first thing you need to do is create the folder to which you will attach the folder script. I've created a folder on the Desktop called MetaFolder. This script will process images and export them as JPEGs, so you also need a folder in which to put the processed images. I've created a folder within the Meta-Folder folder called MetaDone to store the finished images.

This is the basic structure of a folder action that triggers when any file is added to the folder:

```
on adding folder items to ThisFolder after receiving AddedItems

    tell application "Adobe Photoshop CS3"
      activate

      repeat with i from 1 to (count of items of AddedItems)
        -- rest of code will go here
      end repeat

    end tell
end adding folder items to
```

The first line sets up the trigger (on adding folder items), a variable (This-Folder) that is the file path to the folder to which the script is attached, and a variable (AddedItems) containing a list of all items added to the folder. The last line (end adding folder items to) is the closing tag for the first line.

The second line (`tell application "Adobe Photoshop CS3"`) directs everything until the `end tell` line (the closing tag to the "tell application" line) at Photoshop. The next line (`activate`) brings Photoshop to the front so that you can watch it do its thing.

The line beginning with `repeat` sets up your loop. The code `with i from 1 to` starts the loop counter (`i`) to begin at 1 and `end` at (`count of items of AddedItems`). Remember that the variable `AddedItems` contains a list of all the files (or, more accurately, their file paths) added to the folder. This means that the code (`count of items of AddedItems`) simply counts those files and makes that the number at which the loop stops. This ensures that every file added is taken through the loop.

You will now replace the line `-- rest of code will go here` with the rest of the script.

OPENING THE IMAGE AND COPYING METADATA

The following lines open the current image and copy the name of the flower from the Description field (referred to in Photoshop scripting as `caption`) from the File Info window:

```
set FilePath to item i of AddedItems as string
open file FilePath
set FlowerName to caption of info of document 1
```

The first line loads the file path of `AddedItems`' first item. (Remember that `AddedItems` is the variable name for the list of files added to the folder.) The second line opens that first file. The third line grabs the flower name from the file's metadata and stores it in the variable `FlowerName`.

BUILDING AND TRIGGERING THE FIRST ACTION

At this point, you've opened the first file and copied the flower name into a variable. Next, you need to build a black bar at the bottom of the image to contain the flower name. Even though you could do this with a script, it's much faster to build an action in Photoshop and trigger it from the script.

To create the black bar, you must first reset the default foreground and background colors to black and white and increase the canvas size with the image anchored to the top.

> **Tip**
>
> The two hyphens in front of `rest of code will go here` make everything on that line a nonexecuting comment. Comments are most often used to briefly describe what a script is doing. If you come back to a script you wrote weeks or months earlier, it may take you some time to figure out exactly how it works. Comments can quickly get you (or anyone editing your code) up to speed.

Create a new action set (Actions panel menu > New Set) and name it MetaSet (**Figure 9.3**). Next, create a new action (Actions panel menu > New Action) and name it MetaAction, then from the Set pull-down menu select MetaSet and click Record (**Figure 9.4**). Photoshop is now recording your mouse movements. Press the *D* key to reset the foreground and background colors to black and white, respectively. Press the *X* key to switch the two colors (so that black is now the background color). The flower images you'll work with are 2 inches wide and 2.125 tall at 72 dpi. Choose Image > Canvas Size, set the height to 2.5 inches, and anchor the image to the top (**Figure 9.5**). Click the square at the bottom of the Actions panel to stop recording.

All you need is one line in the script to trigger this action:

```
do action "MetaAction" from "MetaSet"
```

Figure 9.3 *From the Actions panel menu (left), choose New Set, and in the resulting New Set window (right) name the set MetaSet.*

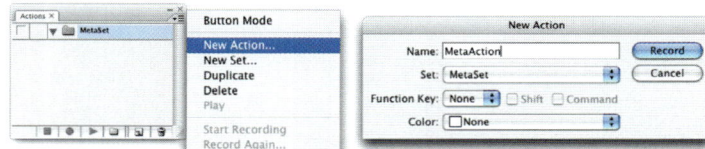

Figure 9.4 *From the Actions panel menu (left) choose New Action, and in the resulting New Action window (right) name the action MetaAction.*

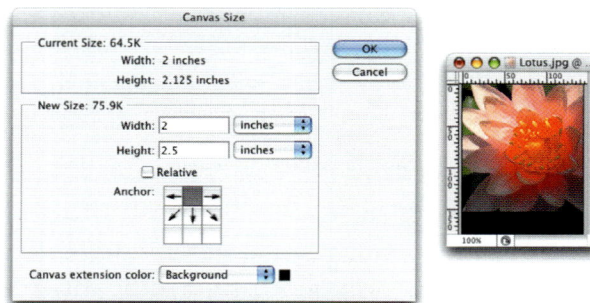

Figure 9.5 *The settings in the Canvas Size dialog box (left) produce a black bar across the bottom of the image (right).*

CREATING THE TYPE

The next block of code creates the text for the flower name and sets its properties line by line.

```
set TextLayer to make new art layer of document 1 with properties¬
{kind:text layer}
set contents of text object of TextLayer to FlowerName
set position of text object of TextLayer to {1 as inches, 2.375 as¬
inches}
set justification of text object of TextLayer to center
set stroke color of text object of TextLayer to {class:RGB color,¬
red:255, green:255, blue:255}
set font of text object of TextLayer to "MyriadPro-Regular"
set size of text object of TextLayer to 15
set antialias method of text object of TextLayer to sharp
```

The first line of the above code creates a new type layer. This is like clicking the image with the Text tool. The next line "sets" the contents of that type layer to the flower name contained in the Description field of the File Info window. Each subsequent line sets another property of that type layer: position, justification, color, font, size, and the anti-aliasing method (it makes a difference). The file now looks like **Figure 9.6**.

SAVING THE FILE

Now it's time to save the file. Again, you could do this via the script, but it's much faster and easier to create an action: From the Actions panel menu, choose New Action; name the action MetaSave; put it in the MetaSet set; and click Record. Photoshop is now recording your mouse movements.

Flatten the image (Layers panel menu > Flatten Image). Save the image as a JPEG (using whatever quality settings you wish) into the MetaDone folder that you created in Step 1. Now, close the file and click the square at the bottom of the Actions panel to stop recording (**Figure 9.7**).

One line in the script will trigger the action (do action "MetaSave" from "MetaSet"), and you're finished writing the script.

ATTACHING THE SCRIPT TO THE FOLDER

It's important that you save your script in the correct folder (Applications > AppleScript > Example Scripts > Folder Action Scripts) so that it will be available for attaching to the MetaFolder (created in Step 1). I've saved the script with the name MetaScript.

Figure 9.6

Figure 9.7

To attach the script to the folder, open the Folder Actions Setup application (Applications > AppleScript > Folder Actions Setup) and make sure the Enable Folder Actions box is checked (**Figure 9.8**). Click the Plus button in the lower-left corner to navigate to the MetaFolder on the Desktop, then click Open (**Figure 9.9**). Once you've done so, you'll be presented with a list of all of the available folder action scripts. Select the MetaScript script, click the Attach button, and quit Folder Actions Setup (**Figure 9.10**).

Figure 9.8

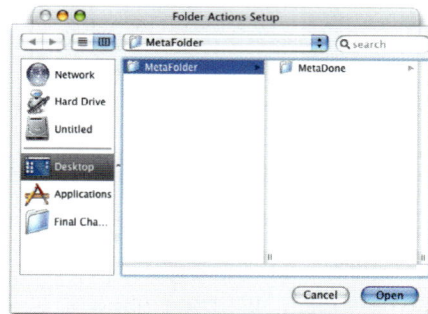

Figure 9.9

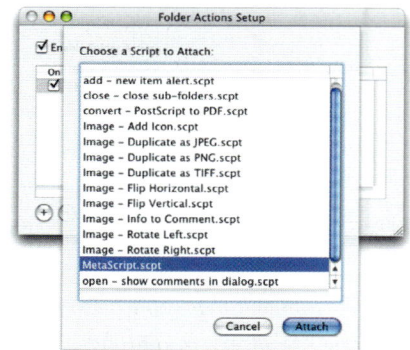

Figure 9.10

That's it. To test your script, drag an image (of the specified size) onto the MetaFolder. Frankly, few automations work the first time out—meaning you'll probably need to do some tinkering to get yours to run. If for some reason your script doesn't work, notice at what point the process halts: This will provide a clue to the error's location.

Some examples of things that might go wrong include mistyped Photoshop action names (resulting in an error message stating the application isn't currently available) and flower names missing from the file's metadata (preventing a caption from appearing with the image). And if the text *starts* to be added to the image but then disappears, you might have forgotten to type "in inches" on the set position of text object line. (If no units are specified, the units set in Photoshop's Preferences will be used.)

Project 2: Bridge Mini Projects

Bridge is a stand-alone application that acts as a centralized tool for managing and organizing Creative Suite files. You can search for files using filenames and metadata as well as run certain Creative Suite automation agents from this single location. Although most of the automation agents are for Photoshop (seven in all), there are also two agents for Illustrator and one for InDesign.

Bridge offers three advantages over standard OS dialog boxes (such as those you see when selecting Open from the File menu): You can use thumbnails to organize files (you can also view thumbnails in Adobe's dialog boxes); you can select files from different folders; and you can easily see and manage metadata for one or many files.

But how useful is Bridge when it comes to automation? Using Bridge, you can run a limited group of Photoshop scripts (Batch, Contact Sheet, Image Processor, Merge to HDR, PDF Presentation, Photomerge, and Picture Package). The advantage of running these scripts from Bridge rather than Photoshop is the flexibility it provides in selecting multiple images. True, you can also select multiple files in Photoshop, but you can't select files from different folders and/or based on searches. In contrast, you can do both by searching for files in Bridge—and you can save the searches for later use. You can also set the metadata and filenames for multiple files in Bridge.

MINI PROJECT 1: BATCH RENAME

Bridge has a great feature for renaming groups of files (whether or not they're of Adobe origin). To open it, choose Tools > Batch Rename. A quick tour of Bridge's Batch Rename window (**Figure 9.11**) reveals that the Destination Folder area at the top contains three radio button selections (**Figure 9.12**):

The first ("Rename in same folder") renames the files and leaves them where they are. The second ("Move to other folder") moves the files to another location (which you specify by clicking the Browse button) and renames them there. The last ("Copy to other folder") copies the files, moves the copies to another folder, and renames them.

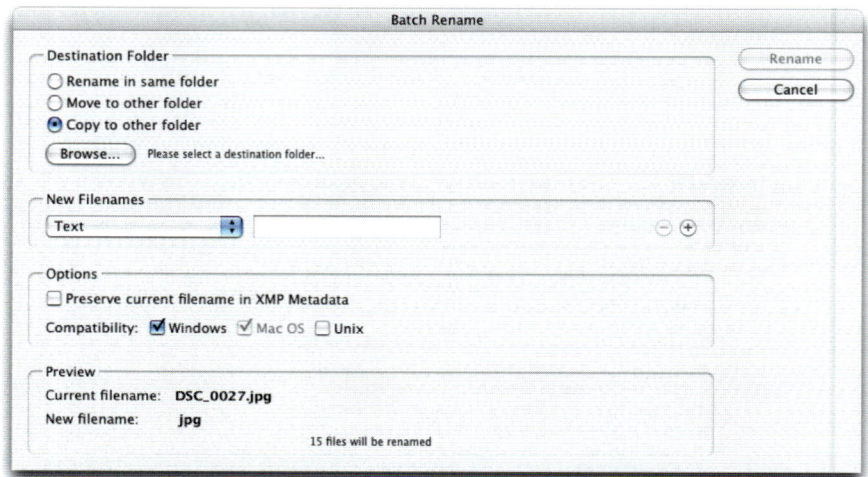

Figure 9.11

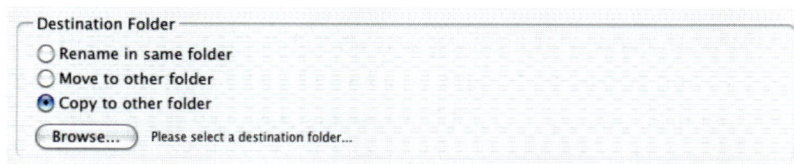

Figure 9.12

The New Filenames area is where you specify the naming elements (**Figure 9.13**). The elements are combined in the order they appear to create the new filename. You can add as many name elements as you want, but be careful because filename lengths can get out of hand pretty quickly. You can add or delete elements by clicking the Plus or Minus buttons to the right of each.

Figure 9.13

The Options section allows you to store the current filename in the metadata field called Preserve Filename (**Figure 9.14**). This gives you a historical record of the previous filename.

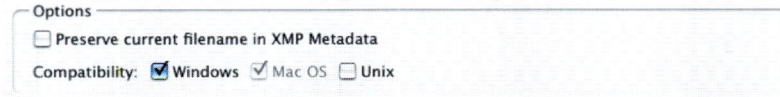

Figure 9.14

For this project you'll select a group of files by running a filename search and then renaming all the resulting files. Imagine this scenario: You've taken some digital photographs for next month's newsletter, and they've all ended up in different folders. You know, however, that you color-corrected and saved them all on the same day (May 3, 2007). The camera has started the name of each file with the letters *DSC*. You'll use both pieces of information in the file search. After the search, you'll rename all of the files with the same name (JuneNews) and number them sequentially.

To create a search, choose Edit > Find (**Figure 9.15**). You can quickly build a complex search by using multiple search criteria. Use the pull-down menus to choose the first set of criteria: Filename, "starts with," and DSC. You'll add a second set of criteria by clicking the Plus button to the right of the first criteria fields. Select Date File Modified, "equals," and 05/03/2007 (**Figure 9.16**). In the Results section, make sure "If all criteria are met" is selected in the Match pull-down menu, and then click Find. The results will look like **Figure 9.17**. (Note that these files are located in multiple folders.)

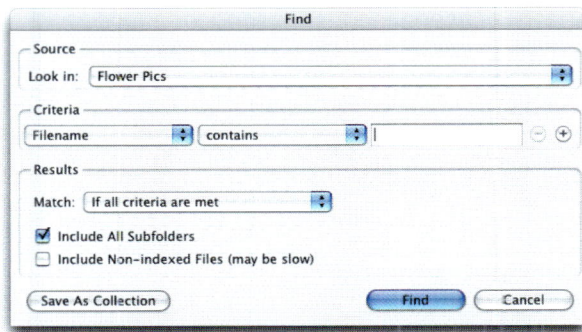

Figure 9.15

Tip

Once you've built a search, you can save it by clicking the Save As Collection button in the lower-left portion of the Find window. This will save an actual search file that you can use for future searches. A cool thing to do is drag that file into Bridge's Favorites column; then, all you need to do is click it to perform that search again.

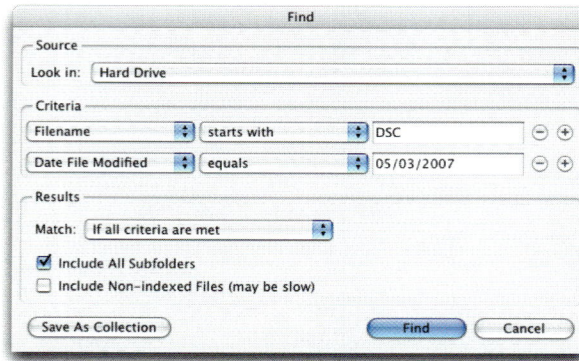

Figure 9.16

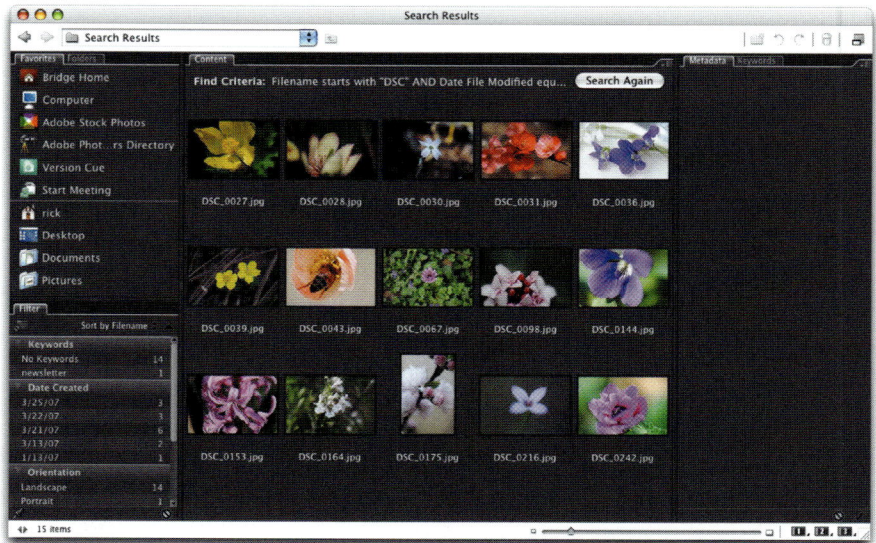

Figure 9.17

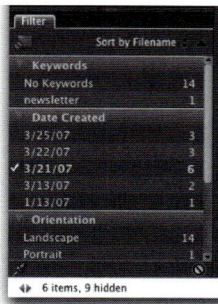

Figure 9.18

You can further refine and sort the search results using the Filter panel (**Figure 9.18**). By selecting various filter criteria (such as Date Created, Date Modified, Orientation, and Aspect Ratio), you can weed out undesirable search results. You can quickly sort the search results by choosing Sort Manually in the Filter panel title bar and selecting from the pop-up list (**Figure 9.19**).

Select all the files in the Search Results window and open the Batch Rename window (Tools > Batch Rename). In the Destination Folder area, select "Copy to other folder," then click the Browse button and create a new folder on the Desktop called Flowers Redux. In the New Filenames area of the Batch Rename dialog box, first create the text element JuneNews-. Click the Plus button to create a new name element. Then use the pull-down menus to choose Sequence Number, 1, and Three Digits. Note that at the bottom of the window you can see a preview of the filenames; the preview should read JuneNews-001.jpg (**Figure 9.20**).

In the Options area, click "Preserve current filename in XMP Metadata" and select both Windows and Mac OS (whichever platform you're currently using will be selected and grayed out). Click Rename, and you're finished.

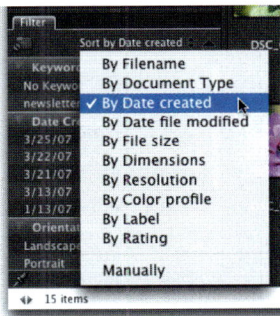

Figure 9.19

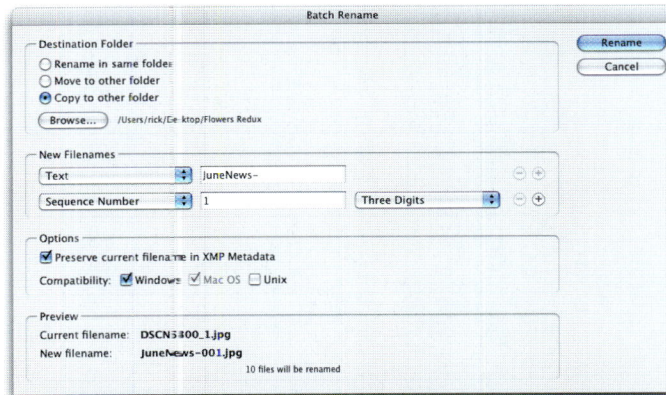

Figure 9.20

MINI PROJECT 2: PDF PRESENTATION

Imagine you want to quickly send a batch of photographs for your customer to review. You could send individual JPEGs, but that's not very professional. Alternatively, you could build a custom slide show in Flash, but that takes a lot of time. Adobe Acrobat PDF files, on the other hand, make great slide shows, *and* you can build them right out of Bridge.

PDFs provide both great image compression and slide transitions. By using the PDF Presentation Photoshop script in Bridge, creating a slide show becomes a matter of a few painless clicks.

In Bridge, select the photos you want to include (this works for almost any image file format). This selection process could follow the lines of that described in Mini Project 1 (searching, filtering, and sorting), or you could simply select a group of images by clicking or dragging. Unfortunately, you have to select individual images (rather than a folder) for this script.

Go to Tools > Photoshop > PDF Presentation, and you'll see what must be the tallest Creative Suite dialog box (**Figure 9.21**). In the Source Files area at the top, you'll see the files you selected in Bridge. (By the way, at this point Bridge has switched you to Photoshop.) You can select and drag files to reorder them, add more files by clicking the Browse button, and duplicate and remove files by clicking the appropriate buttons.

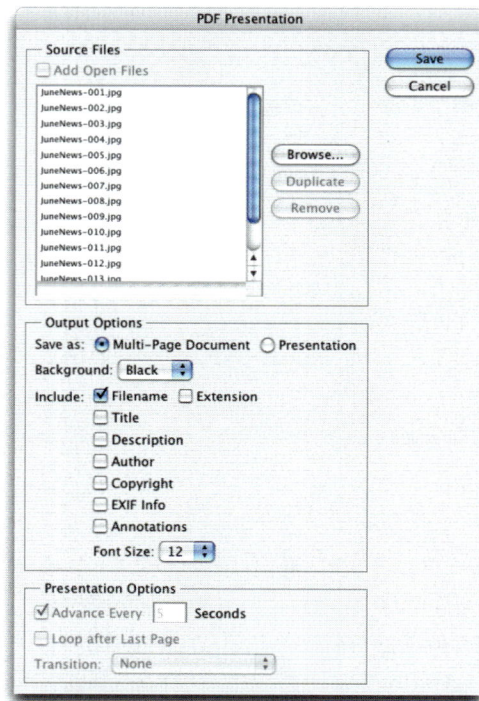

Figure 9.21

In the Output Options area, you can specify how you want the PDF document to be built. A Multi-Page Document is just that: a standard PDF with multiple pages that the user flips through manually. If you select the Presentation radio button, the PDF will open in Slide Show mode and use the slide transitions you've specified in the Presentation Options area of the dialog box.

You have three choices for background color and seven choices for the text that will appear below the file on its PDF page. If you selected the Presentation radio button, you can set additional options in the Presentation Options section at the bottom of the window.

Project 3: Annotations

Photoshop annotations are like sticky notes that you can attach to an image as if you were sticking them to your monitor—except that annotations remain with their files (**Figure 9.22**). Another kind of annotation stores audio instead of written words. You can attach these nonprinting comments to a file for someone else to read or hear.

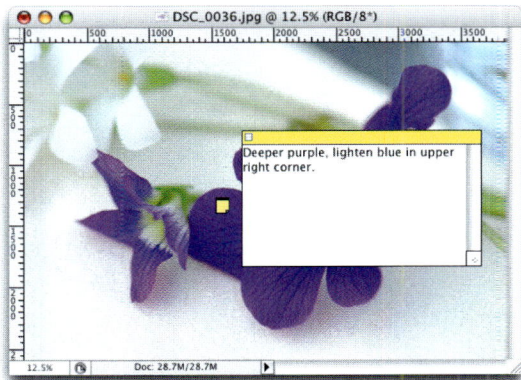

Figure 9.22

Photoshop can import annotations from PDF and FDF (Form Data Format) files—the latter of which store only annotations to PDFs (and the contents of PDF form fields, as you'll see in the next chapter). You may wonder how annotations can be used for graphics automation and how it's done. Production environments often use a handful of similar workflows that require a few standard communications. For instance, product shots might require reminders that the food law department needs to approve them, people shots might require notes to confirm that a model release has been obtained, and shots from a particular photographer might need annotations instructing someone else in the workflow to check them against certain production standards.

You could set up an automated system to attach a prewritten note to Photoshop files based on some characteristic, such as an element of the images' metadata (like date created or creator); you could also use information from a database to determine which images needed a note. For this project, however, you'll use the images' filenames as the trigger to append a note. (Remember the tip in the metadata project about using filenames to convey information about files' contents.) To do so, you'll create a simple file-naming convention with four numbers. Each number identifies that file as requiring a certain prebuilt annotation to be imported or a voice annotation to be created. A file could have none, one, all, or a combination of the four. For the purposes of this project, let's assume that a person examines each image and appends the appropriate number codes to the filename. You could devise a more automated and perhaps less error-prone method of renaming the files, but this project focuses on getting the annotations onto the images.

For our project, you'll create three text annotations for import: Legal, Marketing, and Resolution. If a filename contains the numeral *1*, the Legal annotation will be imported; if it contains the numeral *2*, the Marketing annotation will be imported; if it contains the numeral *3,* the Resolution annotation will be imported; and if it contains the numeral *4,* an action will be triggered leading you to add a voice annotation explaining some special circumstances.

Photoshop cannot selectively import PDF or FDF annotations from a file—it must import all of them. This means that you must set up one annotation per PDF if you're to import them individually.

USING ANNOTATED IMAGES IN A WORKFLOW

After you've used this kind of automation to append notes to an image, your next likely step will be to either send the image around for review or send it along to the next phase of production. To route this kind of annotated image for review, you could save the file in the Photoshop PDF format and send it via e-mail. Reviewers could then use Adobe Acrobat or the free Adobe Reader to review the document and make comments. Routing a PDF of your image for review probably means that you will need to go through a second round of importing comments into the original Photoshop image, and of course you have to maintain two files: the original Photoshop production file and the PDF.

To use an annotated image in a production workflow, you could save the file as a Photoshop PSD file, which reviewers would open and review in

> **Note**
>
> For a reviewer to use the free Adobe Reader, you would need to first open the review file in Acrobat, then select Comments > Enable for Commenting in Adobe Reader, and save the file before distributing.

Photoshop. One potential downside is that all reviewers have to own Photoshop, and the review file will be larger than a typical PDF. But this approach has the advantage of using just one file for both production and review.

TRIGGERING THE SCRIPT

You can choose how and when to trigger the script that annotates the images. How you initiate the script depends on whether you want to annotate individual images as you work on them or batches of images. For individual images, you can use the AppleScript provided below. Copy the script to the Library > Scripts folder (and put it in its own folder, named something like Photoshop), then access it from the Mac's script menu (**Figure 9.23**). You'll first need to make sure the script menu is visible in the menu bar by opening AppleScript Utility and checking the "Show Script Menu in menu bar" check box (**Figure 9.24**). You could, of course, switch from Photoshop to the script editor of your choice and run it from there, but that's not an elegant solution. Note that you cannot trigger an AppleScript (or a VBScript) from either Photoshop's actions or its Script Events Manager.

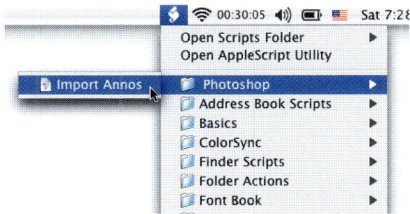

Figure 9.23

Figure 9.24

You can further streamline this process by triggering the script from within Photoshop, if you download and install the JavaScript version (available from www.peachpit.com/apprentice). To do so, place the script in Photoshop's Presets > Scripts folder to make it accessible from the File > Scripts menu. (You'll need to restart Photoshop to get it to appear.) You can also set up a script event in Photoshop's Script Events Manager (File > Scripts > Script Events Manager) so the JavaScript can be triggered by an event, such as a file being opened. Another excellent option is to trigger the JavaScript from a Photoshop action, which you can assign to a Function key. (For a refresher on how to assign Function keys to actions, see Chapter 3.)

If you want to run the script later on a batch of files, you can do so by using Photoshop's Batch feature (File > Automate > Batch). As a hybrid approach, you could arrange to trigger the AppleScript whenever a new file is added to a particular folder, using the Mac's Folder Actions (see the "Setting Up the Folder Action Wrapper" section of Project 1).

BUILDING THE ANNOTATION FILES

After being imported, annotations are placed in the same location as they were in their files of origin. Since there's a chance that all three types of sticky note annotations could be imported (and the audio annotation has a icon position as well), it would be nice if they didn't overlap. You will position the annotations as if the image were divided in quarters.

All the images you'll be working with are 5 inches wide by 3.75 inches high at 150 dpi, so you'll create a new document with those dimensions (**Figure 9.25**). You'll drag two guidelines out to make it easier to see the quadrants and save the file as Anno Template.psd (**Figure 9.26**). This is the template you'll use to create the three annotation files.

Using the Notes tool, click in the top-left quadrant (**Figure 9.27**). A sticky note will appear; type Get Legal's signoff in it (**Figure 9.28**). Save this file as a Photoshop PDF named LegalAnno.pdf and put it in a new folder on the Desktop named The Four Annos.

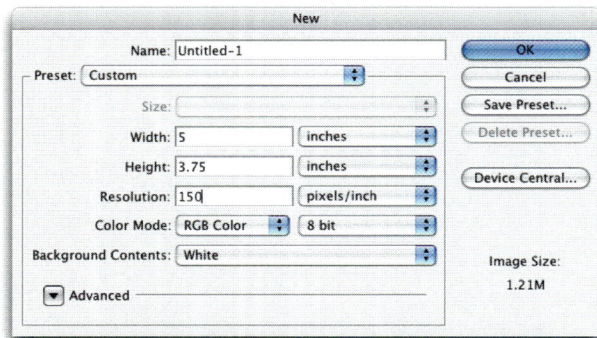

Figure 9.25

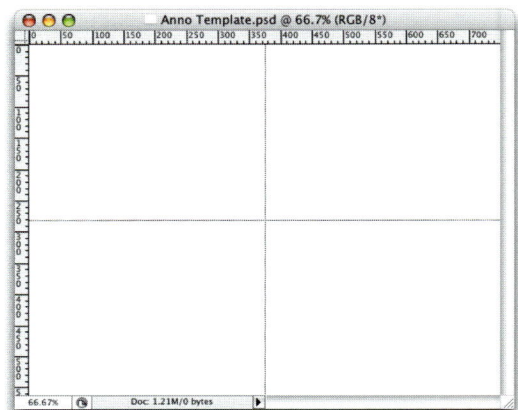

Figure 9.26

Figure 9.27

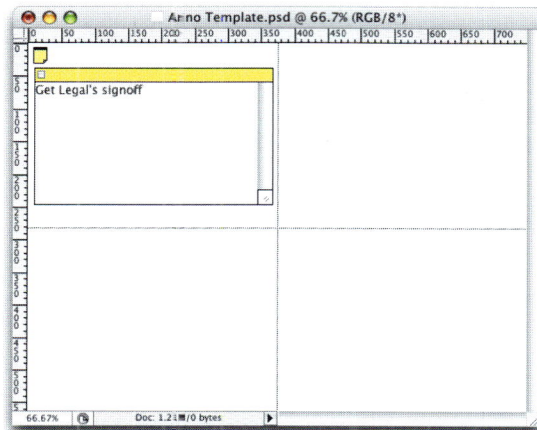

Figure 9.28

Open the Anno Template.psd file again (remember, it contains no annotations) and with the Notes tool, click in the upper-right quadrant. Type Run by Marketing in the resulting sticky note (**Figure 9.29**). Save the file as Market-Anno.pdf in the same folder as the first one.

Open the Anno Template.psd file again and add an annotation in the lower-left quadrant that reads Confirm 300 dpi at 100%, and save it as dpiAnno.pdf (**Figure 9.30**).

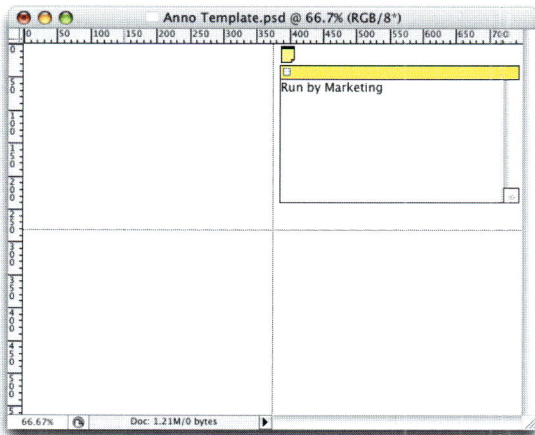

Figure 9.29

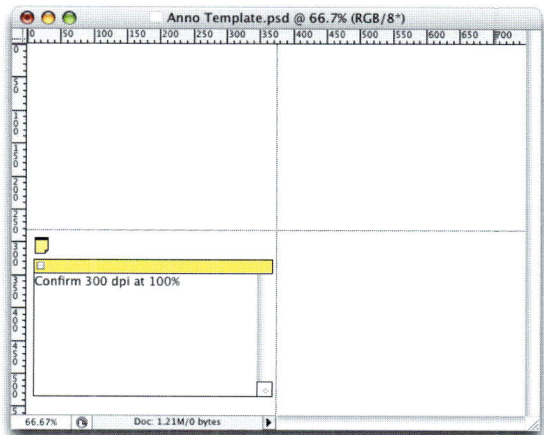

Figure 9.30

BUILDING THE AUDIO ANNOTATION ACTION

The action you are about to build will add an audio annotation icon in the lower-right quadrant of the file. It will then prompt the user to record a voice annotation—handy when a file includes peculiar issues best explained with a voice message.

Open the Anno Template.psd file, create an action set (Actions panel menu > New Set), and name it AnnoSet. Create a new action, name it VoiceAnno, and click Record. Make sure you have a microphone plugged into your computer's audio-in port.

With the Voice Annotation tool, click in the center of the lower-right quadrant of the file (it will add only a speaker icon); an Audio Annotation dialog box will appear (**Figure 9.31**). Click the Start button, record your message into the microphone, and when you're finished, click Stop. Now, click the Stop Recording button (the small square) at the bottom of the Actions panel to finish the action (**Figure 9.32**). This action will be triggered if the filename contains the numeral *4*.

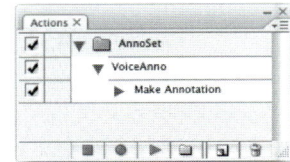

Figure 9.32

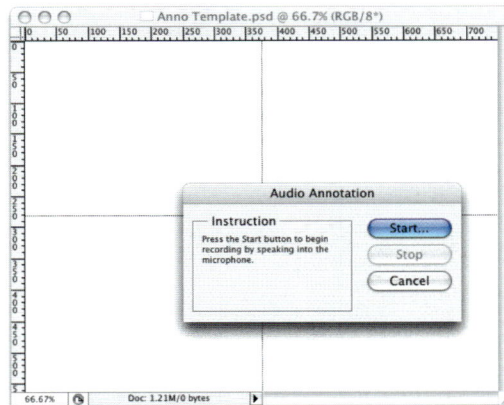

Figure 9.31

WRITING THE SCRIPT

Writing this AppleScript is going to be easy. Take a look at the entire script below before proceeding:

```
set LegalAnno to "/Users/zorro/Desktop/The Four Annos/LegalAnno.pdf"
set MktgAnno to "/Users/zorro/Desktop/The Four Annos/MarketAnno.pdf"
set dpiAnno to "/Users/zorro/Desktop/The Four Annos/dpiAnno.pdf"
```

```
tell application "Adobe Photoshop CS3"
   activate
   set FileName to name of current document

      if FileName contains "1" then import annotations current document¬
      from LegalAnno
      if FileName contains "2" then import annotations current document¬
      from MktgAnno
      if FileName contains "3" then import annotations current document¬
      from dpiAnno
      if FileName contains "4" then do action "VoiceAnno" from "AnnoSet"

end tell
```

The first three lines of the script (all of which start with the word *set*) assign the path to the annotation files to the variables. The `tell application` line indicates that Photoshop will execute the following lines. The `activate` line makes Photoshop the active application (bringing it to the front). And the `set FileName` line assigns the name of the current document (whichever file is open in Photoshop and frontmost) to the variable `FileName`.

Now that the `FileName` variable stands for a particular file, you can "ask" that file if it contains any of the four numbers—and the next four lines do just that. For the first three of these lines, if the answer is yes, the annotation will be imported from the respective annotation PDF files. If it contains the numeral *4*, the VoiceAnno action will be triggered and the user will be prompted to record a voice annotation.

Create a few test files with various combinations of the four digits in their filenames and run them through the script (**Figure 9.33**).

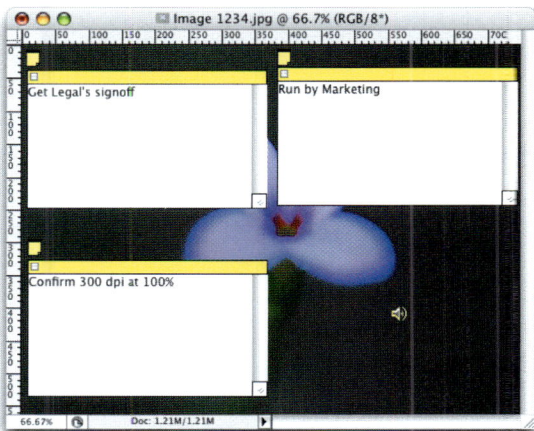

Figure 9.33

10
Beautiful Geometry

The Illustrator Projects

If the solution is not beautiful, I know it is wrong.

—*Buckminster Fuller*

I remember the exact moment I discovered the possibilities afforded by automating Illustrator: I had opened version 10 and found that I could name objects in an Illustrator file—exciting stuff. While earlier versions had let you refer to objects by number (using a command like "Move path item 10 over to the right"), this quickly became confusing since adding a path item to the document meant that item 10 would become item 11 (and so on). This made it impossible to keep track of objects and made the process seem hopelessly frustrating.

With Illustrator 10, however, for the first time I was able to name my object something like BlueCircle and it would always be BlueCircle, regardless of how many other objects I added to the file. I could now move and change BlueCircle and know which object I was manipulating—a simple persistence of names that began my graphics automation journey.

Goofing around with files in this way started as a hobby but quickly became more when I realized I could use automation to produce multiple production files for printing—that is, *honest-to-goodness production files that people pay good money for.* Then the Web came along, and I found I could export raster images from Illustrator for online use. When I started working in a production environment creating packaging files, I soon realized that there were seemingly thousands of little repetitive tasks that I could use automation to handle. I realized that if I could name the piece of type that contained, say, the sodium content, I could set that number with scripting. While it would be a ton of work to edit just one file with scripting, if I could somehow apply that automation to a batch of files, I could automatically edit the sodium content for 20 files at a time. Furthermore, I figured, I should be able to automate the use of templates to build whole files anew—placing graphics, setting text, and changing colors. It's not an overstatement to say that I felt like I'd entered a brave new world: *It was magic.*

That, of course, was before actions and Automator and InDesign and XML and Adobe's data-driven graphics capabilities. Illustrator has grown considerably in the intervening years, adding tools and capabilities that make it particularly interesting for graphics automation. For instance, you can create live (editable) type that's distorted in ways that you could previously achieve only by converting that type to outlines or raster art. And you can match that distorted type to the perspective of an image, making it appear part of it (because it's live), and change it via scripting (or some other method).

The following projects—which employ the same scenario as the Photoshop projects in Chapter 9 (and are for the same gardening and nursery client)—should help you discover the magic of using automation with Illustrator.

Project 1: Direct-Mail Image

Star & Fey went out on a limb a couple of years ago and added in-store coffee shops in an attempt to capture some of the additional traffic that bookstores have enjoyed. All in all, the concept worked, but the company found that casual and potential customers didn't even know the coffee shops existed. So the company asked your studio to create a direct-mail piece using customization. After some back and forth, you and the client decided to use the customer's first name and the name of his or her local Star & Fey retail store in a direct-mail piece.

The client wanted the image to convey the European feel Star & Fey strives for in its coffee shops and retail spaces. You came up with a design showing cups and glasses from Star & Fey's coffee shops, and the client bought it (**Figure 10.1**). The piece is designed so that the first thing the customer sees is his or her name on a coffee cup. Drawn into the image in this way, the customer will then notice the name of his or her town on the napkin. The idea is to make customers feel that the images have been created just for them.

Figure 10.1

To keep this project to a manageable size, you'll concentrate on the image that appears in this mailer, not the entire two-sided piece, and export the output files as TIFFs. Note, however, that if you were producing the whole two-sided piece, you would probably export PDF files.

Creating the Template File

The photograph I used in my example shows no printing on the coffee cup or beneath the logo on the napkin (**Figure 10.2**). To build the template, you need to add type to both locations, matching the curve of the cup and the perspective of the napkin. You'll tackle the cup first.

Draw a path on the face of the coffee cup and type in `Christy` (**Figure 10.3**). With the type selected, use the Eyedropper tool to sample the green in the logo on the napkin.

To match the curve of the cup, you'll need to skew the type a little (Type > Type on a Path > Skew). You'll probably need to adjust the line to get the skewed type to match the cup. In the Transparency palette, I chose the Multiply blending mode and an opacity of 96 percent to get the type to look more like it was actually printed on the ceramic cup (**Figure 10.4**). Play with the blending modes (depending on your image, you might try Darken, Hard Light, or even Normal, the default) and transparency to get the right mix for your image.

Figure 10.2

Figure 10.3

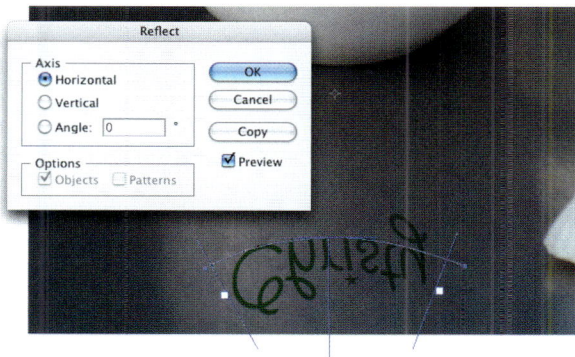

Figure 10.4

Although you could use envelope distortion (Object > Envelope Distort) to achieve the same effect, simply distorting type on a path is much easier. If doing it this way doesn't work for your particular project, try Envelope Distort, but be aware that it doesn't work as well with dynamic text (as I'll explain later).

Since the cup is reflected in the surface on which it sits, it will add to the realism if you can also get the variable text to reflect. Select the type on the cup, and then choose the Reflect tool. While holding down the Option key, click under the type, and then in the Axis section of the dialog box choose Horizontal and then click Copy (**Figure 10.5**). Drag the type into place, and in the Transparency palette choose the Color Burn blending mode and a 25 percent opacity (**Figure 10.6**).

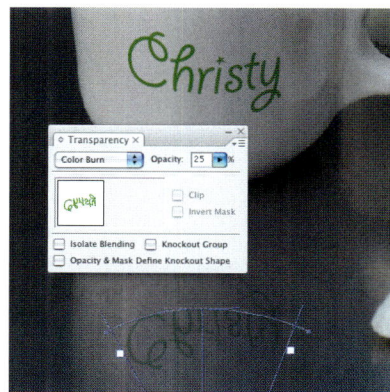

Figure 10.5

Figure 10.6

Now, on to the napkin: Draw a straight line and add type to it—in this case, Lenexa (or whatever you like) for the location. To match the perspective of the napkin, use a combination of rotating the line and skewing the type with the Shear tool. Adjust the combination until it fits the perspective. In the Transparency panel, choose the Multiply blending mode and a 75 percent opacity (**Figure 10.7**).

Figure 10.7

Creating the Variables

Taking advantage of Illustrator's data-driven graphics capabilities, you will now create an external file that contains your variable text in a specialized file format called XML (Extensible Markup Language). XML provides a way to structure and identify data in a text file so that different systems on different platforms can read and understand it. Each piece of data is "tagged," or labeled, so that XML-aware systems can identify it and determine how to handle it. Since our project has only three pieces of variable data, editing the XML file should be fairly easy.

Using the Selection tool, select the type that appears on the cup. Then open the Variables panel (Window > Variables), and from the Variables panel menu choose Make Text Dynamic (**Figure 10.8**). Variable 1 will now appear in the Variables panel. The T symbol means the variable type is Text String (there are other variable types, which I'll describe later). Double-click Variable 1 in the panel and change the name to CupText, then click OK (**Figure 10.9**). Giving this variable a descriptive name here will help you find it when you're editing the XML file. Now that you've made this type object variable, you can change its text in the Variables panel—and you can set up as many instances of the text as you'd like.

Repeat this same process for both the reflection type, naming it ReflecText, and the napkin type, naming it NapkinText (**Figure 10.10**).

> **Note**
>
> Now that you've learned how to make your text into a variable, here are the pitfalls to using it with envelope distortion. First, you must assign a variable to the text before applying the distortion. After you've distorted the text, you can edit it (Object > Envelope Distort > Edit Contents), but if you physically move it in either Contents or Envelope mode, the link to the variable will break. You can relink the text to a variable by choosing both the text and the variable in the Variables panel and choosing Make Text Dynamic from the Variables panel menu.

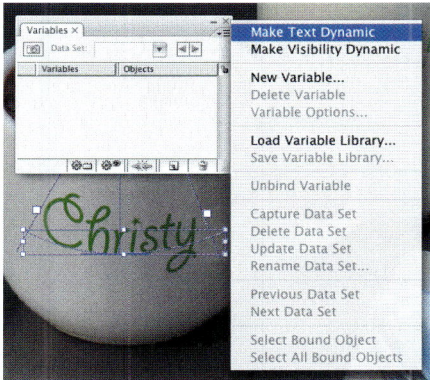

Figure 10.8

Figure 10.9

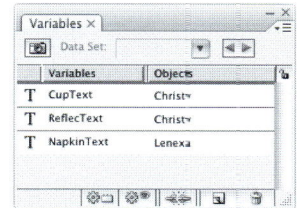

Figure 10.10

Building the Data File

The next step in our project may *seem* complicated, but it's not. To start, you must create what Illustrator calls a *data set,* which contains variables (like the CupText, ReflecText, and NapkinText objects you just created) and their associated values. To do so, open the Variables panel and click the camera icon in the upper-left portion (**Figure 10.11**). Data Set 1 will appear in the window next to the camera.

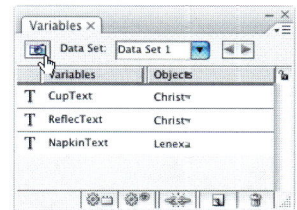

Figure 10.11

To see how this works (and to help when it comes time to edit the XML file), change the text in the three variables. (I've used *Shawn* for the name and *St. Elmo* for the location.) Then click the camera icon again to create a second data set. Both sets of text are now stored in the Variables panel, and you can jump back and forth between them by clicking the Previous and Next Data Set arrows (**Figure 10.12**). Presto, the different states, or data sets, will appear in the file.

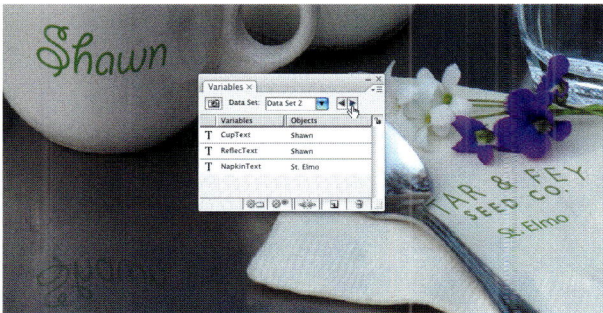

Figure 10.12

If you wanted to make only a handful of iterations of your illustration, you could just keep entering sets of text and capturing the different data sets. It would all be stored in the Variables panel, so you could work completely within Illustrator (meaning you wouldn't have to export a data file in XML format or edit in a separate text editor). But if you need to create many data sets, it's faster to export an XML file, edit it, and import it back into the Illustrator file. You could also have a programmer populate your XML file with additional data using scripting or XML-editing software, and then return the file to you to import back into Illustrator. That scenario—a tagged text file working with a graphics file—demonstrates one of the greatest benefits of data-driven graphics (and XML): *the separation of design and content.*

To write an XML file out of Illustrator, from the Variables panel menu choose Save Variable Library (**Figure 10.13**). Illustrator will then ask you where you'd like to save the file (which is referred to as a *library*). Keep in mind that it's fine to change the name, but you should keep the .xml file extension.

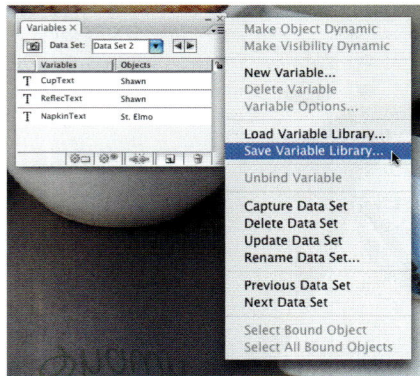

Figure 10.13

Editing the XML File

When you open the XML file in a text editor, such as WordPad in Windows or TextEdit on the Mac, you can ignore most of its contents—particularly what appears at the top and bottom of the file—but be careful not to remove or modify anything except the section that relates to your variables (lest you break the document) (**Figure 10.14**). The first section, which you can ignore, identifies the XML version, how the characters are encoded, and some housekeeping stuff for Illustrator (**Figure 10.15**).

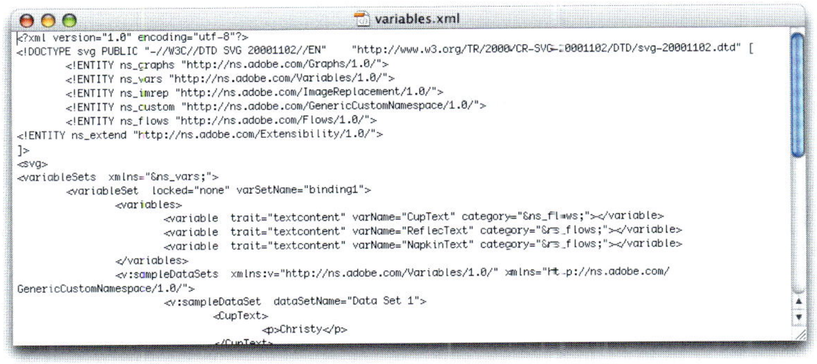


```
<?xml version="1.0" encoding="utf-8"?>
<!DOCTYPE svg PUBLIC "-//W3C//DTD SVG 20001102//EN"    "http://www.w3.org/TR/2000/CR-SVG-20001102/DTD/svg-20001102.dtd" [
	<!ENTITY ns_graphs "http://ns.adobe.com/Graphs/1.0/">
	<!ENTITY ns_vars "http://ns.adobe.com/Variables/1.0/">
	<!ENTITY ns_imrep "http://ns.adobe.com/ImageReplacement/1.0/">
	<!ENTITY ns_custom "http://ns.adobe.com/GenericCustomNamespace/1.0/">
	<!ENTITY ns_flows "http://ns.adobe.com/Flows/1.0/">
<!ENTITY ns_extend "http://ns.adobe.com/Extensibility/1.0/">
]>
<svg>
<variableSets  xmlns="&ns_vars;">
	<variableSet  locked="none" varSetName="binding1">
		<variables>
			<variable  trait="textcontent" varName="CupText" category="&ns_flows;"></variable>
			<variable  trait="textcontent" varName="ReflecText" category="&ns_flows;"></variable>
			<variable  trait="textcontent" varName="NapkinText" category="&ns_flows;"></variable>
		</variables>
		<v:sampleDataSets  xmlns:v="http://ns.adobe.com/Variables/1.0/" xmlns="http://ns.adobe.com/
GenericCustomNamespace/1.0/">
			<v:sampleDataSet  dataSetName="Data Set 1">
				<CupText>
					<p>Christy</p>
```

Figure 10.14

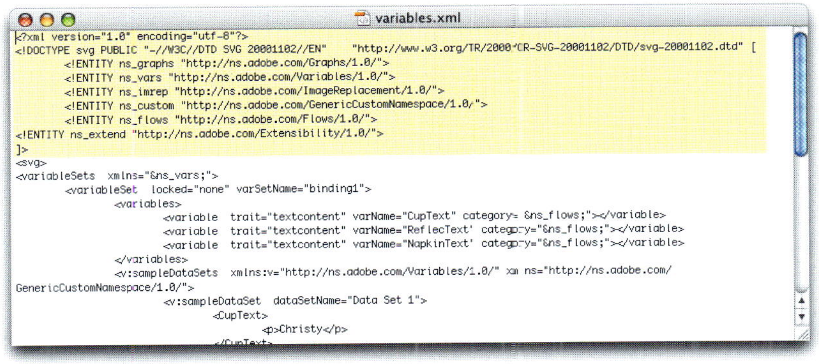


```
<?xml version="1.0" encoding="utf-8"?>
<!DOCTYPE svg PUBLIC "-//W3C//DTD SVG 20001102//EN"    "http://www.w3.org/TR/2000/CR-SVG-20001102/DTD/svg-20001102.dtd" [
	<!ENTITY ns_graphs "http://ns.adobe.com/Graphs/1.0/">
	<!ENTITY ns_vars "http://ns.adobe.com/Variables/1.0/">
	<!ENTITY ns_imrep "http://ns.adobe.com/ImageReplacement/1.0/">
	<!ENTITY ns_custom "http://ns.adobe.com/GenericCustomNamespace/1.0/">
	<!ENTITY ns_flows "http://ns.adobe.com/Flows/1.0/">
<!ENTITY ns_extend "http://ns.adobe.com/Extensibility/1.0/">
]>
<svg>
<variableSets  xmlns="&ns_vars;">
	<variableSet  locked="none" varSetName="binding1">
		<variables>
			<variable  trait="textcontent" varName="CupText" category="&ns_flows;"></variable>
			<variable  trait="textcontent" varName="ReflecText" category="&ns_flows;"></variable>
			<variable  trait="textcontent" varName="NapkinText" category="&ns_flows;"></variable>
		</variables>
		<v:sampleDataSets  xmlns:v="http://ns.adobe.com/Variables/1.0/" xmlns="http://ns.adobe.com/
GenericCustomNamespace/1.0/">
			<v:sampleDataSet  dataSetName="Data Set 1">
				<CupText>
					<p>Christy</p>
```

Figure 10.15 *Do not edit or delete any part of the top section of an XML file (highlighted in yellow). This will render the file unusable to Illustrator.*

The second section lists the three variables you created in the Variables panel in Illustrator (**Figure 10.16**). The last section in the middle of the file is what you will edit, because it contains your actual data.

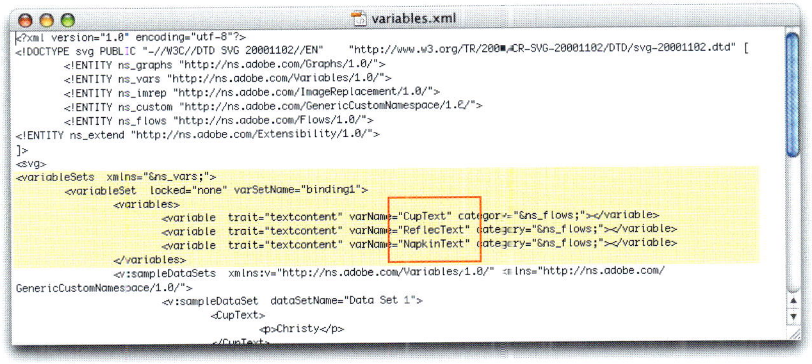


```
<?xml version="1.0" encoding="utf-8"?>
<!DOCTYPE svg PUBLIC "-//W3C//DTD SVG 20001102//EN"    "http://www.w3.org/TR/2000/CR-SVG-20001102/DTD/svg-20001102.dtd" [
	<!ENTITY ns_graphs "http://ns.adobe.com/Graphs/1.0/">
	<!ENTITY ns_vars "http://ns.adobe.com/Variables/1.0/">
	<!ENTITY ns_imrep "http://ns.adobe.com/ImageReplacement/1.0/">
	<!ENTITY ns_custom "http://ns.adobe.com/GenericCustomNamespace/1.0/">
	<!ENTITY ns_flows "http://ns.adobe.com/Flows/1.0/">
<!ENTITY ns_extend "http://ns.adobe.com/Extensibility/1.0/">
]>
<svg>
<variableSets  xmlns="&ns_vars;">
	<variableSet  locked="none" varSetName="binding1">
		<variables>
			<variable  trait="textcontent" varName="CupText" category="&ns_flows;"></variable>
			<variable  trait="textcontent" varName="ReflecText" category="&ns_flows;"></variable>
			<variable  trait="textcontent" varName="NapkinText" category="&ns_flows;"></variable>
		</variables>
		<v:sampleDataSets  xmlns:v="http://ns.adobe.com/Variables/1.0/" xmlns="http://ns.adobe.com/
GenericCustomNamespace/1.0/">
			<v:sampleDataSet  dataSetName="Data Set 1">
				<CupText>
					<p>Christy</p>
```

Figure 10.16 *In the second section of the XML file (highlighted in yellow), you can see the three variables (inside the red box) that you created in Illustrator.*

Tip

Like HTML files, XML files use tags to identify file parts such as title, body, and individual elements (for example, paragraphs and names and addresses). Each part, or element, must be enclosed in opening and closing tags, and tags must be surrounded by angle brackets (< >). For example, our project has a <NapkinText> tag for the type on the napkin. The associated closing tag is </NapkinText>, which has a forward slash between the first angle bracket and the tag's name (see **Figure 10.17** on the next page). The text between these two tags is that variable's content. Note that in the first data set the text between these two tags—<p>Lenexa</p>—includes its own tags, which indicate a paragraph. The entire file is built in this fashion.

Beginning with the line that starts <v:sampleDataSet dataSetName="Data Set 1">, you'll see your first data set and part of the second, including the three variables (which appear twice, once in each data set) and the text you typed listed between them (**Figure 10.17**). From here, it's just a matter of copying, pasting, and editing the right part of this file to create new data sets.

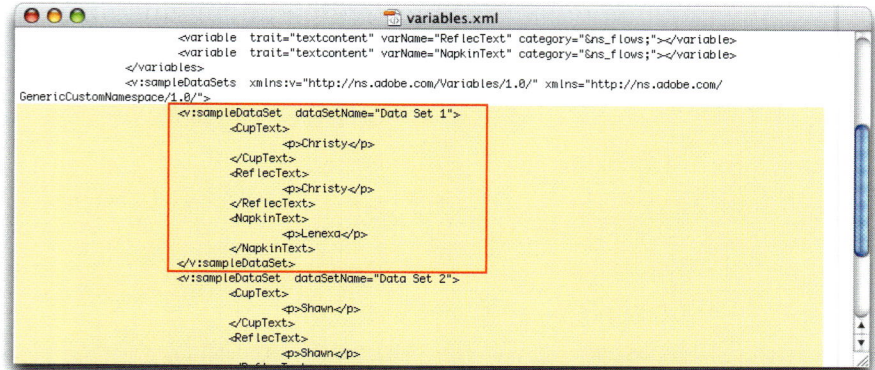

Figure 10.17 *The third section of the XML file (highlighted in yellow) shows the first data set (inside the red box) and part of the second.*

To begin, select and copy Data Set 1 as shown below:

```
<v:sampleDataSet  dataSetName="Data Set 1">
  <CupText>
    <p>Christy</p>
  </CupText>
  <ReflecText>
    <p>Christy</p>
  </ReflecText>
  <NapkinText>
    <p>Lenexa</p>
  </NapkinText>
</v:sampleDataSet>
```

Immediately beneath the closing tag for Data Set 2 (</v:sampleDataSet>), press Return to insert a line space, then paste the block of text you copied: This will become Data Set 3. Now, change the data set name to Data Set 3 (making sure to leave the quotation marks in place), and then change CupText to Bonnie, ReflecText to Bonnie, and NapkinText to Decatur. It should now look like the following:

```
<v:sampleDataSet  dataSetName="Data Set 3">
   <CupText>
      <p>Bonnie</p>
   </CupText>
   <ReflecText>
      <p>Bonnie</p>
   </ReflecText>
   <NapkinText>
      <p>Decatur</p>
   </NapkinText>
</v:sampleDataSet>
```

You can keep pasting the same code block and modifying the text to create as many data sets as you wish, but I'll stop at three for this project. Save the file in plain-text format with the .xml extension.

Importing the New XML File

Now you'll need to import the new XML file back into Illustrator and generate the individual Illustrator files. To import the file, open the Variables panel menu and choose Load Variable Library (**Figure 10.18**). If the XML file is up to snuff, Illustrator asks if you want to overwrite the current variables and data sets (**Figure 10.19**); click Yes. The Data Set 1 name does not appear in the Data Set window in the Variables palette, but you can put the data sets into play by clicking on the Data Set pull-down menu and selecting one. You can flip through the data sets by clicking on the Previous and Next Data Set arrows to the right of the Data Set window (**Figure 10.20**).

Figure 10.18

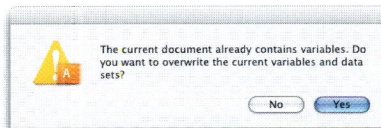

Figure 10.19

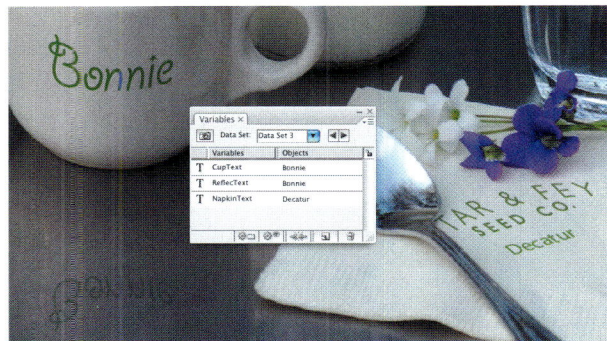

Figure 10.20

Generating the Output Files

You will now use Illustrator's Batch feature to output the data-driven graphics files. Make sure your Illustrator file is open, and then open the Actions panel and its panel menu, and choose New Action. In the window that appears, type the name BatchExport and click the Record button (**Figure 10.21**) to record your action. This action has just one step—exporting the file as a TIFF—so all you have to do is choose File > Export, and from the pull-down menu choose TIFF. In the next window (TIFF Options), select CMYK and High Resolution, and then click OK. After the file finishes writing, click the Stop Record button in the bottom-left portion of the Actions panel (**Figure 10.22**).

Figure 10.21

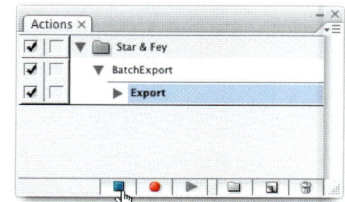

Figure 10.22

Now, from the Actions panel menu choose Batch (**Figure 10.23**), and in the Play area of the Batch window that appears, select the Set and the Batch-Export Action you just created (**Figure 10.24**). In the Source area, choose Data Sets, and in the Destination area, click the check box next to Override Action "Export" Commands so that you can specify the kind of filename you want to associate with the radio buttons. Under File Name, choose File + Number to use your original Illustrator filename plus sequential numbering. This option appends numbers by thousands (001000, 002000, 003000, and so forth), and there's no way to change the numbering scheme. Before you leave the dialog box, click the Choose button (above the Override Action "Export" Commands check box) to specify where you want files to be saved.

When you've set up the Batch window to your satisfaction, click OK. You can now watch as Illustrator runs through the data sets, plugging in the different text and exporting the files—a pretty cool thing to witness. You'll end up with a batch of TIFFs; the number of output files will depend on the number of data sets you built in your Illustrator file (**Figure 10.25**).

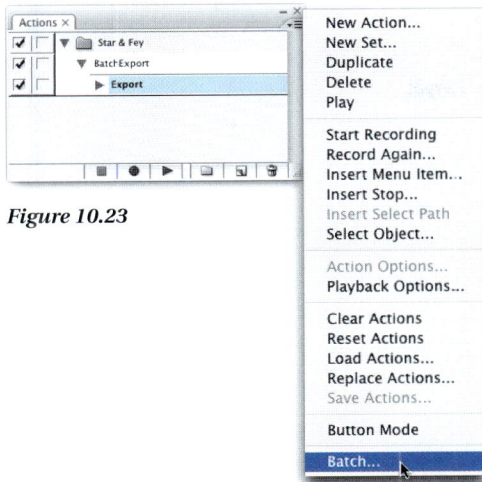

Figure 10.23

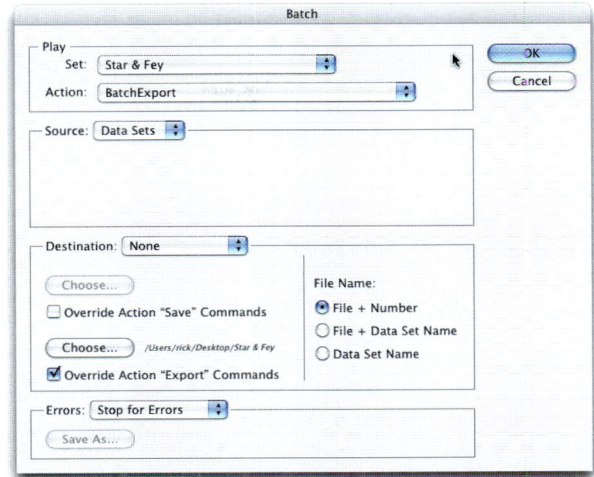

Figure 10.24

Figure 10.25

Project 2: Seed Packets

This is another data-driven graphics project, but it produces Illustrator production files for printing instead of TIFFs, like the first project. For this project, you'll be working with seed packet production files in their flat, unfolded form (**Figure 10.26**). The flower name, flower description, two photos, and the

Figure 10.26

"NEW" graphic will be your variables. Since I covered most of the mechanics of setting up an Illustrator data-driven graphics file in the preceding project, I'm going to focus on different aspects here.

Creating the Template File

Since this template file is a straightforward Illustrator file—no warping or skewing of type needed—you can build it as you would any other Illustrator file. Note that you'll be placing the same image twice. For the first data set, you'll use the Morning Glory name and description and two instances of the morning glory image; the "NEW" graphic will also be visible.

Creating the Variables

In addition to the text variables we created in Project 1, this project will include two other types of variables: placed (or linked) images and visibility (which determines whether an object is visible or hidden). The value for a text variable is text; the value for a linked image is the path to the image; and the value for a visibility variable can be either True, for visible, or False, for hidden.

You'll set up the text variables the same way you did in Project 1. In this project the flower name variable is Name, and the description variable is—hold on to your hats—Description. To create a linked image variable, select the image (using the Direct Select tool—which resembles a hollow arrow—if the image is masked or grouped), open the Variables panel menu, and choose Make Linked File Dynamic (**Figure 10.27**). Do this now, and name the variables LgPhoto (for the vertical image) and SmPhoto (for the horizontal image). Even though these are the same linked image, we need two variables for the two instances in the file.

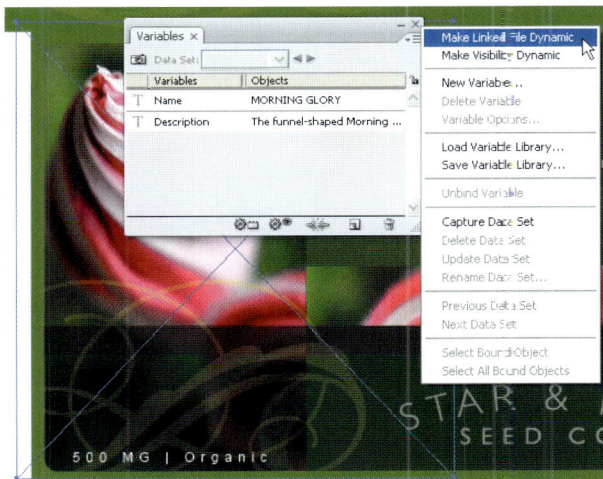

Figure 10.27

Now it's time to create the visibility variable. Visibility variables work for single objects, groups, and images. Since the "NEW" graphic will only appear on new products, you will manually designate "newness" for each data set. Keep in mind, however, that you could also set "newness" automatically. For example, if you were pulling the product data from a company database, you could evaluate each product by how long (based on date entries) the product had been in the company system.

The starburst and type in the illustration are already grouped, so select them with the Selection Tool (solid arrow), and from the Variables panel menu choose Make Visibility Dynamic and then name the variable NewBug (**Figure 10.28**). Click the camera icon in the Variables panel to create the data set for the first flower. Your Variables panel should now look like **Figure 10.29**.

Figure 10.28

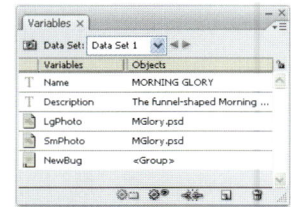

Figure 10.29

Building, Editing, and Importing the XML File

As in Project 1, you will add data sets to your XML file in an external text editor, keeping in mind that it will be easier to see what's going on in the XML file if you create more than one data set in Illustrator. The second data set you need to create will be for a daylily seed packet (containing the appropriate name, description, and images). Since daylilies are not a new item for Star & Fey, you'll need to hide the "NEW" graphic by choosing Object > Hide > Selection. After you've set up this version, click the camera icon in the Variables panel to create Data Set 2 (**Figure 10.30**). Note that you don't have to create more than one data set before you export the XML file; I've just found it's easier to figure out the structure of the XML file if it contains more than one data set.

Save the XML file the same way you did in Project 1 (that is, from the Variables panel menu, choose Save Variable Library) and open it in a text editor. The data set will look a little different than the one in Project 1, but it's still basically the same animal (see below).

```
<v:sampleDataSet  dataSetName="Data Set 1">
  <Name><p>MORNING GLORY</p></Name>
  <Description>
```

```
    <p>The funnel-shaped Morning Glory flowers open in the morning and
    die by the afternoon. New flowers bloom every day.</p>
  </Description>
  <LgPhoto>file:////Users/zorro/Flower Pics/MGlory.psd</LgPhoto>
  <SmPhoto>file:////Users/zorro/Flower Pics/MGlory.psd</SmPhoto>
  <NewBug>true</NewBug>
</v:sampleDataSet>
```

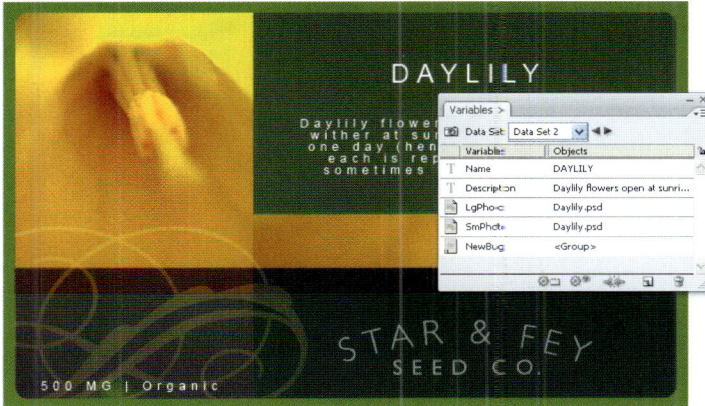

Figure 10.30

Tip

Notice that in this file the opening and closing tags are generally on the same line as the content (except for the Description). In Project 1 the opening tags, contents, and closing tags were all on different lines. In XML land either is acceptable, and Illustrator may arrange them all one way, all the other, or a combination of both.

Now copy and paste this data set to create one for the Winter Daphne, which has the "NEW" graphic hidden. Remember to make a line space and paste your new data set underneath Data Set 2.

```
<v:sampleDataSet  dataSetName="Data Set 3">
  <Name><p>WINTER DAPHNE</p></Name>
  <Description>
    <p>An evergreen shrub, the Winter Daphne produces wonderfully
    fragrant, light pink flowers with spreading lobes and glossy
    foliage. Propagate by semi-ripe cuttings in summertime.</p>
  </Description>
  <LgPhoto>file:////Users/zorro/Flower Pics/WDaphne.psd</LgPhoto>
  <SmPhoto>file:////Users/zorro/Flower Pics/WDaphne.psd</SmPhoto>
  <NewBug>false</NewBug>
</v:sampleDataSet>
```

Save the XML file in plain-text format with the .xml file extension, and then import the new XML file back into Illustrator (from the Variables panel menu, choose Load Variable Library). Now you can click through the data sets to view your handiwork.

Figure 10.31

Generating the Output Files

Generating the output files for this project works about the same as it did for the previous one, with the exception that you need to create an action to save the files in the Illustrator format. To do so, open the Actions panel menu and choose New Action, then name your new action SaveAsAI. Now click the Record button to begin recording. Save the file in Illustrator format to anywhere you want (you'll change the location in the next step) and then click Stop (**Figure 10.31**).

Now open the Actions panel menu and choose Batch. The Batch setup is the same as in Project 1, with the following exceptions: In the Action pull-down menu, choose SaveAsAI, and in the Destination area choose Override Action "Save" Commands (instead of "Export" Commands). The Choose button above the "Save" option should now be highlighted. Click it and select your preferred location (**Figure 10.32**).

Note

If you wanted to take this packaging project one step further, you could script a bar-code application to automatically generate the bar code. Some bar-code applications generate EPS files; others generate vector art. I prefer working with EPS files, which can be linked to the Illustrator file and dynamically updated.

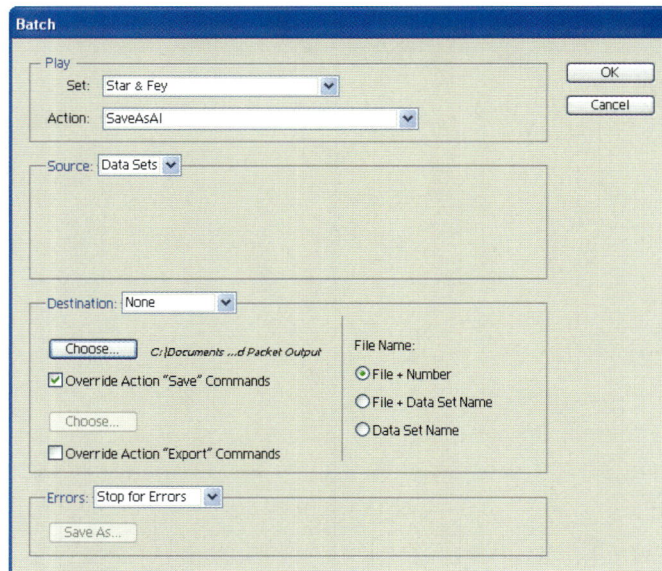

Figure 10.32

Project 3: E-Mail Invitation

In this project you'll use scripting to automatically create an e-mail invitation (**Figure 10.33**). Specifically, your script will create a custom image in Illustrator (incorporating a customer's first name), save the file and attach it to an e-mail, and fill the e-mail's To, Subject, and Body fields with custom text. Although you could arrange to send the e-mails automatically, you're going to inspect each image first, then send it off.

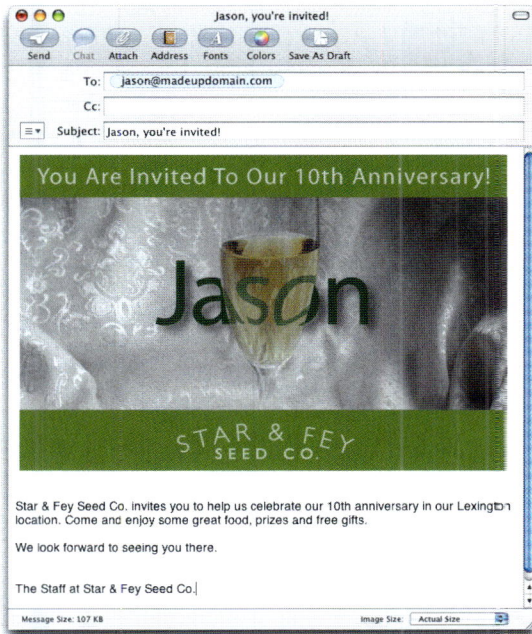

Figure 10.33

Your client, Star & Fey, is having 10th anniversary celebrations at each of its retail locations and wants to invite its customers via customized e-mails. To create and distribute this piece, you will work with three pieces of data per customer (which you will export from the company's customer database): first name, e-mail address, and the retail location the customer has previously visited.

This relatively easy project demonstrates how to build a graphics automation system that involves more than one application—in this case Illustrator and the Mac Mail application.

Note

This project demonstrates why you should always look at a file before sending it out. If a name is too short (like Hal or Jen), it may not be legible because the undistorted part won't stick out far enough. And if the name is too long, it will run off either side of the image. You can handle such situations by adding routines to adjust the horizontal scaling, tracking, or size, but this requires more advanced scripting.

Setting Up the Illustrator File

In your invitation design, the customer's name is displayed to make it look as if it were being viewed through a champagne glass. One name is masked to the inside of the glass using a bulge warp (choose Effects > Warp > Bulge) so that it will appear refracted by the liquid. A second piece of type is masked to the outside of the glass to appear as if it's the undistorted type peeking out from either side of the glass (**Figure 10.34**). A standard drop shadow has been applied to this type to make it appear more anchored to the rest of the image and as if it's behind the glass. In the Layers palette, name these pieces of type *BackName* (for the undistorted type) and *FrontName* (for the distorted type) (**Figure 10.35**).

Figure 10.34

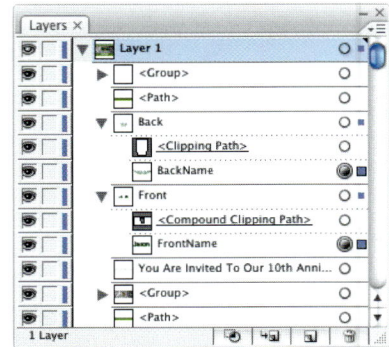

Figure 10.35

Writing the Script

Your script will be divided into two parts: The first will insert the names into and export the Illustrator file; the second will build the e-mail. I created this project using AppleScript and Mac Mail on the Macintosh platform, but you can rewrite it for another scripting language or platform. (Keep in mind, however, that although Apple's Mail program is scriptable, not all are—which means you'll need to learn about your e-mail application's capabilities. Microsoft Outlook can be easily scripted using VBScript.)

First, you need to do a little setup by *declaring* your variables—that is, loading up your variables with lists of customers' names and e-mail addresses as well as the store locations where they shop. Although our example uses only five customers, the script will handle a virtually unlimited number of records.

One limiting factor may be the need to review the e-mails with the images attached: To avoid overloading your system's memory by opening too many files at once, you may want to approach this project in batches.

The following portion of the script declares the first three variables:

```
set nameList to {"Jason", "Clara", "Daniel", "Mandy", "Alex"}
set emailList to {"jason@madeupdomain.com", "clara@madeupdomain.com",¬
"daniel@madeupdomain.com", "mandy@madeupdomain.com",¬
"alex@madeupdomain.com"}
set localList to {"Lexington", "Summerdale", "Milton", "Farmington",¬
"San Francisco"}
```

In this tutorial, the lists of names, e-mail addresses, and locations have been entered by hand, but often you will receive this kind of data as comma- or tab-delimited text files that have been exported from a database. It's easy to build the lists from these text files by cycling through each record (that is, each set of data, such as the personnel information for one employee), picking out the specific data from each, and compiling and storing them in a variable, as in the script above.

Since you want your script to loop through the code for each customer, you'll start the repeat loop with the following line (the end repeat companion line is the last one in the script): `repeat with i from 1 to count of items of nameList`

Now that you're in a loop, you'll set up the `thePerson` variable (which will be filled with a different first name with each iteration of the loop) as follows:

```
set thePerson to item i of nameList
```

Then you'll set the `theFile` variable (which is a file path telling Illustrator where to export the file) as follows:

```
set theFile to ((path to desktop folder as string) & thePerson &¬
".png")
```

The file path is made up of three parts: `path to desktop folder as string` is AppleScript shorthand for the Desktop; the variable `thePerson` will insert whatever person's name is active for that iteration of the loop; and `.png` is the file extension. On my computer, the "path to desktop folder as string" is Hard Drive:Users:zorro:Desktop: and the first customer's name is Jason, so the variable `theFile` will be Hard Drive:Users:zorro:Desktop:Jason.png for the first time through the loop.

The following code instructs Illustrator to insert the customer's name in two pieces of type and export the file to the desktop in the .png format:

```
tell application "Adobe Illustrator"
    set contents of text frame "BackName" of document 1 to thePerson
    set contents of text frame "FrontName" of document 1 to thePerson
    export current document to file theFile as PNG8 with options¬
    {class:PNG8 export options, color count:128}
    end tell
```

Note that BackName and FrontName are what you named the two pieces of type in the Illustrator template.

Now it's time to build the e-mail and plug in the image, though first you have to do something that may seem a bit crazy: You must declare the file location variable again, this time as an alias. This is because even though Illustrator works with direct file paths, Mail likes aliases, which provide a way for the Mac operating system to keep track of files even after they've been moved in the Mac file hierarchy. Call this second location variable theFile2, and Mail will be happy.

```
set theFile2 to alias ((path to desktop folder as string) & thePerson¬
& ".png")
```

Now it's time to talk to Mail: Activate it to bring it to the front (so that you can watch the action—though this isn't mandatory) and then declare the variables for the e-mail address, subject line (which includes the customer's name), body, and From line (theSender), as follows:

```
tell application "Mail"
        activate
    set theAddress to item i of EmailList
    set theSubject to thePerson & ", you're invited!"
    set theLocale to item i of localList
    set theBody to return & return & "Star & Fey Seed Co. invites you¬
    to help us celebrate our 10th anniversary in our " & theLocale & "¬
    location. Come and enjoy some great food, prizes and free gifts."¬
    & return & return & "We look forward to seeing you there." & return¬
    & return & return & "The Staff at Star & Fey Seed Co."
    set theSender to "Star & Fey <info@starandfey.com>"
```

Next, you'll build the e-mail and attach the image using the following script:

```
set newMessage to make new outgoing message with properties¬
{subject:theSubject, content:theBody & return & return}
tell newMessage
```

```
    set visible to true
    set sender to theSender
    make new to recipient at end of to recipients with properties¬
    {name:thePerson, address:theAddress}
        tell content
      make new attachment with properties {file name:theFile2} at¬
      before the first character

end tell
end tell
end tell
end repeat
```

If you read the chapter on scripting, you should recognize many parts of this AppleScript. See if you can make sense of AppleScript's English-like commands. For instance, even though at before the first character sounds silly, it describes precisely where the image will be attached (before any characters already in the e-mail). Also note how the subject line and message body combine hard-coded, static text with variables to further customize this communication.

If you really want to see this puppy fly, insert two words into the code—send newMessage—on the line before the last end tell line, so that the last three lines of code appear as follows:

```
send newMessage
end tell
end repeat
```

Inserting this code will automatically send the e-mails, so for testing you might want to change the whole list of e-mail addresses to your own e-mail address (in all five places).

Although the customer won't necessarily think you wrote the e-mail by hand it shows that you think enough of them to use a system like this. In that moment you hope to make a positive connection and plant a seed, so to speak.

Project 4: Unused Swatch Cleanup

Since it's good housekeeping to clean up files before you send them to anyone—for example, deleting unused swatches (colors), stray points, empty or useless layers, and unused objects—this project creates an action to delete unused swatches. Assigning a keystroke to this small but important task will make it even faster to execute.

To get started, open the Actions panel and create a new action (or a new Set, if needed). (I've named my new action Unused Swatches; you can name yours whatever you want.) Now, from the Function Key pull-down menu choose F1, and click the check box next to Command (for Mac) or Control (for Windows) (**Figure 10.36**). Now, whenever you want to run this action, you simply press Command-F1 (Control-F1 on Windows). Click the OK button to begin recording the action.

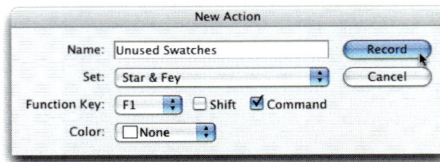

Figure 10.36

Open the Swatches panel and its panel menu and choose Select All Unused (**Figure 10.37**). Illustrator will now highlight all of the unused swatches. From the same menu, choose Delete Swatches (**Figure 10.38**). A dialog box will appear, asking if you really want to delete the swatch; click Yes.

When you play this action back, the same dialog box will appear, asking (once again) if you really want to do this. To get rid of this potentially annoying step, go to your action and click the Toggle Dialog On/Off icon to the left of the second step in your action called Swatches—OK, they're both called Swatches, so it's the second one (**Figure 10.39**). Run the action again, and the dialog box won't appear.

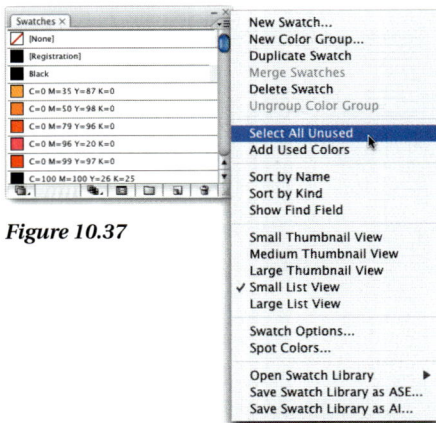

Figure 10.37

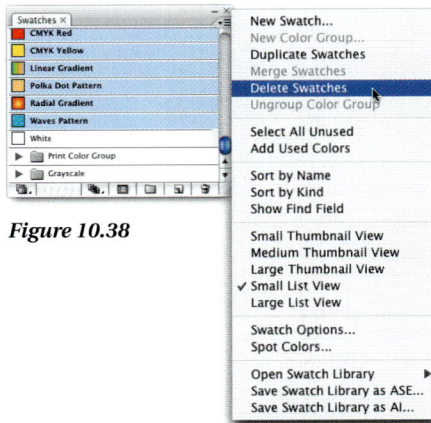

Figure 10.38

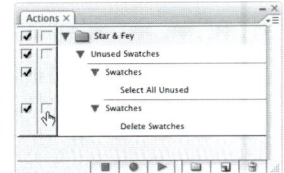

Figure 10.39

11
The Art of Composition

The InDesign Projects

Design is the method of putting form and content together.

—*American graphic designer Paul Rand*

If, as Paul Rand asserts, design is the marriage of form and content, and automation, as it's sometimes described, is the *separation* of form and content, together they can be considered a sort of yin and yang. They aren't opposites; rather, they complement each other. Nowhere is this more evident than with InDesign. Page layout is the last step in many design projects—the place where images, type, shapes, and interactivity come together.

Despite this, InDesign's automation possibilities have not been exploited as much as those in Photoshop and Illustrator have. For example, InDesign is mysteriously lacking actions—unlike Photoshop and Illustrator—yet it's highly scriptable and includes a data-driven publishing mechanism called Data Merge, so it's no slouch either.

Automating page layout in InDesign works a bit differently than image or illustration automation in Photoshop or Illustrator and tends to involve multipage documents and more page elements, and is typically text-heavy. The projects in this chapter reflect these differences and show how InDesign interacts with applications like Adobe Acrobat, Microsoft Excel, and Adobe Bridge as well as the types of InDesign documents that lend themselves to automation.

Project 1: Ad Generator

Imagine that you're the regional manager of several retail stores. Every quarter you manage the creation of magazine ads for all of the stores. The ads share the same basic layout, differing only in their copy. The variable text frames in the ad represent the store location, a promotional item, and the promotional item's price. You collect all of the information from each store, create each individualized ad, and send each store a publishable PDF (**Figure 11.1**).

Figure 11.1

The slow and error-prone way to produce the stores' ad copy would be to call or e-mail each location to collect the information and then manually type or paste the data into the ad layout. The fast and *less* error-prone method—which this project will demonstrate—would be to collect the variable ad copy via a PDF form that you e-mailed to each store.

In the latter method, the stores customize their ads by picking options from pull-down menus in the PDF form before e-mailing the data back to you. You then assemble the collected data into a spreadsheet that you can import into InDesign and automatically generate each store's ad.

Building the Base InDesign Ad

To begin, set up your base ad in the standard InDesign CS3 document format. The background rectangle is 4.625 inches square (the sale-price oval over-hangs the rectangle on the left by one-eighth inch), and the text frames you'll make variable are price, special, and store location (**Figure 11.2**). Save the file as SandF_SpringAd.indd (or use the file provided on this book's companion site, www.peachpit.com/apprentice).

Building and Distributing the PDF Form

Acrobat PDF forms provide an efficient means of collecting data and auto-matically assembling it in a tabular format that InDesign can use. Like Photo-shop, InDesign can import data from tab- or comma-delimited text files.

Figure 11.2

> **Tip**
>
> Although you'll only be working with variable text in this tutorial, you can set up variable *images* as well.

PDF forms are standard PDF documents that contain fillable form fields. In this scenario, users complete a form, save their responses in a special Acrobat file format called FDF (Form Data Format), and then return the FDF file to you via e-mail. The FDF export and e-mailing happen in one step because of the way you're going to set up the form. Since an FDF file contains only what's captured in the form fields, it's a much smaller file than the entire document. (Comments exported from a PDF in Acrobat are also saved in the FDF format.) FDF files can be imported into another copy of the same PDF form, and the contents will show up in the right place. For this project, you'll use Acrobat to assemble multiple sets of form data in a single location.

Start building the form by creating a document 6.5 inches wide and 4.5 inches tall in InDesign. You'll add a background, some type, and the client's logo (**Figure 11.3**) and then save the document as a PDF (by choosing File > Adobe PDF Presets > Smallest File Size). Now open it in Acrobat.

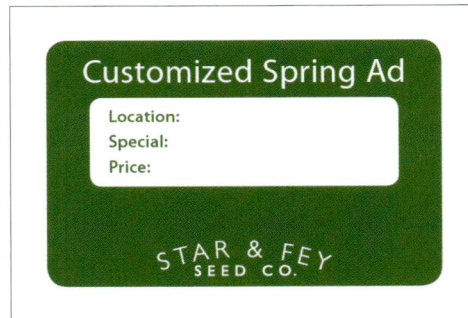

Figure 11.3

In Acrobat, choose the Combo Box tool (Tools > Forms > Combo Box Tool) and drag and release to create a field next to the Location label (**Figure 11.4**). In the Combo Box Properties dialog box that appears, you will need to specify three properties for your combo box: Name, Border Color, and Item List (**Figure 11.5**).

If the General tab isn't active, select it, and then replace the default text (Combo Box1) in the Name field with the name for your field: Location. Next, click the Appearance tab and choose black for the Border Color by clicking the Border Color icon and choosing the black color chip (**Figure 11.6**). To

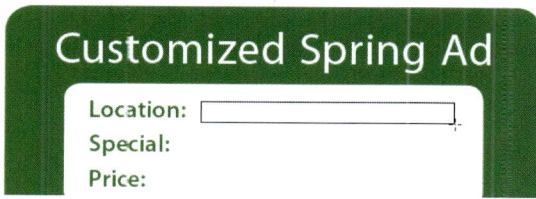

Customized Spring Ad

Location:
Special:
Price:

Figure 11.4

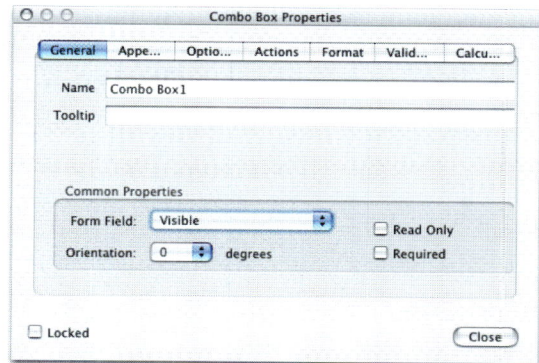

Figure 11.5

create the choices that will appear in the Location pull-down menu, click the Options tab. This combo box will contain a list of five store locations. Type a city name, such as Atlanta, in the Item text field and then click the Add button. The city name you entered will appear in the Item List field below. Enter four more locations and click Close (**Figure 11.7**). (I used Decatur, Salem, Athens, and St. Elmo, but you can enter any towns you like.)

Following the same process, create combo boxes next to your Special and Price labels. Give the Special field the name Special and set up the following list items for it: Garden Tools, Gloves, Wildflower Seeds, Straw Hat, and Knee Pads. Give the Price field the name Price, and for list items, enter $4.99 to $14.99 in $1 increments.

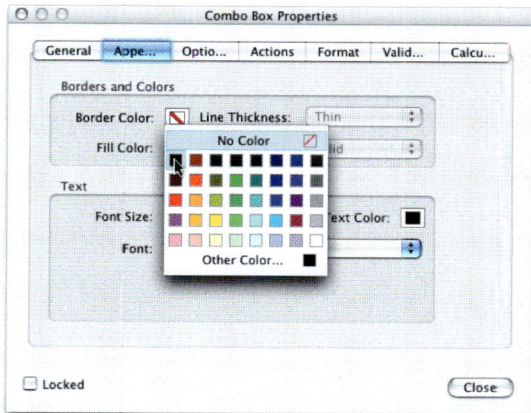

Figure 11.6

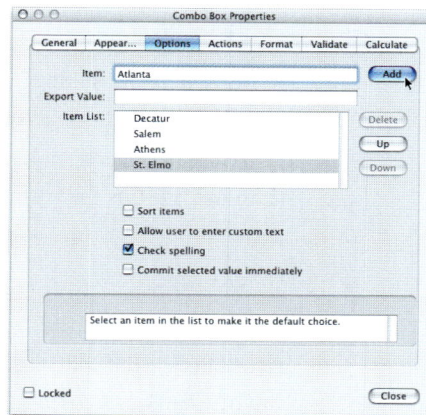

Figure 11.7

Tip

You might find that Acrobat's Forms toolbar speeds up designing forms (**Figure 11.8**). It also makes testing forms easier, thanks to the Preview/Edit Layout toggle button.

Figure 11.8

Now you'll add a Submit button, which will collect the data, save it in an FDF file, create an e-mail message, and attach the FDF file to the message. To do this, choose the Button tool (Tools > Forms > Button Tool) or select the tool from the Forms toolbar (the button icon with OK on it). You can either double-click the document to produce a default-size button, or you can click and drag to make a custom-size button.

Click and drag above the Star & Fey logo so that the button looks something like **Figure 11.9**. The Button Properties dialog box (which looks a lot like the Combo Box Properties dialog box) should appear. Select the General tab and name your button Submit. Now click the Appearance tab and for Border Color select No Color and for Fill Color choose white.

Figure 11.9

Next, open the Actions tab so that you can specify what you want the button to do. From the Select Trigger pull-down menu, choose Mouse Up. For Select Action, choose "Submit a form." Now click the Add button, and you'll see the Submit Form Selections window. In the "Enter a URL for this link" field, type mailto:info@starandfey.com. Better yet, type in your own e-mail address after mailto: (like all of the client info in this project, info@starandfey.com is a made-up e-mail address). In the Export Format area, select the FDF Include radio button, and in the Field Selection area, click the "Only these" radio button and then click the "Select fields" button.

In the Field Selection dialog box, you'll see a list of the three combo boxes and the button that you created. Click the check boxes next to Location, Price, and Special (**Figure 11.10**). Make sure the Include Selected radio button is selected, and click OK. This will take you back to the Submit Form Selections dialog box. Click OK again, and you'll return to the Button Properties dialog box. Click Close to save and close the file.

To distribute the form, create a new e-mail and attach the form to it (**Figure 11.11**).

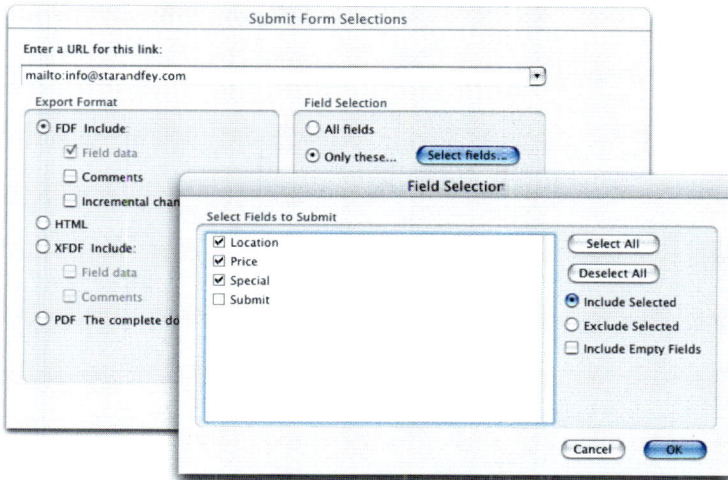

Figure 11.10

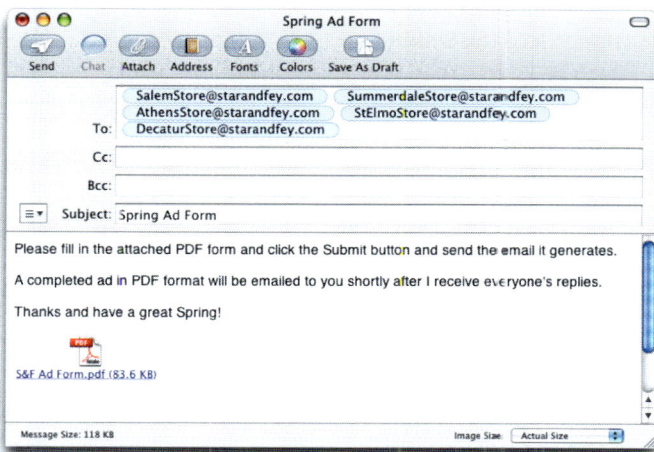

Figure 11.11

Note

It's possible to write a script that saves all FDF files in a mailbox with unique names based on the sender's name. Download the project files for this chapter at www.peachpit. com/apprentice and open the MailAttachments Apple-Script for an example.

Collecting Form Data

As you receive the e-mail replies, detach the FDF files and save them in a folder. Since every FDF file you receive will have the same name (something like SandF_SpringAd_data.fdf), this is a good time to save them using the different store names (**Figure 11.12**). You'll now use Acrobat to combine the FDF files into a single, comma-delimited text file that can be opened in either a spreadsheet application or text editor.

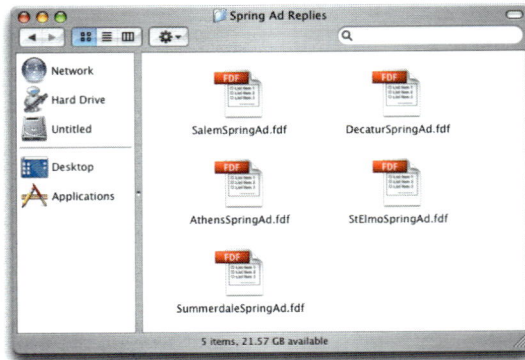

Figure 11.12

After you've received and saved all the FDF files, open Acrobat and from the Forms menu, choose Manage Form Data > Merge Data Files into Spreadsheet (**Figure 11.13**). In the Export Data From Multiple Forms dialog box, click the Add Files button, navigate to the folder where you've saved the FDFs, select all of them, and click the Select button. The files will be listed in the Export Data From Multiple Forms dialog box (**Figure 11.14**). Click the Export button. In the Select Folder To Save File dialog box, choose a location and click the Save button. The filename defaults to report.csv.

Figure 11.13

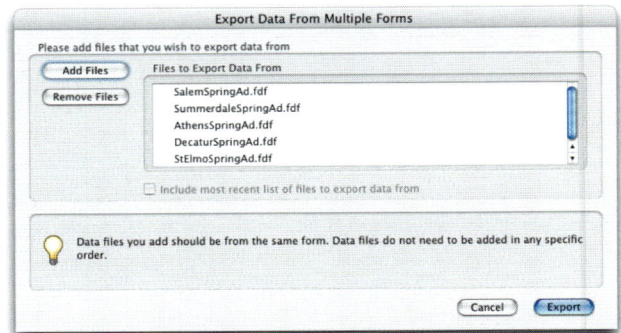

Figure 11.14

When Acrobat is finished exporting the form data, it displays the Export Progress dialog box, which gives you the option of opening the report.csv file (**Figure 11.15**). If you click View File Now, the file automatically opens in whichever application has been set up to open .csv files by default; usually that's a spreadsheet program, such as Excel, or a text editor (**Figure 11.16**). Using a spreadsheet for the task is preferable because it's easier to see individual data points and modify them as needed. In a text editor, all the data seems to run together, making it harder to read and work with (**Figure 11.17**).

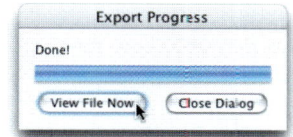

Figure 11.15

Figure 11.16

Figure 11.17

Now, you will need to edit your form data before it can be fed to InDesign. In order for the data to import correctly, every header in your data file must have an entry in every field beneath it. And every column of data must have a header. The data file from your form violates both of these rules, but it's easy to fix.

Open report.csv in a spreadsheet application. The A column, which contains the names of all the exported FDF files, lacks a head (**Figure 11.18**). You can remedy this situation by either deleting all text in this column (since you won't need it) or adding a head to make InDesign happy. Let's make InDesign happy and add the head Store in cell A1. Column E, in contrast, has a head but no text beneath it. Therefore you should delete the Submit head in cell E1 (**Figure 11.19**), and then save and close the file.

> **Note**
>
> If you plan to simulate the process of receiving multiple FDF files, you have a few options: You can send yourself multiple FDFs via e-mail; you can manually build a text file like the report.csv file; or you can download an example report.csv file with this chapter's project files.

Figure 11.18

Figure 11.19

Merging the Data and Generating the Ads

Now you'll link to the report.csv file and associate its three fields with the three text frames in the InDesign ad template. After that, it's a simple matter of generating the five output files (one for each store)—InDesign calls these *merged* files.

Open the Spring Ad template SandF_SpringAd.indd in InDesign and choose Window > Automation > Data Merge (**Figure 11.20**). If you don't see the Automation menu item, you might need to select Show All Menu Items at the bottom of the Window menu. The Data Merge panel is one of the few in Creative Suite 3 that contains instructions for its use (**Figure 11.21**).

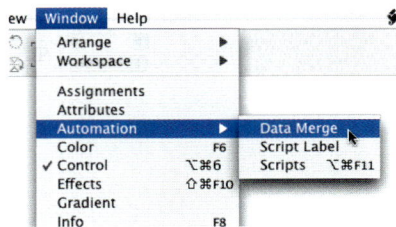

Figure 11.20

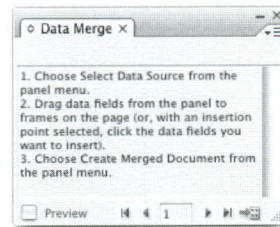

Figure 11.21

Follow the panel's first instruction and choose Select Data Source, navigate to the report.csv file, and then click Open (**Figure 11.22**). The Data Merge panel should now display report.csv (the name of your data file), as well as the four column heads it contains (**Figure 11.23**). Remember that you won't be using the Store column. InDesign is actually linking to report.csv—you can find it in the Links panel.

Now comes the cool part—dragging the headers from the Data Merge panel onto the text frames in your layout to associate the text frames with the

Figure 11.22

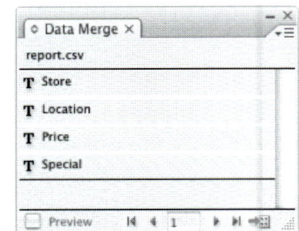

Figure 11.23

corresponding data from the report.csv file. Using the Type tool, click in the Price text frame and select all. With the Price text selected, drag the Price tag from the Data Merge panel onto the Price text frame. This will replace the text in the frame with <Price> to show that the text frame is now associated with the Price column of data in the linked report.csv file (**Figure 11.24**). Do the same for the Special and Location text frames, and the InDesign template file should look like **Figure 11.25**.

Figure 11.24

Figure 11.25

In the Data Merge panel, click the Preview box in the lower-left corner and the data from the Athens store should appear (**Figure 11.26**). You can flip through the other four versions of the ad by clicking the Next and Previous buttons at the bottom of the Data Merge panel (**Figure 11.27**). You'll see right away that the Special text frame will need some adjusting for each file, but that's all right.

Figure 11.26

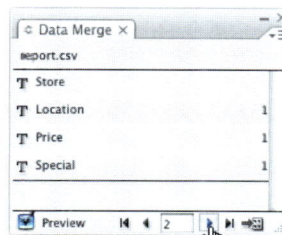

Figure 11.27

To generate the merged files, open the Data Merge panel menu and choose Create Merged Document (**Figure 11.28**). Under the Records tab, make sure to click the All Records radio button in the Records To Merge area. In the area below that, you can choose how InDesign will lay out your output document: Single Record puts each version on its own page in a multipage document, while Multiple Records puts the different versions onto one page (based on settings you specify under the Multiple Record Layout tab). For this project, you want one document per page, so in the Records per Document Page pull-down menu choose Single Record (**Figure 11.29**).

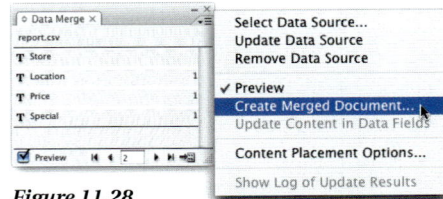

Figure 11.28

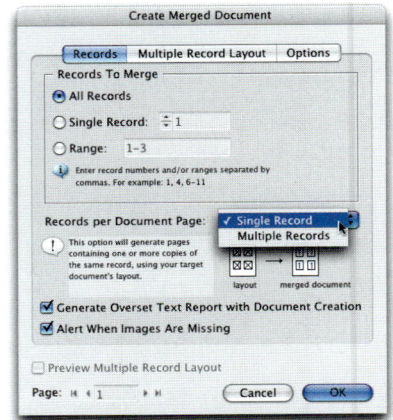

Figure 11.29

The two check boxes at the bottom of the dialog box alert you when there is overset text (known as *overflow text* in Photoshop and Illustrator; both terms refer to text that's too long to fit in its frame) in any of the merged files and when images specified in the data file are missing. Leave both boxes checked (even though you don't really need an alert for missing images with this project), and click OK. After InDesign generates a document with each version on a separate page, make any necessary adjustments to the text (such as resizing text boxes if the type is overset). Then export each page by choosing File > Export, name the file (in this case using the store names), and click Save. In the next window (Export Adobe PDF), type the page number in the Range, select any other needed settings, and click Export. You've just created the final files to e-mail back to each store location.

Project 2: Contact Sheet

With a little help from Adobe Bridge, InDesign can automatically lay out a contact sheet of a selected group of images (**Figure 11.30**). When done in a custom template, a contact sheet can be an excellent way to present a group of images to a client. The template can contain logos, contact information, and copyright notices. This project combines automation capabilities that are built into Bridge with a customized template that you will create. It's a little different from most projects in this book in that it uses a prefabricated auto-mation agent with limited customizability. However, it's important to know about the tools that Creative Suite provides, and isn't the point of graphics automation to avoid doing unnecessary work?

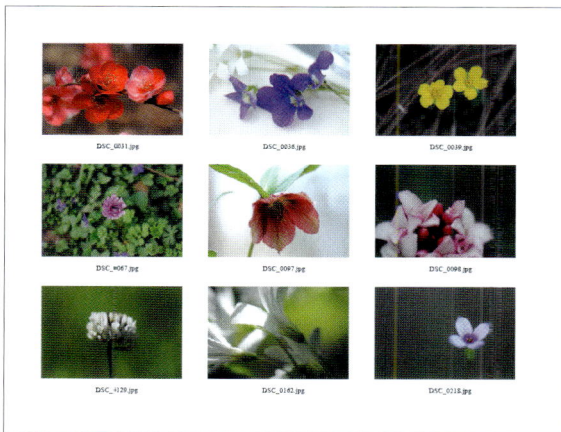

Figure 11.30

Creating the Template

You'll set up your contact sheet template by creating a regular InDesign document and saving it in InDesign's template format. As with most of the projects in this book (and indeed most automations), it's virtually impossible to set up a system that doesn't require a final inspection of your output. In the case of this contact sheet project, you should expect to look over your results and reposition some elements to fit, but that doesn't negate the productivity gained by setting up the template. It still saves plenty of labor in the long run.

For this project, you want a green bar running across the bottom of the con-tact sheet containing the client's logo centered within it. Thus, on a letter-size page, you'll create a green bar that's 11 inches wide by 0.5 inches tall, move it to the bottom of the page, paste your client's logo, and then center it within the bar (**Figure 11.31**). To make your document into a template, choose File > Save As and from the Format pull-down menu choose InDesign CS template. Name the template S&F Contact Sheet.indt.

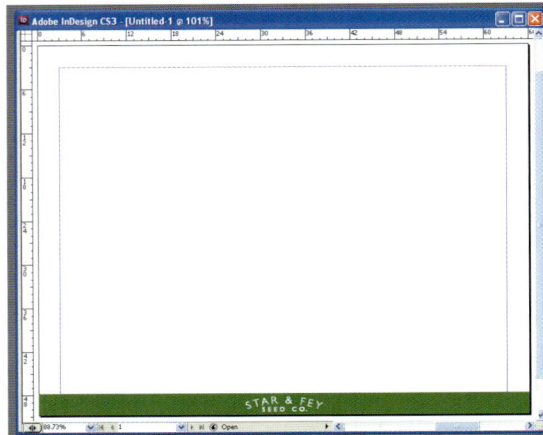

Figure 11.31

Creating the Contact Sheet

Open Adobe Bridge and select nine images (**Figure 11.32**). If you don't select any, Bridge will use all the images in the current content pane. And you must select individual images, not just a folder.

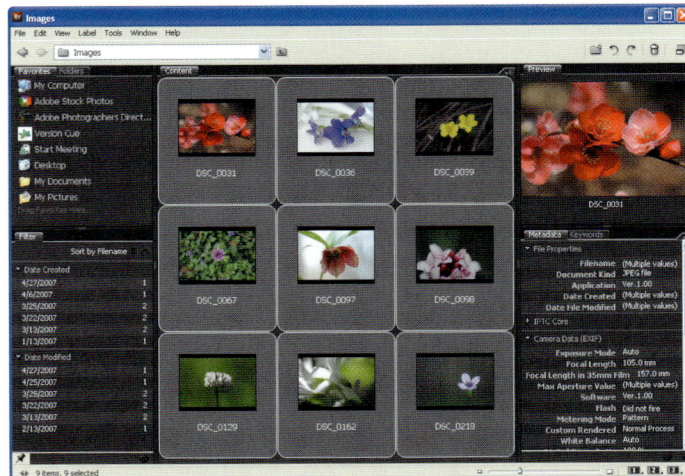

Figure 11.32

Choose Tools > InDesign > Create InDesign Contact Sheet (**Figure 11.33**), and the Contact Sheet dialog box will appear (**Figure 11.34**). The top Presets area is for loading, saving, and removing presets by name. If you like your settings and plan to reuse them, click the Save Settings button in this area to make them a preset.

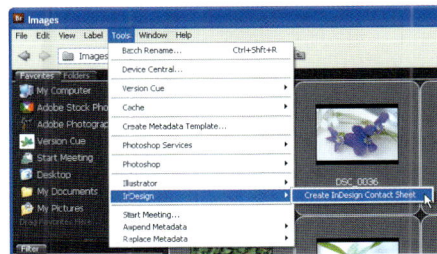

Figure 11.33

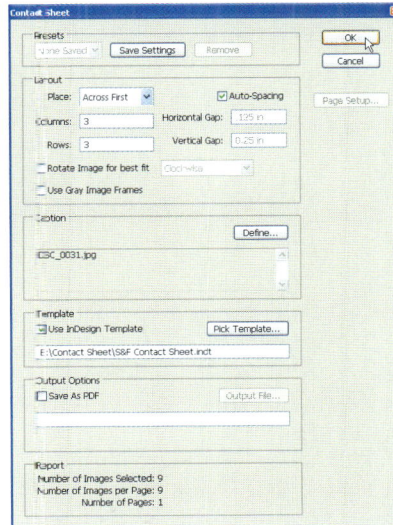

Figure 11.34

The Layout area is where you'll set up the appearance of your image grid (**Figure 11.35**). The Place pull-down menu determines the order in which images appear: You can choose Across First or Down First. Check the Auto-Spacing box, so you don't have to calculate the gaps between the images. Since you're using nine images, you'll type in three columns and three rows. You don't want to rotate the images or use gray frames, so you'll leave those boxes unchecked.

Figure 11.35

In the Caption area of the Contact Sheet dialog box, you'll specify what kind of text appears under each image (**Figure 11.36**). The first time you use the Contact Sheet tool, the caption defaults to filename, displaying the filename of the first image you selected in the Content pane.

In the Caption area of the dialog box, click the Define button. The resulting Create or Modify Caption dialog box can be a little confusing, since rather than just letting you type some text, it forces you to *assemble* the caption out

Figure 11.36

of various elements, such as the images' filenames (**Figure 11.37**). This works a lot like creating a header or footer in Microsoft Word or Excel, where you set up variable fields to display information about the file, such as its creator, page number, or filename. As in the Contact Sheet dialog box, you can save your settings as a preset so you can easily reuse them later.

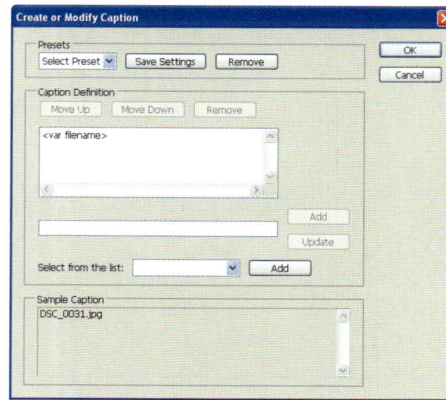

Figure 11.37

A caption can consist of a single element (such as the filename), multiple elements on a single line, or multiple lines of elements. Captions are built out of variables such as the file's name.

The Caption Definition area is divided roughly into the upper half, which contains a text display box and three buttons, and the lower half, which contains a text field, a pull-down menu, and three buttons for rearranging caption elements (**Figure 11.38**). The Sample Caption area at the bottom of the dialog box shows a preview of the elements in the display box (**Figure 11.39**).

Building a caption is an odd, two-step process: You choose caption elements from the "Select from the list" pull-down menu and click Add to make them

Figure 11.39

Figure 11.38

appear in the single-line blank in the middle. You then pick as many variable elements as you want to appear on one line of your caption, insert spaces between them, and then click the upper Add button to put your line into the bigger text display box. The line is editable, so it's possible to make typos: If you type a variable name incorrectly (or if, by a slip of the mouse, you change one that you selected), Bridge calls out the error in the sample caption with the word *undefined*. You can select and reorder or delete lines from the list using the three buttons above the list window. This feature is poorly documented, so you'll need to experiment a bit to get comfortable with it.

Now that you've learned the minutiae of constructing complex, dynamic captions for your contact sheets, for this project you'll keep it simple and build a caption consisting just of the images' filenames. Make sure both of the dialog box's text fields are empty, and from the pull-down menu select File Name. First click the lower Add button, then click the upper Add button, and finally click OK (to save your work and close the dialog box). You'll now be returned to the Contact Sheet dialog box.

One more setting to go. In the Template area of the Contact Sheet dialog box, choose the template you created in the first step. Click the Use InDesign Template box and click Pick Template. Browse until you locate the desired template and then click Open (**Figure 11.40**). You could automatically save the contact sheet as a PDF by clicking the Save As PDF check box, but since you'll need to tweak the document before sending it to your client (see the next section), you'll leave the box unchecked. If you were going to use these particular settings again, you could save them as a preset.

Click OK in the Contact Sheet dialog box and watch InDesign generate the file.

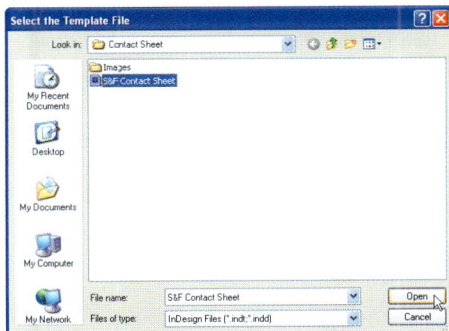

Figure 11.40

A Little Cleanup

After having so much control over the contact sheet's captions, it comes as a bit of a surprise to learn that you have *no* control over three other things: the placement of the grid of images, the orientation of images within their frames, and whether you want strokes around the frames. Thus, you need to do a bit of post-automation cleanup.

First off, your template has a bar running across the bottom, so you'll need to shift the images up a little. Since the bar and logo are on the master page, you can select all and get just the image boxes. Now move everything up an eighth of an inch.

Don't deselect your image grid just yet, though: With the group still selected, choose Object > Fitting > Center Content to center the images within their frames and eliminate the strokes around the photos. If Adobe ever includes actions in InDesign, these cleanup steps could be accomplished with a simple action. And while I'm dreaming, Adobe could also include in Bridge's Contact Sheet window the ability to automatically trigger said action after the contact sheet has been built**.**

But back to business! Now it's time to save the contact sheet as a PDF (File > Export > Format: Adobe PDF) and e-mail it to your client (**Figure 11.41**).

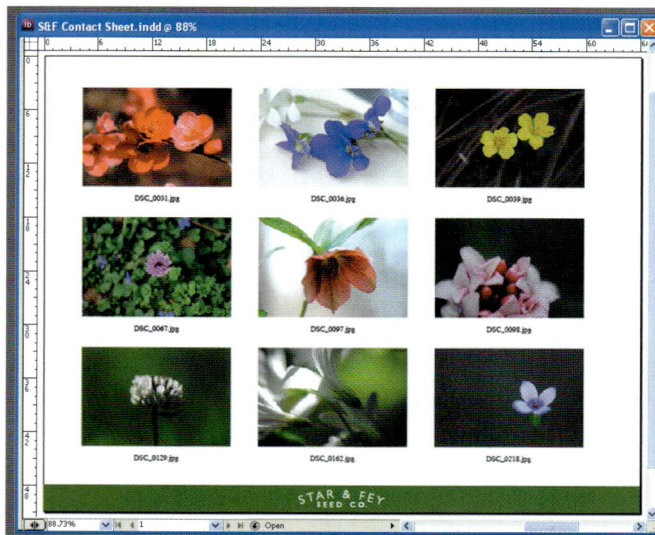

Figure 11.41

Project 3: Step and Repeat

Step and repeat refers to the process of duplicating an object (or objects) to fill a page—usually done to gang objects on a sheet and thus save on printing costs. InDesign includes a Step and Repeat feature; however, it has limitations. (To access the Step and Repeat feature, select an object then choose Edit > Step and Repeat. Note that you may need to choose Show All Menu Items at the bottom of the Edit menu for Step and Repeat to appear.)

Usually a step-and-repeat process produces a grid (columns and rows) of objects on a page (**Figure 11.42**). InDesign's Step and Repeat feature, however, only steps and repeats in one direction—columns *or* rows, not both. (It will also step and repeat diagonally, but still in only one direction.) This means that to produce a grid of objects, you must go through the process *twice,* once for each direction. In addition, after the first run-through of the process, you must stop and select all objects for the second run-through—not a huge deal, perhaps, but you can do a little better with a small script.

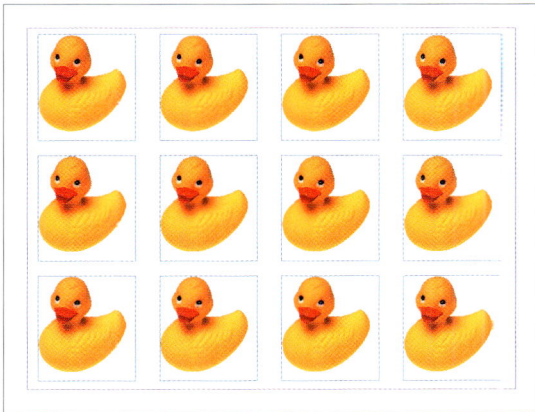

Figure 11.42

Your project is to step and repeat a single ticket so that you end up with six tickets per letter-size sheet. Thus, you will create an AppleScript that asks the user to enter the number of copies for the rows and the horizontal distance between objects, and then asks the user for the number of copies for the columns and the vertical distance between the objects. The script will then automatically select all objects in the row produced by the first step before duplicating them vertically to produce the columns.

Note

You'll use the product of this project (a six-up grid of tickets) for your next project (building a sequentially numbered ticket generator).

Here's a brief overview of the steps carried out by the script:

1. It first checks to make sure something is selected and displays an error if nothing is.

2. It asks the user how many horizontal copies he or she would like and how far apart it should place them.

3. It asks the user how many vertical copies he or she would like and how far apart it should place them.

4. It duplicates the object horizontally per the user's input.

5. It selects everything on the page.

6. It duplicates everything vertically per the user's input.

When I go through the script section by section, you'll see that it's not that complicated. But first, let's take a look at it in its entirety:

```
repeat 1 times
    tell application "Adobe InDesign CS3"
        set mySelection to selection
        if mySelection = {} then
            display dialog "Please make a selection and try again."
            exit repeat
        end if

        set SavedDelims to AppleScript's text item delimiters
        set AppleScript's text item delimiters to ","

        set HorizSpecs to text returned of (display dialog "Horizontal¬
        copies? / Distance apart (in inches)?" & return & "[ Separate the¬
        two numbers with a comma. ]" default answer "3,2")
        set HorizNum to text item 1 of HorizSpecs
        set HorizInch to text item 2 of HorizSpecs

        set VertSpecs to text returned of (display dialog "Vertical¬
        copies? / Distance apart (in inches)?" & return & "[ Separate the¬
        two numbers with a comma. ]" default answer "3,2")
        set VertNum to text item 1 of VertSpecs
        set VertInch to text item 2 of VertSpecs

        repeat HorizNum times
            duplicate mySelection
            move mySelection by {HorizInch, 0}
        end repeat
```

```
      select all
      set mySelection to selection

      repeat VertNum times
         duplicate mySelection
         move mySelection by {0, VertInch}
      end repeat
   end tell

   set AppleScript's text item delimiters to SavedDelims
end repeat
```

The first line (repeat 1 times) sets up a loop for the entire script. But, you may be asking, what's the point of a script that repeats only once? A loop provides a structure to "escape," or stop, the script without resulting in an error. The upcoming section of the script, which checks to see if anything is selected, needs a way to gracefully bow out of the overall script if nothing is, in fact, selected. As you will see, that graceful out is provided by exiting the repeat (or loop), which effectively exits the entire script.

The next line (tell application "Adobe InDesign CS3") directs everything that follows to InDesign until it encounters the closing end tell line (the third line from the bottom).

The next section of our script tests to see if anything is selected in the InDesign document:

```
      set mySelection to selection
      if mySelection = {} then
         display dialog "Please make a selection and try again."
         exit repeat
      end if
```

The line set mySelection to selection stores whatever the user has clicked in InDesign as the variable mySelection. The next line (if mySelection = {} then) tests whether mySelection contains anything; if the user has not selected anything in InDesign, the script goes on to display the message "Please make a selection and try again." The exit repeat line ends the repeat (or loop) and stops the script without displaying an error. The end if line closes the if block and ends this section.

Note

AppleScript doesn't actually have any formal structure called a *section*, but I like to think of scripts in chunks because they're easier to analyze that way.

The next section serves as a bit of housekeeping that will help us decipher user input (the number of columns and rows, and the distance between each):

```
set SavedDelims to AppleScript's text item delimiters
set AppleScript's text item delimiters to ","
```

Text item delimiters are characters that separate different text items, such as tabs or commas (for example, the comma-separated values file in Project 1). In this script, the first line saves AppleScript's current delimiters to the variable SavedDelims, which means that the value of SavedDelims is stored in RAM until another value is assigned or the script editor is closed. You'll use the value of SavedDelims to restore the current delimiters after you change them for this script. You don't absolutely have to do this, but it's a good way to keep from breaking other scripts. The second line sets the delimiters to commas. (Note that you can set this to anything that's convenient for a user to input, such as a colon, asterisk, or tab.)

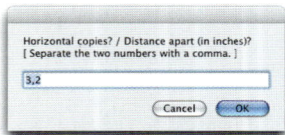

Figure 11.43

The next section displays a dialog box that asks for the number of horizontal duplicates and the distance between them, separated by a comma (**Figure 11.43**):

```
set HorizSpecs to text returned of (display dialog "Horizontal¬
copies? / Distance apart (in inches)?" & return & "[ Separate the¬
two numbers with a comma. ]" default answer "3,2")
set HorizNum to text item 1 of HorizSpecs
set HorizInch to text item 2 of HorizSpecs
```

Plain-vanilla AppleScript does not provide a way to present a dialog box with two or more text-entry boxes; thus, we're finessing our script by entering two values separated by the text delimiter.

The first line of this section displays a dialog box with some text—Horizontal copies? / Distance apart (in inches)? and Separate the two numbers with a comma—which asks the user to input some data.

```
(set HorizSpecs to text returned of (display dialog "Horizontal copies?
/ Distance apart (in inches)?" & return & "[ Separate the two numbers
with a comma. ]" default answer "3,2"))
```

The script then stores the user's input in the variable HorizSpecs. The default answer "3,2" portion of the script puts the text "3,2" in the text field to give the user an example to follow.

Note

The unit of measure for both distances entered by the user comes from InDesign's Preferences (InDesign > Preferences > Units & Increments) for ruler units. For this project, the unit of measure is inches.

The next line (set HorizNum to text item 1 of HorizSpecs) takes the first number stored in the variable HorizSpecs (whatever the user entered as the number of horizontal duplicates) and stores it in the variable HorizNum. The line after that (set HorizInch to text item 2 of HorizSpecs) takes the second number stored in the variable, HorizSpecs (the distance between horizontal objects), and stores that in the variable HorizInch.

The next section does the same thing, but for the vertical data:

```
set VertSpecs to text returned of (display dialog "Vertical¬
copies? / Distance apart (in inches)?" & return & "[ Separate the¬
two numbers with a comma. ]" default answer "3,2")
set VertNum to text item 1 of VertSpecs
set VertInch to text item 2 of VertSpecs
```

The following section sets up a loop that repeats the number of times stored in the variable HorizNum:

```
repeat HorizNum times
    duplicate mySelection
    move mySelection by {HorizInch, 0}
end repeat
```

The second line duplicates whatever is stored in the variable mySelection (which is whatever you originally selected in the InDesign document), and the subsequent line (move mySelection by {HorizInch, 0}) moves it the distance stored in the variable HorizInch. Notice that the zero in the brackets indicates that there is no vertical movement.

The next two lines select everything on the page (which should be the first row) and store it in the variable mySelection.

```
select all
set mySelection to selection
```

The next section does the same thing as the previous section, only vertically:

```
repeat VertNum times
    duplicate mySelection
    move mySelection by {0, VertInch}
end repeat
```

And now, instead of duplicating a single object, the script is duplicating *all* of the objects in the first row, thus creating the columns.

The last three lines close the InDesign tell block, restore the delimiters to their previous setting, and close the repeat block:

```
end tell

    set AppleScript's text item delimiters to SavedDelims
end repeat
```

The object that you'll step and repeat in this project is a raffle ticket (**Figure 11.44**). Open the document in InDesign and select all (Edit > Select All), then switch to the script editor and click the Run button. In the first dialog box type 1,5 (1 horizontal duplicate and 5 inches, because the ticket is 5 inches wide). In the second dialog box, type 2,2.5 (2 vertical duplicates and 2.5 inches, because the ticket is 2.5 inches tall). Your results should look like **Figure 11.45**.

Save this document as S&Ftickets-6up.indd and leave it open since you'll be using it in the next project.

Figure 11.44

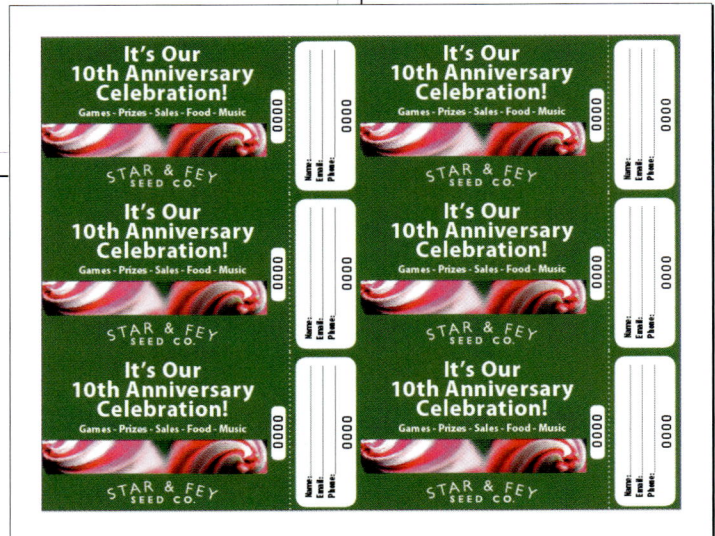

Figure 11.45

Project 4: Ticket Generator

If it's not already open, open the tickets file you created in the last project, S&Ftickets-6up.indd. In this project you'll create another script that automatically duplicates this page of tickets and sequentially numbers each ticket based on two pieces of user input: number of tickets and the starting number.

Your script will use InDesign's Script Labels feature to identify the text frames that contain the numbers. A script label in InDesign is like a layer name in Photoshop or Illustrator: It names the object so a script can find it. Each ticket has a main body and a tear-off stub, both of which contain the same sequential number. You'll give both text frames the same script label so that they'll be assigned the same number.

To prepare the file for this project, you need to do two things: Put everything but the numbers on a master page, and apply script labels to the sequential-number text frames (so that your script can identify and change their contents). Placing the graphics on a master page will create a much smaller final file (because the pages with only the number text frames will be duplicated) and will allow us, if need be, to quickly change all the ticket graphics by editing only the master page.

Make sure the Pages panel is open (Window > Pages). To move everything but the numbers to a master page, select all, then Shift-click to deselect all of the number text frames. Choose Edit > Cut, double-click the A-Master page in the Pages panel, and choose Edit > Paste in Place (Figure 11.46).

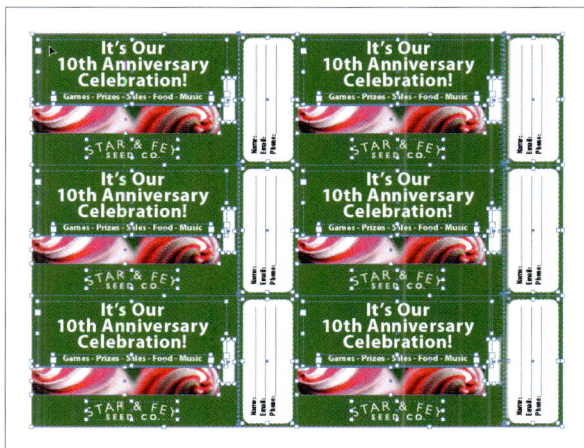

Figure 11.46

Now return to Page 1 by double-clicking its icon in the Pages panel. Select the two sequential-number text frames on the first ticket on the top left (**Figure 11.47**). If the Script Label panel is not visible, choose Window > Automation > Script Label. With both text frames selected, type one in the Script Label panel and press the Tab key to assign the label to both frames (**Figure 11.48**). Give the two sequential-number text frames for the second ticket (top right) the label two. Label the text frames for the third ticket (middle left) with three, the fourth ticket (middle right) with four, the fifth ticket (lower left) with five, and the sixth ticket (lower right) with six. Save the file.

Figure 11.47

Figure 11.48

Now let's move on to the script, which is going to seem very short and simple after the previous one. This script includes three sections: The first presents a couple of dialog boxes for user input; the second duplicates the page of tickets (based on user input); and the third sequentially numbers the tickets. Here's the script:

```
tell application "Adobe InDesign CS3"

   set StartNum to text returned of (display dialog "Starting number:"¬
   default answer "1001")
   set TotNum to text returned of (display dialog "How many tickets?"¬
   default answer "100")
   set TextFrames to {"one", "two", "three", "four", "five", "six"}
   set PageNum to (TotNum / 6 as integer)

   repeat (PageNum - 1) times
      duplicate spread 1 of document 1
   end repeat

   repeat with i from 1 to PageNum
      try
         set contents of text frame "one" of page i of document 1 to¬
         (StartNum as string)
         set contents of text frame "two" of page i of document 1 to¬
         (StartNum + 1 as string)
         set contents of text frame "three" of page i of document 1 to¬
         (StartNum + 2 as string)
         set contents of text frame "four" of page i of document 1 to¬
         (StartNum + 3 as string)
         set contents of text frame "five" of page i of document 1 to¬
         (StartNum + 4 as string)
         set contents of text frame "six" of page i of document 1 to¬
         (StartNum + 5 as string)
         set StartNum to (StartNum + 6)
      end try
   end repeat

end tell
```

The first line (`tell application "Adobe InDesign CS3"`) directs this script to InDesign.

The second line displays a dialog box asking the user which number he or she wants to use to start the sequential numbering:

```
set StartNum to text returned of (display dialog "Starting number:"¬
default answer "1001")
```

The number 1001 appears as the default in the text field as a suggestion.

The third line displays a dialog box asking the user how many tickets he or she needs (the default number displayed is 100):

```
set TotNum to text returned of (display dialog "How many tickets?"¬
default answer "100")
```

The fourth line stores the list of script labels that you assigned to text frames (one, two, three, four, five, and six) in the variable TextFrames:

```
set TextFrames to {"one", "two", "three", "four", "five", "six"}
```

The last line in this section (set PageNum to (TotNum / 6 as integer) divides the number of tickets requested by the user by six (since there are six tickets per page) to provide the total number of pages needed. The phrase as integer is interesting and helpful: Here, it converts the value of TotNum-divided-by-six from a real number (a number with a decimal point) to an integer (a whole number). This ensures that the result is rounded up to a whole number of pages (rather than left as a fraction).

The next section sets up a loop to duplicate the page of tickets:

```
repeat (PageNum - 1) times
    duplicate spread 1 of document 1
end repeat
```

The first line instructs the program to repeat this loop by the number stored in the variable PageNum (which is the number of tickets requested divided by six, or the total number of pages of tickets needed) minus one, because your document already contains one page of tickets. The duplicate spread 1 of document 1 line does the actual duplicating. If the user goes with the default 100 tickets, this script will create 16 pages (100 tickets divided by 6 tickets per page = 17 [16.667 rounded up] minus the one page you started with). The last line closes the repeat block.

The next section does the same thing six times per page—namely sequentially numbering the tickets:

```
repeat with i from 1 to PageNum
    try
        set contents of text frame "one" of page i of document 1 to¬
        (StartNum as string)
        set contents of text frame "two" of page i of document 1 to¬
        (StartNum + 1 as string)
        set contents of text frame "three" of page i of document 1 to¬
        (StartNum + 2 as string)
```

```
            set contents of text frame "four" of page i of document 1 to¬
            (StartNum + 3 as string)
            set contents of text frame "five" of page i of document 1 to¬
            (StartNum + 4 as string)
            set contents of text frame "six" of page i of document 1 to¬
            (StartNum + 5 as string)
            set StartNum to (StartNum + 6)
        end try
    end repeat
```

The first line—repeat with i from 1 to PageNum—sets up a loop to repeat
the number stored in the variable PageNum. That means that the code inside
this loop will operate on each page in turn. The next line (try) sets up a try
block that says if there is an error in this loop the script should keep going
rather than stop and present an error. Try blocks are great because they allow
a script to handle errors gracefully (that is, without stopping); on the other
hand, they don't provide feedback when there's an error.

Take a look at the next line:

```
set contents of text frame "one" of page i of document 1 to (StartNum¬
as string)
```

This line is instructing the program to set the contents of the text frame with
the script label "one" of page 1 (the first time through the loop—it would
be page 2 the second time, and so on) to the number stored in the variable
StartNum. The first ticket gets the number the user entered as the starting
number. Since both numbers on the first ticket have the same "one" script
label, both their contents are set to this same number.

The second line does the same thing for the second ticket, and so on through
all six tickets. The line set StartNum to (StartNum + 6) increases the value
stored in the variable StartNum by six each time through the loop because
there are six unique numbers per page. If the user goes with the default starting number of 1001, the first page of tickets will be numbered 1001 through
1006. At the end of the first time through the loop, the value stored in StartNum
is increased to 1007 (1001 + 6), and that becomes the first ticket number on
the second page. And so on.

As mentioned earlier, if the user keeps the defaults (100 tickets starting at
1001), the script will produce 17 pages of tickets numbered from 1001 to 1102.
This produces 102 tickets, but that's probably OK.

12

A Symphony of Automations

The System Project

We are what we repeatedly do.

—*Aristotle*

To produce rich, complex documents, it's possible to create graphics automation *systems:* groups of agents that work together to act on multiple applications. Systems are the symphonies of graphic automation—with much going on and many different modules—and you are both composer and conductor (with a bit of the ringmaster thrown in). Within these exciting organisms, the modules have to perform flawlessly (meshing and communicating with others) if they're to produce the document you planned.

The first part of this book covers automation concepts; the second covers tools; and the third provides recipe-type projects. This last chapter focuses on the experience of planning and building a multipart system. Although the project described here is larger than anything covered thus far in this book, its components are no more complex than those you've seen in previous chapters. And the process is pretty similar to building a single, small agent: You must plan what you're going to do (breaking the project down into manageable sections), select your tools (that is, which form of automation you'll use), and solve the problems that will inevitably crop up along the way.

Since you're by now familiar with available automation technologies—you know how to use the tools, and you know where to look for technical details you don't remember—this chapter is less about the nitty-gritty techniques of automation and more about planning and problem-solving strategies. When you're building a large project, the most useful knowledge you can apply is an understanding of automation concepts, tools, and problem-solving techniques.

Go to www.peachpit.com/apprentice to download the scripts and project files described in this chapter.

The Project

Since this book covers Photoshop, Illustrator, and InDesign, I originally conceived of a project that would link the three programs and add some capabilities from other applications to build a large-ish graphics automation system. As it turned out, this automation uses seven applications, and it took nine applications to produce it: The automation uses the three Creative Suite applications, an e-mail client, a script editor, the Mac's Finder (to build the audio file), and a Web browser. Producing the automation required an HTML editor and a text editor as well. Despite all of these tools, the individual automation agents are not all that complicated.

The project is to build a personalized, interactive PDF newsletter for our fictitious client—Star & Fey Seed Co.—to send to its customers (**Figure 12.1**). The newsletter contains personalized text, a photo of a garden rock with the customer's first name (as if chiseled there), a map of the customer's region of the United States with his or her state highlighted and showing the state's U.S. Department of Agriculture hardiness zone (a climate-based code for planting guidance), and a customized spoken greeting incorporating the season and the customer's first name and state.

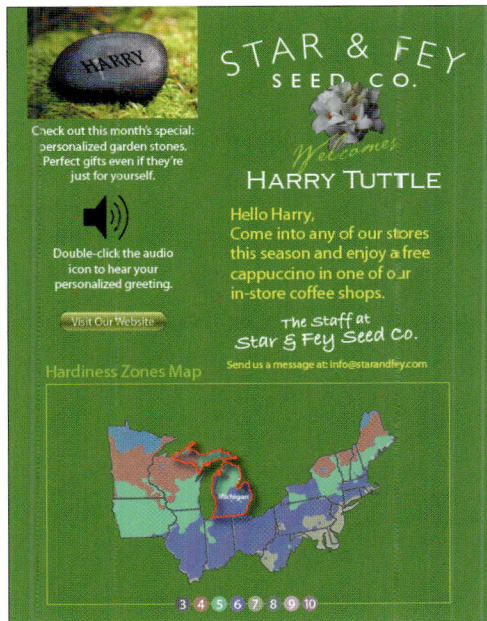

Figure 12.1

Customers enter their contact information in a Web form, and that data is sent to an e-mail box; receipt of these messages triggers a script that collects the data from each e-mail as it is received and writes it to a text file. Later, a person triggers another script that reads all of the customers' data from the text file and uses it to build files in Photoshop, Illustrator, and InDesign, as well as to build the audio file. Finally, the whole thing is saved as an interactive PDF and e-mailed to the customers using the addresses they provided.

I wanted to design an automation that would send a newsletter to customers almost immediately after they submitted their information, but it wasn't practical, because the Creative Suite license doesn't allow the kind of end-to-end, unattended automation I envisioned. A licensed Creative Suite user (that is, someone who has a legal copy of the software) must initiate the automation to create the images and the newsletter with the Creative Suite applications. I worked around this by having the graphic designer step in after the customer's information is received but before any Creative Suite documents are generated.

Planning

You should always sit down and scope out your project before beginning work on it. Like any design project, this one has a goal, restrictions (intended usage, budget, and so on), and a timeline. When you are getting started, this phase often gets neglected. The first step is to write out the project's workflow, which will look a little like the following:

1. Build templates for dynamically generated personalized communications, including determining which elements will be personalized.

2. Solicit customer information needed for contact purposes and for personalized elements of the newsletter (including name, home state, and e-mail address).

3. Receive and store customer data.

4. Parse customer data into tabular format for reuse in dynamically generated communications.

5. Combine customer data with templates to generate personalized communications.

6. Send personalized communication to customer via e-mail.

For this project I physically listed on a pad (almost like a to-do list) the modules I needed to build for my system. You'll notice that most of this system's application agents are scripts; in the Tools section later in this chapter, you'll find out why, as I demonstrate how scripting (and AppleScript in particular) fulfills all of the automation needs for this project. The modules I built for this project include the following:

- Photoshop, Illustrator, and InDesign templates
- Web form to collect customer data and transmit it via e-mail
- E-mail rule (in Apple Mail) to intercept the e-mail generated from the Web form and trigger a script to process it
- A script to gather data from each e-mail and write it to a text file for storage
- A script to read the data from the above-described text file (to be triggered by a person when it's time to send out the newsletters)
- A script that creates a personalized audio file (like the one I created in Chapter 2)
- A script to build a personalized Photoshop file
- A script to build a personalized Illustrator map file
- A script to open an InDesign template, plug in all of the other files, and export the PDF
- A script to build a new e-mail with customized text, attach the PDF, and send it to the customer

Note that the scripts described in the last five bullets will become one big script in the end.

Strategy

I laid out the scope of the project as described in the previous section because that's exactly how I intended to build the system—one module at a time. I would later link them in a chain to produce the system. Working in discrete units serves as an efficient way to build a system: For starters (as I mentioned earlier in the book), it's easier to build and test smaller agents because there are fewer issues to deal with and fewer things to go wrong; consequently, when something does go wrong, it's easier to track down the problem. Also, you should think of these modules as a library of parts that can be adapted and reused for other projects—and it's easier to reuse self-contained modules that do just one task. This building-block approach is very similar to the way Automator works (see Chapter 5).

Finally, the sense of satisfaction you get from successfully finishing a module can keep you going when you're in the middle of a big project. You will undoubtedly encounter thorny problems, and although problem solving can actually be fun (it's true), too many problems in a row will drag you down. This approach prevents that from happening.

The risk in building projects a module at a time is that if the system is dependent on a particular module (say, inserting files into an InDesign template), the whole system is in danger if that module proves unworkable. If that module isn't produced until later in the project cycle (like the InDesign module), it might be too late in the process to rescue the system. Yet this also points up the virtue of breaking a workflow into the smallest possible units—because most of your modules are probably reusable. It also reinforces the importance of identifying and isolating tasks in your workflow before picking the automation tools to accomplish them (if you're too wedded to one of your tools, you could miss finding a work-around). After you get a few automation projects under your belt, you'll find it easier to identify potential trouble spots early and tackle them head-on. For instance, since I'd never linked an audio file to an InDesign document before this newsletter project, I decided to test it early so that I could cross it off my potential issue list. (This is not to say you won't come across potentially deal-killing issues as you move through your projects; you will. Later, you'll learn of one in particular that I had to handle for this project.)

Another timesaving strategy I employed was adapting previously created agents, including the spoken-word audio file (Chapter 2) and the script for generating e-mail messages (Chapter 10). Reuse and adaptation is a tried-and-true method that will greatly reduce the time you spend building and troubleshooting a system.

DEAD ENDS

On this project I wasted a good amount of time trying to figure out how to use a zip code to place a town marker on a map in Illustrator. My original idea was to have the person's town indicated on his or her state map. I would then convert zip codes into latitude and longitude and use those coordinates to create objects in Illustrator. I found a free 1999 database file from the Census Bureau with zip codes and corresponding latitudes and longitudes, and imported it into a FileMaker Pro database. This done, it was pretty easy to write a script to locate the database record containing the person's zip code and to get their coordinates.

But that scheme was for naught. Latitudes and longitudes are derived from lines drawn on a sphere, which when represented in a 2D space such as an Illustrator file, turns out to be curved. Coordinates in Illustrator are based on straight lines and therefore cannot be used to locate a position on a flat map. You can get approximate locations with this method, but the margin of error is too big to, say, accurately mark towns near state lines. I knew all that in the back of my mind, but I was so interested in solving the problem that before long I was on a caffeine-fueled quest to triumph at all costs. Before I crashed and burned, I discovered that you can script Google Earth and other mapping services. You can send a URL containing a zip code or address to Web sites like Yahoo Maps via scripting, then trigger a screen-capture utility to take a screen shot of the map it produces. (These were unusable because they cannot be redistributed for commercial purposes.) So I couldn't use any of this in my newsletter, but it's almost certain to come in handy somewhere down the line.

So don't despair when something doesn't work. Even if you fail, as I did, you will have at least learned what *doesn't* work, and that goes into making you a better graphics automation developer. In other words, *enjoy the journey.*

Tools

The automation techniques I used to build this project had to meet three requirements: They needed to work across multiple applications (including a couple that aren't part of Creative Suite); they had to pass data from the beginning of the process all the way to the end; and they had to continually trigger each module in turn (with the caveat that a person has to trigger Module 4, as described in the Planning section earlier in this chapter).

In this case, I opted to use one tool that can communicate with multiple applications (including non-Adobe applications). To work across multiple applications, your choices are Automator and scripting. I don't have enough Automator actions for what I need to do (and it wouldn't be efficient to write as many as this would take), so scripting won on this criterion.

Passing data from the beginning to the end of the system presents similar challenges. You could conceivably use different tools for different modules, but not all tools are good at interfacing and sharing data. Adobe's actions, for instance, don't interface with other agents at all, and it's difficult to pull data out of an Automator workflow from another agent. To pass data all the way through the system, you can't avoid using scripting. To keep the process moving (triggering each module in turn), scripting again represents the only workable solution. But how do you know *which* scripting language? Ideally, you'd want this to work on both Windows and Mac. But ExtendScript (Adobe's cross-platform flavor of JavaScript) only links Adobe applications (and only when run from Adobe's ExtendScript Toolkit). And VBScript only works on Windows, and only within one application at a time. So I went with AppleScript.

To keep the process moving, you could conceivably use a variety of tools, such as Creative Suite's actions, scripts, and Automator. But this approach presents a different problem, requiring you to repeatedly leap from tool to tool. Graphics automation tools are typically written to operate within a relatively small environment (say, a single application) and don't generally communicate very well with other tools. For example, actions can't accept data from outside the application in which they reside (either Photoshop or Illustrator); Automator can trigger some other tools but is somewhat limited in how it can pass data to them; and so on. You would have to continually jump through hoops to make this approach work.

If you've been following the bouncing ball, you'll know that AppleScript is the winner. It's unfortunate that it only works on Macs, but AppleScript fulfills all my project's automation requirements.

Getting Started

Although I always write up a plan like the one described earlier in this chapter, I have to admit that I don't always follow it to the letter. I sometimes go off on tangents, and I definitely hit my share of dead ends. But there's a difference between losing your way when you have a map to lead you back on track and being just plain lost. So give yourself a good map—a constantly updated to-do list—and do your best to stick with the plan. But don't beat yourself up for getting a bit sidetracked. I guarantee the experience will prove useful in time, no matter how useless it feels in the moment.

The Templates

This project uses six templates: a photograph in Photoshop on which type is placed, four maps in Illustrator dividing the contiguous United States into four regions, and the final InDesign newsletter. Both the Photoshop and Illustrator files will be placed into the InDesign document. Templates are easy environments in which to work because you know where everything is and what it's named.

A well-built template will be flexible enough to handle issues that crop up in automated design, such as type whose length changes in different iterations of a document. You can use your automation technology (for example, scripting) to handle some of the variability, but you can make it easy on yourself by compensating for variations during the design phase as much as possible.

PHOTOSHOP TEMPLATE

This project's Photoshop image consists of a rock onto which I have placed type that (hopefully) appears to be chiseled into the stone (**Figure 12.2**). One of the most common issues when dealing with type is how to make variable-length type fit within a given space—in this case, the length of a rock. Because Photoshop doesn't have text-measuring capabilities, I had to improvise them. A good way to anticipate potential design issues is to insert the extremes of your content into the template. For the rock text, I inserted the shortest name (*Al*) I planned to use and then subsequently tried inserting incrementally longer names (*Brigid, Nicholas, Alexandria,* and so on). By so doing, I discovered ways I could build the template file to compensate for varying name lengths.

Figure 12.2

On my rock photo I've set up three text layers, each of which is a different font size to accommodate varying numbers of letters. Names of 10 or more characters just don't look good on the rock, so I had to come up with a different solution for them (more on that in a subsequent section).

The rock image is 3 inches wide by 2 inches high at 120 dots per inch. I created a text layer by using the Text tool to click the image; then I named it ShortName. I typed a three-letter name *(Jez)* and used Free Transform to distort the type to match the position and perspective of the rock. I applied the Bevel and Emboss layer style (Layer > Layer Effects). Thirty-five-point type looked best for the three-and-under letter crowd.

I duplicated the ShortName layer twice, naming one MedName (for medium) and the other LongName. I found that 28-point type worked best for medium (4 to 6 letters) and that 19-point type worked best for names of up to 9 letters. I hid all three text layers by clicking the eyes on the far left of each layer in the Layers panel and saved the file, naming it RockFile.psd.

ILLUSTRATOR TEMPLATES

The Illustrator maps were the most difficult to produce. I had to assign each of the 48 state layers their full state names rather than abbreviations. I overlaid the map with the USDA hardiness zones (www.usna.usda.gov/Hardzone/ushzmap.html).

I wanted my newsletter graphic to highlight the recipient's home state, labeled with the state's name—but when I used a map of the contiguous United States, the individual states were too small. So I decided to divide the U.S. map into four regions (Northwest, Southwest, Northeast, and Southeast). I divided the map into quarters pretty much by eyeball; I didn't use one of the many accepted region divisions.

I duplicated the state layers and used these to create each state outline and state name (**Figure 12.3**).

INDESIGN TEMPLATE

InDesign offers a few bells and whistles when it comes to exporting interactive PDF files: You can add audio (and video) files, interactive buttons, hyperlinks, and PDF bookmarks.

Figure 12.3

The Layout

First, I built the layout, creating and placing placeholder images for both the rock and map images and creating two text boxes. The first text box contains the customer's first and last names (with a space in between); my script will pull these from my data (**Figure 12.4**).

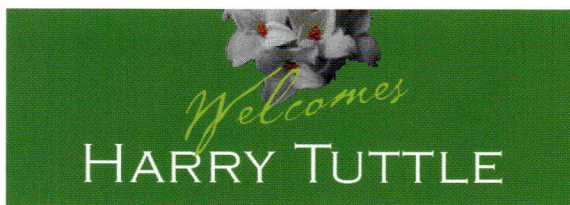

Figure 12.4

I needed to name this text frame so that my script would be able to identify it. I selected the full-name text frame and chose Window > Interactive > Script Label. I then clicked in the Script Label panel, typed `CustName`, and pressed the Tab key to accept it (**Figure 12.5**).

Figure 12.5

In the text frame directly beneath the preceding one (which begins with the text *Hello Customer)*, there are two words that will be replaced in each iteration. I needed to name this text frame by giving it a script label. I selected the Hello Customer text frame and chose Window > Interactive > Script Label. I then clicked in the Script Label panel, typed `CustLetter`, and pressed the Tab key to accept the label (**Figure 12.6**).

The word *Customer* will be replaced by the customer's first name, and the word *season* will be replaced by the current season (spring, summer, fall, or winter). (The script gets the current month from the computer to determine which season it is.) While the customer name runs the risk of oversetting the text frame, I estimated that it would take a first name of about 20 letters to do so—*not* very likely.

Figure 12.6

Interactive Features

As mentioned previously, I'm using three of InDesign's interactive features: the audio file, the Multistate button (with a Web page hyperlink), and a text hyperlink to e-mail. I wouldn't ordinarily use so many interactive elements on one page, but in a rich, multipage document, a range of interactive features can be very effective.

I built a temporary audio file and placed it in the InDesign template (File > Place). The icon for an audio file is what InDesign calls a *poster* (**Figure 12.7**).

In setting up this part of my layout, I ran into one of those unforeseen problems. The standard poster for an audio file is pretty ugly, so I wanted to replace it with a graphic of my own design (**Figure 12.8**). To replace the poster, I double-clicked the placed audio file. Then, from the Poster pull-down menu, I selected Choose Image as Poster and clicked Choose (**Figure 12.9**). Even though I used the same Web-safe green for the background of both the audio poster and the newsletter, they didn't match when I exported the document to PDF.

Figure 12.7

Figure 12.8

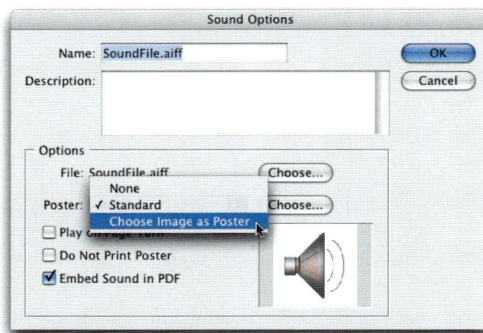

Figure 12.9

Figure 12.10

After about 40 minutes of trying everything I could think of (copying and pasting from Illustrator and triggering the audio from a button), I found that if I set Poster to None, the exported PDF would contain a black audio icon that I hadn't seen before (**Figure 12.10**). Even if this didn't make sense, given my other choices, I decided it wasn't so bad. I gave this rectangle the script label AudioFile and then saved the file.

With InDesign, you can create interactive buttons that change their appearance according to whether they're idle (the Up state), being moused over (the Rollover state), or being clicked (the Down state). This is part eye candy, part user feedback; I added a hyperlink to the button so that when a user clicks it, he or she is taken to a Web site.

InDesign lets you create multistate buttons in two ways: You can either convert your own graphic to a button or use InDesign's Button tool and appearance effects. I chose to create the button-state graphics in Illustrator. To do so, I created three PNG files in Illustrator (File > Export > PNG format) and placed the Up button in InDesign. (While the Rollover and Down states are optional, all buttons in InDesign have the Up state.) I then converted it to a button (by selecting the Button graphic and choosing Object > Interactive > Convert to Button).

By bringing up the States pane (Window > Interactive > States), I created the other two states and imported the graphics for them. From the States pane menu (**Figure 12.11**), I chose New State to add the Rollover state, where I specified which graphic would appear when a user hovered his or her mouse over the button. I then returned to the States panel menu and selected Place Content into State (**Figure 12.12**). I browsed until I located the rollover graphic and clicked the Open button. I repeated the process for the Down state.

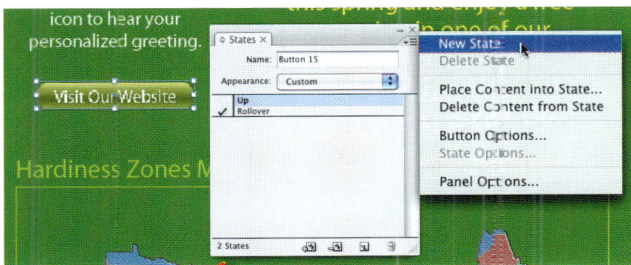

Figure 12.11

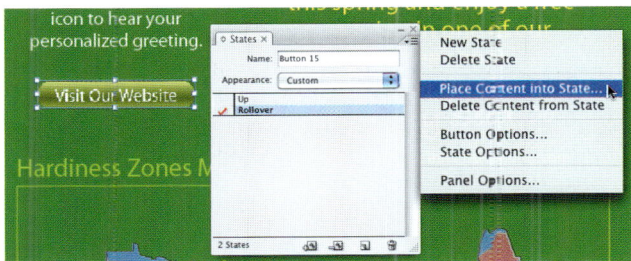

Figure 12.12

Although I couldn't test the button states by mousing over and clicking the button in InDesign, I was able to see the states in play by clicking each in the States panel to make them appear in the InDesign document. To really test the button, I had to export to PDF. To actually get the button to do something (in this case opening a Web page), I selected the button and chose Object > Interactive > Button Options (you can also double-click the button to bring up the same window). I clicked the Behaviors button at top center and in the Event menu chose Mouse Up. (Mouse Up means "click and release the mouse button.") In the Behavior menu, I chose Go To URL and entered my Web page address, http://www.starandfey.com (**Figure 12.13**). Note that you can specify multiple behaviors per event.

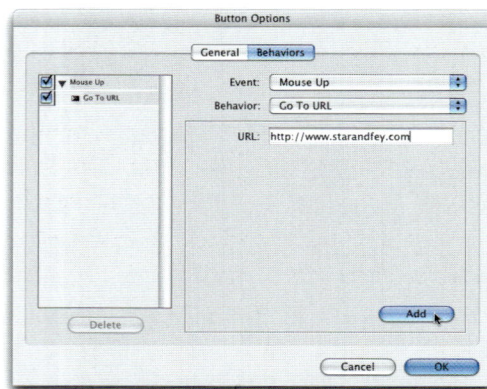

Figure 12.13

The last interactive feature I added to my InDesign template was an e-mail hyperlink. After bringing up the Hyperlinks panel by choosing Window > Interactive > Hyperlinks, I selected the text I wanted to associate with the hyperlink (in this case the entire "Send us a message" text frame). Then, from the Hyperlinks panel menu, I chose New Hyperlink (**Figure 12.14**).

From the Type pull-down menu, I then chose URL and typed in `mailto:info@starandfey.com`. Note that this URL is formed by combining mailto: (don't forget the colon) plus an e-mail address with no space in between. A few ways to highlight the link are provided in the Appearance area of the New Hyperlink dialog box, but none of them looked very good in this design. I chose Invisible Rectangle in the Type pull-down menu and None for the Highlight (**Figure 12.15**).

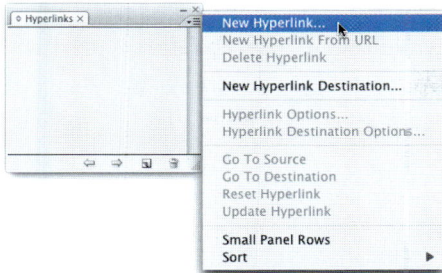

Figure 12.14

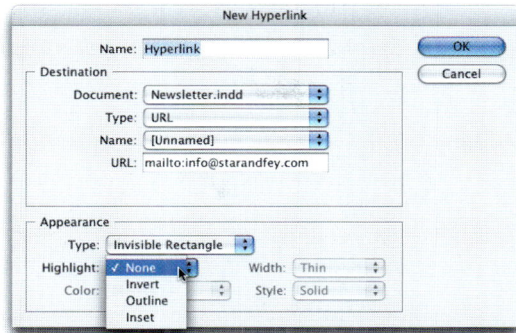

Figure 12.15

Export Setup

Although the script will do the exporting to PDF, I needed to set two important export preferences in InDesign: First, I saved the InDesign document one last time to make sure I wouldn't lose anything. Then I exported the template document by choosing File > Export, selecting Adobe PDF from the Format pull-down menu, and clicking the Save button. In the next window I checked the Hyperlinks and Interactive Elements boxes in the lower right (**Figure 12.16**) to ensure that those elements are included in the PDF.

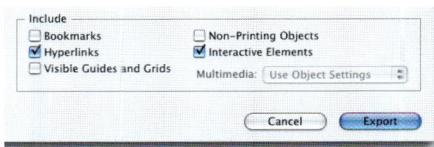

Figure 12.16

The Web Form

A form that resides on a Web page provides a nice means of collecting data: Users simply fill in the form, and the data is collected and sent to you in an e-mail message. You could collect the data in other ways (see the Adobe Acrobat form in the Ad Generator project in Chapter 11 as an example), but none is likely to be as user-friendly as Web forms: All they require is that the user be on the Internet and have a Web browser.

Web forms are surprisingly easy to build. They are fairly simple Web pages and can be built in almost any WYSIWYG Web page editor. (I used Adobe Dreamweaver.) You'll need to check with your Internet service provider (ISP) as setups vary (some even offer templates), and you'll need a Web hosting account. If you're working with a Web producer, you can design the page, and that person will take care of all the back-end stuff.

I downloaded an example form from my ISP's Web site and opened it in Dreamweaver. From there, I added a background color and the client's logo, and deleted all of the fields I didn't need. I also added a pull-down menu with the 48 contiguous states (**Figure 12.17**). Using the same method, I created a confirmation page that read, "Your submission was successful," and an error page that read, "There is an issue with the information you entered. Press the Back button and try again." Then, following my ISP's instructions, I uploaded these forms to my Web site.

Figure 12.17

E-Mail Script and Rule

The cool thing about collecting data this way is that the data is delivered to my mailbox as regular e-mail messages. All I needed to do was figure out a way to automatically copy the data out of each message and compile it in a text file. (I could also have chosen to store the data in a spreadsheet or database.)

THE E-MAIL SCRIPT

To extract customers' information from all the e-mail messages generated by my Web form, I wrote a script (which you can download with the rest of the project files from www.peachpit.com/apprentice). Whenever I receive a message from the Web form, a rule that I set up in Apple Mail recognizes the standard subject line and activates my script. Then the script copies whatever is in the body of the e-mail and appends it to the end of a text file (BrochureList.txt). This is great, because the script lets you write to a text file without ever opening it.

I did, however, have to troubleshoot a couple of unanticipated problems with this script. Invisible characters were being appended to the end of the e-mail messages and ending up in my text file, so I had to write a small loop in the script to delete them. To get rid of the unwanted mystery characters, I copied and pasted the invisible text from a sample e-mail, stored it in a variable called `illegalCharacters` in the script, and deleted them before writing to the text file.

The problem of the invisible characters is an example of something you will encounter time and again when writing automation agents—things that you didn't think about or could not have foreseen. This is plain, old problem solving and can be the bane of your existence or a fun romp, depending on which way the winds blow—and your attitude.

Personally, I find this type of problem solving interesting, because it's like solving a mystery. Take the invisible characters: All I could see was that there was some invisible text written to the text file. Where did it come from? Was I somehow accidentally writing it from the script? I checked but didn't find anything there. So I opened one of the test e-mails written by the Web form, and sure enough there was some invisible text at the end of it. This usually points to the existence of a return or some tabs, but the invisible text remained even after I tried to delete those. I didn't know where the invisible text came from or what it consisted of, but I knew that if I could store it in a variable in my script, I could use that to identify the characters copied from the e-mail and delete them.

After everything was working, I saved the script as EmailRuleScript.scpt.

THE E-MAIL RULE

The e-mail rule that initiates my script operates on the same principle as the junk-mail filter in your e-mail client (and is probably only a bit more complicated). Although common and simple to use, e-mail rules are bona fide automation agents. You can use them to automatically forward, delete, or reply to messages that match criteria you specify, such as recipient, subject line, or date received. Apple's Mail application can also trigger AppleScripts, opening up entirely new vistas. And although it's not as easy, you can script Entourage and Outlook to do something similar. I remember reading about someone who'd figured out she could send a message to her home e-mail, trigger an AppleScript to create a new message, attach a particular file to it, and e-mail it back to her—a weird but cool form of remote control, regardless of the security issues.

In this case I wanted an AppleScript to be triggered whenever an e-mail was received with the Subject line "Star & Fey Newsletter Form Feedback" (as set up in my Web form). In my e-mail application I set up a rule by choosing Mail > Preferences > Rules. E-mail programs (that support rules) vary, but the idea is that you specify one or more criteria (such as subject line, sender, or priority) and then one or more operations that you want to be carried out when the criteria is met. I clicked the Add Rule button and added a new rule, set up as shown in **Figure 12.18**.

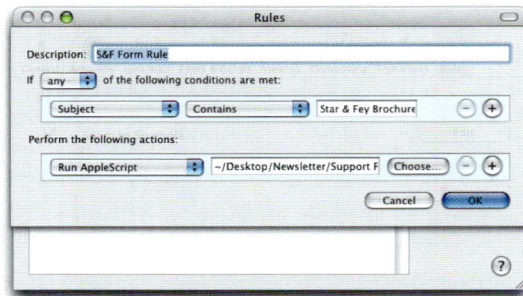

Figure 12.18

I ended up with a text file—each line consisting of one person's first name, last name, state, and e-mail address—that looks something like this:

    Sam,Lowery,California,sam@madeupdomain1.com

    Jill,Layton,Oregon,jill@madeupdomain2.com

    Jack,Lint,Georgia,jack@madeupdomain3.com

    Harry,Tuttle,Maine,harry@madeupdomain4.com

    Ida,Lowery,Iowa,ida@madeupdomain5.com

The Big Project Script

The command center for this project is one large script. It assembles data, builds an audio file, creates Photoshop and Illustrator documents, brings it all together in InDesign, and saves it as a PDF. The script is long, but it's nothing more than a series of individual modules. It's similar to an Automator workflow, where each module accepts data, performs some operation, and then passes the data along to another module.

I won't step through the script line by line but instead will provide an overview of each module and talk a little about the more interesting bits. I manually triggered the script from the script editor, but before I ran it, I opened the BrochureList.txt file containing the customers' data and deleted the first empty line. The e-mail script writes a return before writing customer data, so if left unedited, the first line consists of nothing but a return, which the big script interprets as a customer record, causing it to error out when it tries to gather data that's not there.

SEASONS

Since one of the dynamic text elements in the newsletter is the season, I needed to find a way to determine which season was currently under way. To do so, I used system information (the date, according to the computer's operating system). Among the data you can pull from the operating system is the date, which looks something like the following: *Thursday, June 12, 2008 11:33:05 AM*. I decided to extract the month to determine the current season. Other date elements you can use and act upon include the day of the week (is it the weekend or not?), the day of the month, the year, the period of day (A.M. or P.M., day or night). With two times, you can determine an elapsed amount of time (how long did it take to do something, and is that period of time out of spec?). As you can see, you can often ferret out a considerable amount of information from what seems like a small amount of data.

> **Note**
>
> You can also save the date from the e-mail you received from the Web form and use that to derive the season—plus, knowing the date on which the customer contacted you might be handy for follow-up communications.

The month is June. To determine the season, I built four lists of the months in each season. Here's how that looks in the script:

```
set spring to {"April", "May", "June"}
set summer to {"July", "August", "September"}
set fall to {"October", "November"}
set winter to {"December", "January", "February", "March"}
```

Once you've done this, it's just a matter of finding out which list the current month belongs to (spring).

IMPORTING TEXT FILE AND BUILDING VARIABLES

After importing the text, I separated out the data and stored it in variables. The four variables for this project included each customer's first name, last name, state, and e-mail address. Lists of this nature make it easy to work with data. You can identify this section of the script (the parsing of records and assigning them to variables) because it starts with the comment `-- BUILD THE LISTS OF CUSTOMER DATA.`

I used these four lists (variables)—FirstName, LastName, State, and Email—throughout the script.

Now that the basic data setup is complete, it's time to start building the individual files that make up the final document.

AUDIO FILE

Once I'd created the variables, it was easy to grab personalized text from them and use that to create the audio file. Although the computer voice sounds far from human, it speaks directly to the customer (and no one else), which is a nice touch.

Just as with text in a text frame, I can build an audio file that mixes static and dynamic words. Here's what I wanted the voice to say: *Hello [customer's first name]. Welcome to the Star & Fey [the season] newsletter. Check out the personalized garden stone on sale this month and double-check your hardiness zone for [the customer's state] in the chart at the bottom. Have a great [the season].*

Text-to-speech conversion is available in Windows, Mac, and other operating systems. This is something that computers do pretty well now (this wasn't always the case), and it can be a great help for those with impaired vision or learning disabilities. As I was writing this (in June 2007), Apple announced improvements in its computer accessibility, including a much improved synthesized voice (called Alex, which will be available in Mac OS X 10.5 in October 2007). I hope Alex is a sign of changing times—for all operating systems.

The Mac's available voices, while relatively good, are still sometimes hard to understand, and since Alex won't be available until the fall of 2007, I decided to use a voice from a company called Cepstral (www.cepstral.com). They sell good synthesized voices for about $40, and I chose the UK English voice, Lawrence. The British accent doesn't have anything to do with this project; I just happen to like it.

PHOTOSHOP

As I described in the Templates section, in Photoshop, I put a name on a rock, which isn't all that difficult. All I had to do was replace text in one of three text layers I set up in my template. To determine which layer to display, my script had to count the number of characters in the first name to be displayed and then pick one of the layers.

The script counts the letters in the customer's first name and stores that in a variable called NameLength. The script asks a series of questions to determine which category the name belongs in. The first question, `if NameLength ≤ 3`, is asking if the number of letters is less than or equal to 3. The second question, `if (NameLength > 3) and (x < 7)`, is asking if the number is greater than 3 and less than 7. The third question asks if it is equal to or greater than 7 but less than 10. The last question determines whether the count is 10 or greater.

I found that names with 10 or more letters didn't read well on the rock, so I decided that names of 10 letters or longer would make the LongName layer visible and insert the text *Your Name*—not an ideal solution, but it works. These are the types of work-arounds you'll need to create when designing for data-driven documents. It is a whole new dimension to design for a page where elements may move around and change size, shape, and color.

ILLUSTRATOR

Since there are four Illustrator maps for my four United States regions, I had to determine which one to open and act upon for each newsletter being generated. My approach for this was similar to the one I used to determine the season. I first built four variables (like the four seasons) and listed the states that belong to the four regions (NW, SW, NE, and SE). Here's what the four variables and their lists look like:

```
set SElist to {"Virginia", "Louisiana", "Kansas", "Oklahoma",
"Arkansas", "Missouri", "Mississippi", "Texas", "Kentucky", "Tennessee",
"North Carolina", "Alabama", "Georgia", "South Carolina", "Florida"}
```

```
set NElist to {"Wisconsin", "Minnesota", "Illinois", "Indiana",
"Iowa", "Michigan", "Ohio", "West Virginia", "Maryland", "Delaware",
"Pennsylvania", "New Jersey", "New York", "Vermont", "New Hampshire",
"Maine", "Massachusetts", "Connecticut", "Rhode Island"}

set SWlist to {"New Mexico", "Colorado", "Utah", "Nevada", "Arizona",
"California"}

set NWlist to {"Nebraska", "South Dakota", "North Dakota", "Oregon",
"Washington", "Idaho", "Montana", "Wyoming"}
```

Again, I more or less quartered the lower 48 according to my whim, not by any
official reckoning. So now, as with the seasons, my script must find which list
contains the newsletter recipient's home state. I stored the recipient's state
in the variable StateName. Here again, my script asks a series of four questions, this time along the lines of if StateName is in NWlist. When it finds
the correct list, the script uses the corresponding variable to open the region's
map file.

Once the region map is open, the script makes that state's layer visible and
exports the file in PNG format (**Figure 12.19**).

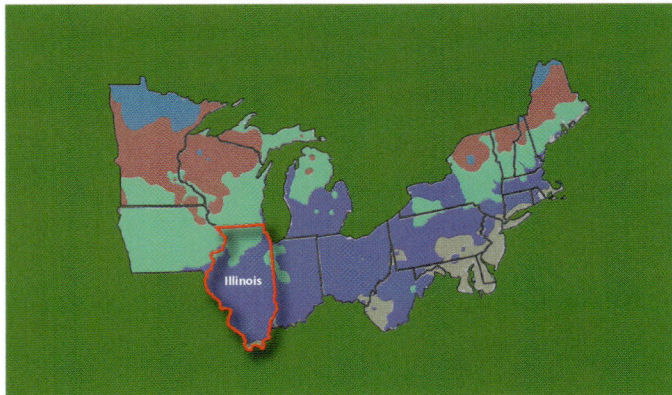

Figure 12.19

INDESIGN

Now it's time to bring it all together. The script opens the InDesign template
file, inserts the two images and the one audio file, changes some text, and
exports the document. Inserting files is accomplished with fairly simple

statements like `place [file path] on rectangle [rectangle name] of document 1`. Because the audio file is contained in a rectangle, setting its icon (or poster, in Adobe-speak) is a little weird: `set sound poster type of sounds of rectangle "AudioFile" of document 1 to none`.

One of the text boxes in my template displays the customer's first and last names (which are made up by combining the first name variable, a space, and the last name variable) in a text frame. Because names can be of different lengths, the script includes some logic to ensure that the full name fits. Here's the code that makes that happen:

```
set contents of text frame "CustName" of document 1 to FullName
repeat
set Overset to (get overflows of text frame "CustName" of document 1)
   if (Overset as string) = "true" then
      set PointSize to point size of text of text frame "CustName" of¬
      document 1
      set contents of text frame "CustName' of document 1 to ""
      set contents of text frame "CustName' of document 1 to ""
      set point size of text of text frame "CustName" of document 1 to¬
      (PointSize - 2)
      set contents of text frame "CustName" of document 1 to FullName
   else
      exit repeat
   end if
end repeat
```

This code inserts the customer's full name (`FullName`) in the CustName text frame and starts a repeat loop that asks if the text frame is overflowing (true or false). If it is, the script sets the text frame to nothing (""), reduces the type size by 2 points, and starts over by inserting the full name again and running through the loop until the text frame does not overflow.

InDesign is a little weird and forces me to do something that doesn't seem to make any sense. When text overflows a text frame and you set that text to nothing, InDesign only acts on the text that's visible in the text frame. Thus, if I insert your full name and your last name disappears because it's overflowing the text frame and I then set the text to nothing, it will only delete your first name. If your last name fits in the text frame, it will pop into view. So to ensure that the script wipes out all of the text in the frame, I have to set it to nothing—twice.

For the longer text block, I replaced only some of the text in the frame: the words *Customer* and *season*. I replaced *Customer* with this line in the script:

```
set (contents of every word of text frame "CustLetter" of document 1¬
whose contents is "Customer") to FirstNameSing
```

`FirstNameSing` is the variable storing the customer's first name.

When all the changes are made, the script exports the InDesign document as a PDF named Star_and_Fey.pdf. The script doesn't have to give each PDF a unique name because the file is overwritten after the previous one has been e-mailed.

FINAL E-MAIL

I won't dissect the e-mail script because it's very similar to the e-mail invitation project in Chapter 10. Note that the body of the message is built in the same way as the audio file—that is, by mixing both static and variable text (**Figure 12.20**).

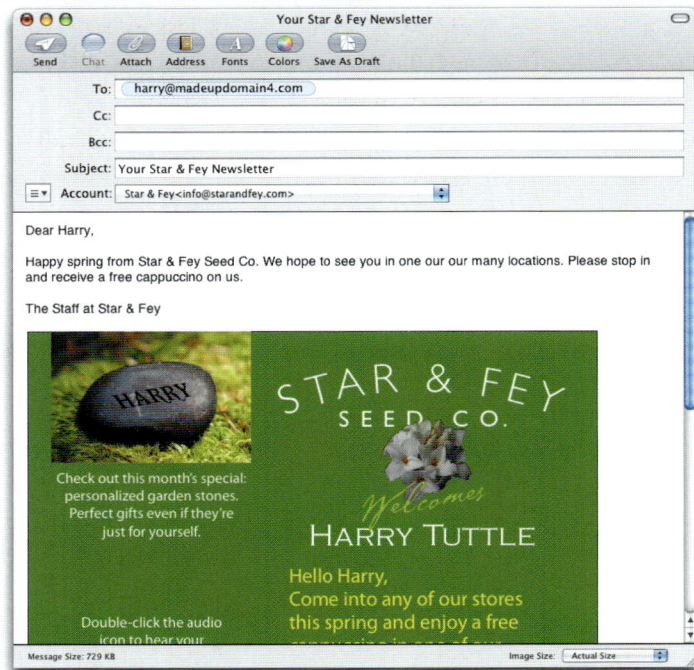

Figure 12.20

Note that there's one little line (the third from the end of the script) that's very dangerous: `send newMessage` can send e-mail to everyone in your data set—before you might be ready. For my testing, I disabled this line in Apple-Script by "commenting it out," which means to change the live code to a comment so the script won't execute it. It's still there, but it's italicized and grayed out. The format of comments varies by scripting language, but in AppleScript you type two consecutive hyphens at the beginning of the line like this: `--send newMessage`.

I tested the script by commenting out the `send newMessage` line and changing the repeat line `repeat with i from 1 to CustDataCount` (it appears in the script right before the Create Audio File section) to `repeat 1 times`. This tells the script to only produce one PDF and not send it, so you can test and tinker until you get your newsletter right. But there will always be errors, bugs, or other unanticipated problems to solve. It's just another part of getting the parts working and playing nice with one another so that the whole thing comes off without a hitch.

This is a data-driven personalized publishing project, but its lessons shouldn't be interpreted narrowly. Think about all its component elements, the different problems each individual agent has to solve, and how everything works together. Keep an eye out for concepts and tricks you can use in other kinds of automation projects. As you gain experience with graphics automation, you'll start analyzing other projects, and through tinkering you'll start to build a knowledge database that will make you an ever more effective automation agent writer. Half the battle sometimes is knowing what is and isn't possible. You can learn some of that by reading books and articles, but a great deal of it will come from your hands-on discoveries.

Appendix: Resources

A healthy amount of reference and training documentation exists for scripting Photoshop, Illustrator, and InDesign—most of which comes in the Creative Suite box. However, if what you're looking for isn't included, go to www.adobe.com and do a search. Be sure to take a look around the scripting forum (www.adobeforums.com/cgi-bin/webx?14@@eea5b36) while you're visiting. If you can't find the information you need there, try Googling it: You'll probably find what you're looking for.

If your needs go beyond scripting, you'll have to do a bit more work: Check out the references listed below for a start, join a local user's group (if available), and troll the forums for your particular subject. (Online graphics automation communities tend to crystallize around specific topics and sub-topics.) If you post a question, make sure you've read the FAQs for that forum first so that you're not wasting people's time. Explain your problem clearly and include any errors you may be getting. More often than not, someone will have encountered the same issue and will be happy to share what he or she has learned.

Keep in mind as you peruse these references that software is constantly changing, so once you've exhausted these resources, do a Google search for new material and tools. I will also maintain an updated resources list at www.peachpit.com/apprentice.

GENERAL
Book downloads and feedback: www.peachpit.com/apprentice
Author contact: apprentice@zumedia.com
Adobe Creative Suite: www.adobe.com/products/creativesuite
Adobe Exchange (downloads): www.adobe.com/cfusion/exchange

CHAPTER 1
Web Sites
Disney's Fantasia: http://disney.go.com/disneyatoz/familymuseum/collection/masterworks/fantasia/index.html
The Sorcerer's Apprentice: http://en.wikipedia.org/wiki/Sorcerer's_Apprentice

CHAPTER 2
Web Sites
Dr. Ann M. Graybiel: http://web.mit.edu/bcs/people/graybiel.shtml

CHAPTER 3
Web Sites
Photoshop actions: http://livedocs.adobe.com/en_US/Photoshop/10.0/
    WSfd1234e1c4b69f30ea53e41001031ab64-7451.html
Illustrator actions: http://livedocs.adobe.com/en_US/Illustrator/13.0/
    WS714a382cdf7d304e7e07d0100196cbc5f-62b3.html
Adobe Exchange (downloads): www.adobe.com/cfusion/exchange
Image Processor in Photoshop: www.russellbrown.com
Adobe Photoshop CS3 JavaScript reference (for events list):
    www.adobe.com/devnet/photoshop/scripting
For scripting guides, see the resources for the next chapter.

CHAPTER 4
Web Sites
Wizard of Oz: http://thewizardofoz.warnerbros.com and
    http://en.wikipedia.org/wiki/The_Wizard_of_Oz_(1939_film)
Photoshop scripting documents: http://partners.adobe.com/public/developer/
    photoshop/sdk/index_scripting.html
Illustrator scripting documents: http://partners.adobe.com/public/developer/illustrator/
    sdk/index_scripting.html
InDesign scripting documents: http://partners.adobe.com/public/developer/indesign/
    sdk/index_scripting.html
Adobe Exchange (downloads): www.adobe.com/cfusion/exchange
Hello World history: http://en.wikipedia.org/wiki/Hello_world
MacScripter: www.macscripter.net
The JavaScript Source: http://javascript.internet.com
Visual Basic Script forums: http://visualbasicscript.com
Jeff Tranberry (Photoshop scripting): www.tranberry.com
Scripting Listener Plug-In: www.tranberry.com/photoshop/photoshop_scripting/
    tips/listener.html
AppleScript: www.apple.com/applescript

Software
Smile: www.satimage.fr/software/en/index.html
Script Debugger: www.latenightsw.com
VbsEdit: www.vbsedit.com
SitePad Pro: www.modelworks.com
AppleScript Studio: www.apple.com/applescript/studio
Adobe Extendscript Toolkit (bottom of page): www.adobe.com/devnet/bridge

Books
Adobe Photoshop CS2 Official JavaScript Reference (Adobe Press, 2006)
Adobe Illustrator CS2 Official JavaScript Reference (Adobe Press, 2006)
Adobe InDesign CS2 Official JavaScript Reference (Adobe Press, 2006)
Adobe Illustrator Scripting with Visual Basic and AppleScript, Ethan Wilde (Adobe
    Press, 2003)

AppleScript: The Definitive Guide, Matt Neuburg (O'Reilly, 2004)
JavaScript: The Definitive Guide, David Flanagan (O'Reilly, 2002)
Microsoft WSH and VBScript Programming for the Absolute Beginner, Jerry Lee Ford Jr.
(Thomson, 2005)

CHAPTER 5
Web Sites
Automator at Apple: www.apple.com/macosx/features/automator
Automator World: http://automatorworld.com
Automator.US: www.automator.us
Type Identifiers (at bottom of page): http://developer.apple.com/documentation/
AppleApplications/Conceptual/AutomatorConcepts/Articles/AutomatorPropRef.html
Working with Automator: http://developer.apple.com/macosx/automator.html
Automator Programming Guide: http://developer.apple.com/documentation/
AppleApplications/Conceptual/AutomatorConcepts/index.html

Books
Mac OS X Technology Guide to Automator, Ben Waldie (SpiderWorks, 2005)

CHAPTER 6
Web Sites
Adobe's Variable Data Publishing Resource Center: www.adobe.com/products/vdp
XML overview: http://en.wikipedia.org/wiki/XML

CHAPTER 7
Web Sites
Apple's folder actions: www.apple.com/applescript/folderactions

Software
QuicKeys: www.cesoft.com (Windows/Mac)
Proxi: http://proxi.griffintechnology.com (Mac)
Quicksilver: www.quicksilver.blacktree.com (Mac)
Butler: www.manytricks.com/butler (Mac)
TextWrangler: www.barebones.com/products/textwrangler/index.shtml (Mac)
UltraEdit: www.ultraedit.com (Windows)
PowerGREF: www.powergrep.com (Windows)
BBEdit: www.barebones.com (Mac)
Nisus Writer Express: www.nisus.com/Express (Mac)
Free Software Foundation (free grep editor): www.gnu.org/software/grep
Microsoft Excel: http://office.microsoft.com/en-us/excel/FX100487621033.aspx
(Windows/Mac)
FileMaker Pro: www.filemaker.com (Windows/Mac)
IDo: www.sophisticated.com/products/ido/ido_ss.html (Mac)
Windows Task Scheduler: http://technet.microsoft.com/en-us/windowsvista/
aa906020.aspx (Windows)
AutoMate: www.networkautomation.com/automate (Windows)
iCal: www.apple.com/macosx/features/ical (Mac)

CHAPTER 8

Weaver D's Delicious Fine Foods: 1016 E Broad St, Athens, GA 30602, 706.353.7797

Web Sites

The origin of Automatic for the People: www.npr.org/templates/story/
story.php?storyId=1071764
Vaughan Pratt (Matchbox server): http://boole.stanford.edu/pratt.html
Adobe SVG Zone: www.adobe.com/svg
DeBabelizer Pro and Server: www.equilibrium.com
Adobe Graphics Server: www.adobe.com/products/server/graphics/overview1.html
Esko: www.esko.com
InDesign Server: www.adobe.com/products/indesignserver

CHAPTER 9

Web Sites

ExtendScript Toolkit (bottom of page): www.adobe.com/devnet/bridge

Books

Secrets of Adobe Bridge, Terry White (Adobe Press, 2006)
Working Smart in Adobe Photoshop CS2, Conrad Chavez (Adobe Press, 2007)

CHAPTER 10

Web Sites

Illustrator's data-driven graphics: www.adobe.com/uk/designcenter/illustrator/articles/
ill10datadrvn.html
http://livedocs.adobe.com/en_US/Illustrator/13.0/
WS714a382cdf7d304e7e07d0100196cbc5f-62a1.html
XML overview: http://en.wikipedia.org/wiki/XML

CHAPTER 11

Web Sites

InDesign's Data Merge: www.adobe.com/designcenter/indesign/articles/
indcs2at_datamerge.html
PDF forms: www.planetpdf.com/developer/article.asp?ContentID=6623

CHAPTER 12

Web Sites

Web forms: http://en.wikipedia.org/wiki/Form_(web)
Cepstral: www.cepstral.com

Index

inserting stops in actions, 32–33
instincts, 16
interactive PDF newsletter, 210–233
    about automation systems, 210
    applications used in, 211
    audio files with interactive buttons, 220–222
    collecting data from via Web form, 223–224
    dead ends in, 214–215
    determining seasons, 227–228
    e-mail script for, 224–226, 232–233
    exporting preferences for, 223
    hyperlinks in, 222–223
    importing text files and building variables, 228
    InDesign templates for, 218–223
    modular development strategy for, 213–214
    overview of final script for, 227
    personalizing audio file, 228–229
    Photoshop photo template for, 217–218, 229
    scope of, 211–213
    setting up regional Illustrator maps, 218, 229–230
    tools for automating, 215–216
Interface Builder (Mac), 78–79

J

JavaScript
    choosing as scripting language, 52
    downloading sample metadata script, 136
    scripting editors for, 53–54
    using, 49
JavaScriptable, 114
Job Status window (DeBabelizer), 126
JPEG files, 175
JScript, 49

L

Lawrence, 229
layers
    building for replaceable clock logo, 101–102
    converting template layers into variables, 102–103
    creating and naming Photoshop, 26

duplicating and flipping, 27
    flattening, 31
Layers panel (Photoshop), 26
Library column (Automator), 68
licensing for Creative Suite users, 129, 212
linked image variables, 168–169
Lives of a Cell (Thomas), 65
loading action sets, 36
Locke, John A., 133
logo
    building layers for replaceable, 101–102
    placing on contact sheet template, 191–192
    varying on image, 100–101
loops
    creating variables and file path for, 175–176
    providing escape in scripts with, 199
    unable to use in Automator, 73
    using with scripts, 62–63

M

Macintosh computers. *See also*
    AppleScript; Automator; Mail
    triggering software for, 117–118
    using AppleScripts, 48
    using Windows droplets on, 37
macro software, 108–110
Mail
    rules for newsletter e-mail scripts, 119, 226
    triggering AppleScript for, 119–120
    using e-mail invitation script with, 173, 176–177
mailing labels, 99
map templates, 218
metadata, 134–141
    adding copyright information to file's, 30–31
    attaching script to correct folder, 139–141
    automating type style, font, and size for, 139
    building and triggering first action, 137–138
    defined, 31
    opening image and copying, 137
    overview of Photoshop project to add, 134–136
    saving with action, 139